HERDWICK COUNTRY COOK BOOK

Heritage, Walks and Recipes

Hugh and Thérèse Southgate

with a foreword by Professor Philip Lowe,
Professor of Rural Economy, University of Newcastle

and photographs by Peter Koronka

Published in association with the

Herdwick Sheep Breeders' Association

HAYLOFT

First published 2003

by Hayloft Publishing Ltd.
Great Skerrygill, South Stainmore,
Kirkby Stephen, Cumbria, CA17 4EU.

Tel. 017683 42300 or Fax. 017683 41568
e-mail: dawn@hayloft.org.uk
website: www.hayloft.org.uk

Paperback - ISBN 0 9540711 7 4
Hardback - ISBN 0 9540711 8 2

Photography © Peter Koronka
Published by Hayloft in association with the Herdwick Sheep Breeders' Association
Produced in Great Britain
Printed and bound in Hungary

CONTENTS

	Page Number
Illustrations	4
Acknowledgements	5
Foreword	7
Introduction	8
The Herdwick Story	9
Cumbrian Cookery	16
Buttermere Valley	23
Borrowdale Valley	34
Ennerdale Valley	40
Ullswater	46
The Langdales and Coniston	58
Wasdale and Eskdale	68
Spinning, Weaving, Dyeing and Felting	76
(including section by Geoff Brown)	
Starters and Soups	94
Main Course Dishes	103
Vegetable Dishes	135
Sweet Dishes	143
Bread, Pastry and Cakes	153
Nutrional Information	166
Cooking Methods	167
Joints and Cuts of Herdwick	169
Oven Temperatures, Weights, Measures and Portions	171
Nutrional Value of Vegetables	172
Advice for Walkers and Countryside Code	173
Food and Wool Trail	174
Bibliography	178
Index	179

ILLUSTRATIONS

	Page Number		Page Number
Eskdale	6	Carrot and Apricot Soup	93
Buttermere	22	Cumberland Curry	96
Wrynose Pass	25	Cumberland Flan	121
Crummock Water and Shepherd's Pie	28	Shallow Fried Leg Steaks & Fell 'n' Tarn	124
Langdale and Old Norwegian sheep	29	Rosthwaite Roast	125
Buttermere walk map	30	Smoked Cumberland Pizza	128
Coniston	32	Crummock Cutlets	129
Borrowdale	33	Herdwick Stuffed Peppers	132
Ennerdale and inset rugs	36	Herdwick Shepherds' Pie	157
Borrowdale walk map	39	Damson Cobbler	160
Ennerdale walk map	45	St. Bee's Delight	160
Ullswater	49	Lemon Meringue Pie	161
Ullswater and wool items	52	Toffee Almond Shortbread	164
Ullswater and Herdwick sheep	53	Borrowdale Teabread	164
Ullswater walk map	54	Maid of Buttermere's Temptation	165
Langdale and felting	56	Keswick Braise	168
Eskdale	57	Joints of Herdwick diagram	169
Eskdale and tea bread	60	Cuts of Herdwick diagram	170
Langdale walk map	66		
Eskdale walk map	74		
Shearing	77		
Wasdale and shearing	85		
Shearing and felt making	88		
Spinning and felt making	89		
Melon and tomato cocktail	92		
Patterdale Paté	92		
Chilled Damson Soup	93		

ACKNOWLEDGMENTS

We would like to extend our thanks to Philip Lowe, Professor of Rural Economy at the University of Newcastle for his kind foreword. Thanks also go to our publisher and photographer for their advice and particularly their patience in surmounting all the sheep hurdles we have encountered along the way!

Our thanks to Geoff Brown and Adrian Banford for their help and advice and to the executive committee of the Herdwick Sheep Breeders' Association for assisting in the financing of the project. Geoff's contribution to the Herdwick history and the chapter on wool are invaluable and bring the story up to date. We would like to thank Tina Linnitt, treasurer of the Herdwick Sheep Breeders' Association, who first mooted the idea of a book. We appreciate the time given to us by farmers Mary Bell, Ian Hall, Mr. Harrison, Anthony Hartley, William Rawling, Mr. and Mrs. J. Relph and Mr. E. Taylforth.

Particular thanks go to David and Lana Norman, Sir Don Curry and Eric Robson for all their support and help. Our thanks to Jeremy Barlow, property manager and Mark Astley, warden of Ennerdale and Buttermere National Trust and Jane Watson at the Trust's office in Grasmere, for their encouragement and belief in the project. Our thanks to Chris Crofts for allowing us to photograph her beautifully crafted Herdwick rugs and to Mr. and Mrs. M. Heelis, for allowing us to photograph sheep being sheared.

Thanks also to Andrew Humphries for the interesting discussions on Herdwick sheep and to Dr. Odne of the Agricultural University, Norway, for his help in giving us new leads for future research into the origins of the Herdwick.

On behalf of the Herdwick Sheep Breeders' Association we would like to express thanks to Barclays Bank for their financial help to the Association for its regeneration activities following foot and mouth disease.

Finally our thanks to all the Cumbrians we have spoken to over our fifteen year association with the county, who have told us so much about the legends, traditions and old recipes of Cumbria.

Hugh and Thérèse Southgate, June 2003

Eskdale

FOREWORD

Herdwick Country Cook Book takes the reader to the heart of the Lake District, its traditions and its economy. The history of Herdwick sheep and that of the Lake District are so closely intertwined that you cannot consider one without the other.

The terrain and climate of the Lake District make it intrinsically difficult on many fronts for those who must make their living from the land. At the same time these very difficulties have served to protect the traditions of the area.

For centuries Herdwick sheep have been the foundation of the Lake District economy. Their ability to thrive on the open fells and to provide valuable wool and meat was not just an economic fact. The landscape itself was shaped by sheep and sheep farmers - grazing keeps the fells clear of trees and the dry stone walls were built to provide lowland enclosures for winter grazing.

Authors Therese and Hugh Southgate have researched the history of Herdwick sheep and their work has won the approval of the Herdwick Sheep Breeders' Association as a reliable introduction to the history of the breed from early times to the present. The book is being published in conjunction with the breeders' association and a portion of the profits will be given to them to further their work on marketing Herdwick sheep.

Cumbrian food has also been strongly influenced by the dominance of Herdwick sheep, and Therese provides a fascinating glimpse into its history. The west coast tradition of trade with the Americas brings an exotic element into local cookery with ingredients such as rum and ginger.

Pride of place in the book are the recipes inspired by the Lake District's culinary traditions. Hugh is a well known and highly respected chef. He has brought his years of experience and obvious love of good food to the subject of traditional ingredients and dishes. The result brings some completely new recipes which will no doubt become old favourites.

Using Cumbrian produce Hugh has devised dishes fit for a Queen (he is a part-time member of the Royal household!). Old favourites such as Shepherd's Pie are included along with exciting new ways of cooking and eating local ingredients. In addition the book contains recipes for almost forgotten foods such as Frumenty and Haver Bread.

To work up an appetite for this glorious food you'll want to be out on those fells. The section on walks gives detailed directions and historical notes about areas of the Lake District particularly associated with Herdwick sheep. For the armchair enthusiast, the book's themes are illustrated with full colour photographs by Peter Koronka.

This is a very special book that brings together landscape, history and food. Fittingly it celebrates the unity of a very special place, its people, culture and living traditions. For the reader it opens up the varied ways - the sights, the sounds and the tastes - to take pleasure from Herdwick Country. Not forgetting the pleasure of a good read.

Philip Lowe, Professor of Rural Economy,
University of Newcastle

INTRODUCTION

The origin of this book came about in the year 2000 before foot and mouth disease hit Cumbria. We attended a number of the agricultural shows helping the Herdwick Sheep Breeders' Association. I was helping to sell the Herdwick meat and Therese was spinning to attract the public over to the stand. The treasurer thought it would be a good idea to give a recipe with the meat purchases. The aim was to highlight the versatility of this speciality meat in the kitchen.

We thought about this and came up with the notion of writing a cookery book with the emphasis on Herdwick meat. The Herdwick is a slow maturing sheep. It matures slowly over a year grazing on the ling heather and bleaberries growing wild on the fells. This allows the special flavours of Herdwick meat to develop. The meat is succulent, tender and tasty and very individual. It has a strong, sweet, gamey flavour resembling venison rather than lamb. This enables the meat to be combined with flavours of a strong and spicy nature. Research by Bristol University has found that the fat is of the omega 3 variety. The fat of the meat has more mono-unsaturated fatty acids than any other lamb and is more akin to olive oil.

The book tells the reader where they can see the Herdwicks in their natural surroundings. Many people are becoming increasingly concerned as to where and how their food is produced. Traceability is now an important issue. Here in Cumbria you can see the food for the table being produced on the fells. You can see it's the best both in terms of animal welfare and the end product. Our aim is also to encourage the use of locally produced food.

This is a cookery book with a difference. It takes you for walks through some of the most beautiful areas of the Lake District where this unique breed of sheep is reared. Some of the history and legends of the area are recounted. The interviews with the farmers are personal views of dedicated men and women concerned about the future of farming and committed to ensuring the survival of this ancient breed. To ensure their survival, the products from these remarkable sheep have to be used. If Herdwick sheep should become extinct, the Lake District landscape, so loved by visitors, would return to scrubland.

The book includes a little of what is known about the history of the Herdwick and its unique instinct, known locally as heafing. A brief history of spinning, weaving and dyeing in Cumbria is included. Modern technology is now being used to make Herdwick wool products more marketable. The book gives information on some exciting new Herdwick wool products and a wool trail detailing where they can be purchased, many by mail order. The social and cultural implications of local recipes and their origins is described together with some traditional local recipes.

There are chapters about the Herdwick strongholds, Lakeland valleys where you can see these native sheep and there are recipes ranging from variations of traditional dishes to innovative recipes created by us. We feel they are within the capabilities of the average cook who enjoys cooking and wants to present dishes with a difference.

The ingredients used are as far as possible local products made and produced in Cumbria. The appendices include a food trail listing where these local products can be purchased, many by mail order so you can try these Cumbrian dishes anywhere in the British Isles.

We also have a selection of starters, simple vegetables dishes. some unusual sweet recipes and cakes and biscuits. This will enable the creative cook to compile a variety of menus for various occasions. We hope you all enjoy these recipes as much we have enjoyed creating and adapting them to use local produce.

THE HERDWICK STORY

Herdwick country, where this hardy breed survives on ancient sheep heafs, is the Lake District. The heart land is the jagged fells around Borrowdale and up over the steep, twisting inclines of Honister down into the Buttermere Valley where Herdwicks quietly munch on the lush, green pastures. Again we climb, surmounting the imposing heights of High Stile and Red Pike into the Ennerdale valley where the Herdwicks face the intruder with that inscrutable gaze. Steeple and Pillar guard the entrance down into Wasdale where the Herdwick still reigns supreme. The soft, rolling beauty of Eskdale and the Duddon Valley gently greet you, whilst the rugged fells of the Langdales and the picturesque charm of Ullswater tempt you to climb the Helvellyn range.

Here in the north west are England's highest mountains: a tough environment where generations of shepherds have nurtured and developed a breed of sheep able to live and flourish at three thousand feet even in the harsh Cumbrian winter. Nowadays some 150-200 farms still farm Herdwick sheep in large numbers. Many of them have flocks going back to time immemorial. A Mrs. Heelis once owned some of these farms. On her death she bequeathed them to the National Trust on condition that Herdwicks were bred on the farms. Mrs Heelis, more popularly known as Beatrix Potter, was a great champion of the breed. She often exhibited her sheep at local shows winning many of the top prizes and was for a time actively involved in The Herdwick Sheep Breeders' Association.

Thousand of years of selective sheep breeding have led to the wools that we know today. Wild sheep were probably originally domesticated to provide a source of meat, their skins being used as protective clothing and the bones being crafted into implements for domestic use. As fibre crafts developed, namely felting, spinning and weaving, man began to select and breed sheep with improved fleece specifically for that purpose. Over the past 8,000 years radical changes have occurred in the fleece.

Wild sheep, namely the Bighorn, related to their prehistoric cousins, still roam the western states of America. Moufflon can be found in Scandinavian countries and much nearer to home at the Otter Trust at Bowes, on the borders of Cumbria and Durham on the A66. The fleece of these sheep consists of coarse outer hairs and a fine short woolly undercoat. The hairy outer coat provides weatherproof protection from the harsh elements of the climate. The hair being very waterproof means the rain just sheds off the top of the outer coat, whilst the fine, woolly undercoat provides insulation.

With man's intervention the fibres of the fleece of the modern sheep have changed, the hairs becoming finer and the wool coarser and longer. Eventually the hairs were eliminated in many breeds leaving a soft crimpy fleece. Initially, wild sheep shed their coats in spring, but the fibres can also be "rooed" or plucked. Soay is a primitive sheep from St Kilda and their fleeces are still rooed. Wild sheep and primitive sheep are mainly brown in colour, a colour which gave them camouflage in their native surroundings.

Herdwicks through the Ages

SOME evidence suggests the Herdwick is related to the dual-coated breeds of Scandinavia such as the Old Norwegian. As you can see from the picture, there is a similarity between the Old Norwegian and the Herdwick. The Spaelsau, Icelandic and Faroes breeds are also believed to have their origins in this ancient breed. The Spaelsau is one of the most spectacular sheep to be found on the western coast of Norway and on the island of Froya. It is one of the most primitive breeds of domestic sheep in Europe. Interestingly, the Herdwick is born either black or very dark brown which perhaps points to his affinity with the wild sheep line, but then as he ages his coat turns to dark grey and becomes lighter with age.

There are two stories as to how Herdwicks came to inhabit Cumbria. One is that they survived a Spanish ship, wrecked off Ravenglass in the 16th century. The other is that in the 9th and 10th centuries, Norsemen brought them here. The latter seems more probable, given their ability to cope with the inclement Cumbrian weather. If they had come from warmer, sunnier climes they are unlikely to have survived. There is also widespread evidence of Norse settlement in Cumbria. This can be found in the local dialect and in place names such as Loweswater,"the leafy lake." This relates to a similar name given to a lake in Sweden, "Lovsjon," also meaning "leafy lake."

The Herdwick's grey face is the result of a gene controlling the blood pigment haemoglobin "A" that shows there is a relationship with the Scandinavian sheep. All have a common ancestry with the primitive, rare breed Soay sheep.

However, the Herdwick is different from Scandinavian breeds which have a long tail and the presence of two types of wool in the fleece. These are coarse in summer, but grow to fine wool in the winter. This seems to suggest that the Herdwick may at some time have been dual coated like the Norwegian breeds. The presence of black hairs suggests interbreeding with the Scottish Blackface somewhere along the way. Other evidence of a Scandinavian connection comes from the fact that we know Norsemen landed in Iceland and then moved to the Isle of Man. When they travelled, Scandinavian historical evidence states they took their sheep with them. In addition to this, Icelandic shepherding terms are the same as Cumbrian. The Isle of Man has an ancient four-horned breed of sheep the Manx Loghtan that is related to the Icelandic four-horned sheep.

The meat of the old Norwegian seems to be very similar to the Herdwick: "the meat from the old Norwegian has very little fat and the taste is more reminiscent of roe-deer or reindeer than mutton."

Herdwick meat is also quite unique and unlike that of any other English lamb. It has a strong, sweet, gamey flavour resembling venison. Both breeds of sheep seem to live in similar conditions, neither require much in the way of additional feeding and both play an important part in maintaining the landscape. In Cumbria the Herdwick feeds on the heather clad fells during the summer whilst for the old Norwegian: "heather is important for feeding and the best maintenance of the heath is careful grazing with old Norwegian sheep."[1]

However, many Herdwick farmers we have spoken to are convinced the Herdwick is indigenous to the area having developed from a primitive Iron Age breed. Other theories are that the Herdwick is a remnant of ancient Celtic breeds isolated in pockets around the British Isles. Such breeds include the Welsh Mountain and Cheviot.

Excavations at Vindolanda on Hadrian's Wall rather support the theory that there was an indigenous hairy sheep in the British Isles. Textiles made from a characteristic, hairy, Herdwick type wool have been found. It is possible the ancestors of the Herdwick were an Iron Age sheep bred by local tribes. The true origins of this monarch of the fells may never really be known; very possibly all theories apart from the Armada one may well have contributed to the present day Herdwick.

For centuries the Lake District was a wooded wilderness. As the population increased, areas of woodland were cleared for agricultural and industrial use. As early as the 12th century cleared areas were known as "herdwykes," derived from the Old Norse, meaning sheep farm. In the 17th century sheep farms in the Lake District were known as "herd-viks" and by the 18th century this name was being used to describe the sheep. An illustration from 1787 shows a sheep with a dark grey, hairy fleece and the characteristic grey/white face, referred to as the Herdwick.

Cloth made from Herdwick used to be called, "hodden grey", for instance Burns wrote:

What tho, on hamely fare we dine,
Wear Hodden Grey and a' that
Gie fools their skills and knaves their wine

[1] Trygve Fjarli, Norway
[1] Henry IV, Part 1

A man's a man for a' that.

Herdwick was referred to in the famous John Peel folk song, recounting the escapades of the Cumbrian huntsman:

D'ya ken John Peel with his coat so grey,

John Peel was a Cumbrian, born and bred in the attractive village of Caldbeck. His grave can be found in the church graveyard along with that of another Cumbrian legend, Mary of Buttermere.

Herdwick was also dyed, and known as "Kendal Green," a colour well known in Shakespeare's time: " three misbegotten knaves in Kendal Green"[1] Exactly what colour Kendal green was, is something of a puzzle. It was probably dyed first with a blue dye, possibly indigo or woad, then a yellow dye was added, one can surmise it was dyers-greenweed (Genista tinctoria) or dyer's-rocket (Reseda Luteola) both of which can be found in the Kendal area.

Both Kendal and Cockermouth were wool towns. Their economy was based on the spinning and weaving of worsted yarn and cloth, which was used for suiting, blankets and carpets. "Pannus Mihi Panis" - cloth is my bread - is the motto of Kendal which had eighty looms making Kidderminster carpets in 1822. One of the oldest Herdwick carpets can be seen in the library at Townend, a yeoman farmer's house at Troutbeck, Windermere. The carpet is reversible and is woven in a three-colour check pattern of red, dark grey and cream. The dark grey is believed to be Herdwick. It was woven in 1768 for the Browne family who were yeoman farmers in Troutbeck.

In addition there were many hand loom weavers meeting local demands. There was a thriving spinning and weaving business at Millbeck Farm in Great Langdale right up until the late 1920's. Caldbeck boasts one of the last hand loom weavers, Tom Sowerby, who died in 1938. There are still a few farmhouses where you can see the old spinning galleries. One is at Yew Tree farm in Coniston and there are two in the hamlet of Hartsop, near Brotherswater.

Through the centuries the Herdwick always seems to have held a special place in the hearts of the men who farmed them. Writing in 1878 to William Gates, editor of *The Shepherds' Guide,* William Abbot said: "There is not a breed anywhere in the world capable of taking the place of the Herdwick, a beautiful and useful animal; stands against rain, hail and snow, braves the strongest blasts that sweep over the northern hills. The hardy Herdwick always to the fore, ready to climb to the summits of the loftiest mountains and proudly look down on less exalted, less beautiful fellow creatures. It is by far the best and sweetest."

The same correspondent also said: "It is by far the best and sweetest meat to eat, fell bred mutton is always preferred by the aristocracy. The Herdwick is well formed and covered with good wool, eagerly sought after by local manufacturers."

The earliest description of a Herdwick is by G. Culley, 1794, who said: "The Herdwick breed have no horns, their faces and legs are speckled; but a greater portion of white, with a few black spots are accounted marks of the purest breed. They have fine, small, clean legs the wool short;

[1] Henry IV, Part 1

the fleeces from 2-2½ pounds. They have thick matted fleece of short wool, which though coarser than that of any other short-woolled sheep, is yet much finer than the wool of the black-faced heath breed."[1] This book also states that it seems fairly clear that the breed was at one time entirely hornless.

A description of 1837 also says they are polled and that the legs and faces are speckled [2] In 1849 T. Rowlandson states some of the rams have horns, but that the ewes should always be polled. William Dickinson writing in 1879 describes the Herdwick as possessing more characteristics of an original race than any other breed in the country and that they show, "no marks kindred with any other race." Again he states the majority are without horns with grey or mottled faces. He also describes the breed as having large manes and beards that suggests a similarity to the Old Norwegian and Spaelsau.

Herdwick fleece has a lot of "kemp," hair that gives it not only its characteristic, coarse quality, but makes it very waterproof. When the lambs are born, the fleece is black and then turns to brown and eventually, as the sheep matures, to varying shades of grey. It is the only breed to change its colour three times during its life span. It is this wonderful range of natural colours, the characteristic broad head and white face with its almost aristocratic, grey, Roman nose; the white, pricked-up ears and chunky legs covered with bristly hairs; the deep well-rounded body and that inscrutable Herdwick gaze, that once encountered captivates you forever.

In the aftermath of the foot and mouth disease outbreak in Cumbria in 2001 it was estimated that 40% of the breed was slaughtered whilst being wintered away from the fells. The loss of this unique breed, so important to the maintenance of the Cumbrian environment, could have been catastrophic. The Herdwick is remarkable in that it is territorial, it has the tendency to heft i.e. to stay in one small area and not wander away. The ewes teach their young to heft and little shepherding is necessary to keep the flock in one area. This hefting instinct is so predominant that young lambs are capable of finding their mothers on the open fell even after being separated for the winter. The hefting instinct is so deeply rooted that Herdwicks don't get lost on the fells. Stories abound of homesick Herdwick ewes making their way back to their place of birth. No distance or obstacles prevent them from achieving their goal.

One story tells of a Herdwick ewe bred at Wasdale and sold in October to a farmer at Caldbeck; within six months she had found her way back home to Wasdale. Another account is from a constable on night duty in Bowness. He saw more than a dozen Herdwicks resolutely making their way through the darkened streets. It seems they were on their back from north Lancashire to the Kirkstone Pass fells where sure enough they were eventually located.

Almost equal to their homing instinct are the tales of their hardiness. Perhaps the most amazing being the one from the county historian Hutchinson, who in 1785, records Herdwicks surviving being buried in snow for fifty days. Despite being recovered blind and having eaten their coats, these sheep became as healthy as the rest of the flock. These combined abilities, of

[1]*Herdwicks Past and Present, A History of The Breed* by R. Lamb.

[2]William Youatt

hefting and survival in extreme conditions in England's harshest weather make this breed irreplaceable.

If the flocks on the fells do get mixed the farmers are able to recognise their sheep by "sheep marks." The sheep are marked in two ways. One with a "lug" mark on the ear, in which a piece of the ear is removed. This shows who the owner of the sheep is. The other is a "smit" mark on the fleece. Smit is a coloured marking fluid. In former times red ruddle obtained from hematite ore mixed with grease or whale oil was used. These marks are then recorded in a shepherds' guide.

The sheep are gathered off the fells four or five times during the course of the year. They have to be dipped or sprayed once a year. Until 1905 when compulsory sheep dipping was introduced the sheep were dipped and washed in deep pools. They were first gathered into the wash fold by the edge of a beck and then "persuaded" into the water where they were dunked and washed.

They then swam to the opposite bank and scrambled out. Later the process of dipping in a sheep dip with a chemical dip was used to ensure the sheep was protected from blowfly and scab. Nowadays, many sheep are sprayed rather than dipped and there is also an injection available.

In July the sheep are gathered off the fells for shearing. Hand shearing was a communal activity where farmers would get together and help each other during shearing time. The farmers would sit astride slatted stools or creels; the sheep upended in front of them. Today most farmers use electric shears though some still do hand clipping. Nowadays, shearing is sometimes put out to a contract shearer who goes round the various farms. After shearing the sheep are re-smitted and returned to the fells.

In November the tups (rams) are put to the ewes. Traditionally, tups were hired at the Autumn tup fairs and kept by the farmer for the winter and returned to the owner in May. Nowadays, most farmers have their own tups. At the local shows you will see these magnificent tups dressed with red colouring to make them more attractive. The tups are also coloured when they are running with the ewes so the farmer knows which ewes have been served by the tup.

Herdwicks are smaller than the average sheep. If a young Herdwick ewe lambs before her third birthday she can die or her growth will be poor and stunted so a form of contraception is used. A "twinter" is a sheep coming up to her second birthday.

Bratting or clouting protects the young ewe from the tup. Brat is the local dialect for apron made from a piece of heavy cloth. A piece of brat or clout is sewn over the rear ends of the twinters from mid November until February.

The mature sheep are returned to the fells for the winter. In previous times, ash and holly trees were pollarded about every twelve years ie., the branches were trimmed off at the top of the trunk and left on the ground for sheep to feed off. The sheep were then able to supplement their sparse diet. Nowadays, food supplements such as hay, silage, sheep cake (a concentrate of vitamin and protein supplements) are put out for them. The young sheep or hoggs are wintered on the lowlands; partly to rest the fells, but mainly to improve their growth.

Gathering again takes place in March when the sheep are brought down to the intakes ready for lambing which starts round the middle of April through until the middle of May. At the end of May the ewes with their lambs are returned to the fells until July when they are brought down again for shearing.

The Herdwick Year[1]

November

Tups, (rams) are allowed to run with the ewes on the in-bye (the valley bottom).

December

Around Christmas the ewes are returned to the fell where they stay, usually without any supplementary feed until April.

April/May

Ewes lamb on the in-bye. Ewes with single lambs go back to the fell in May. Ewes with twin lambs stay on the in-bye until after clipping time.

July/August

Clipping time when all sheep are sheared starting with the geld sheep, (sheep without lambs).

September

Lambs are weaned from their mothers and ewes are returned to the fells until tupping (mating). Those too old to go back onto the fells are either kept on the low ground for further breeding with a crossing tup, ie., Texel, Suffolk or a Cheviot, or sold on to a lowland farmer for the same purpose.

October

Wethers (castrated male lambs) are sold to lowland farmers to fatten or kept on their own farms for fattening.

November

The year has come full circle. Gimmer lambs (female lambs) the breeding stock for the future are sent away to lowland farms. They return in the spring and are put on the fells to find their heaf where as lambs they suckled their mothers and where they in turn will rear their own lambs.

[1]This information is from Geoff Brown, Herdwick Sheep Breeders' Association

CUMBRIAN COOKERY

Food from the fells

Some of the best food in Cumbria must surely come from the fells, the prime product being Herdwick meat. There are numerous speciality food producers in Cumbria. Some produce homemade preserves picked fresh from the hedgerows, whilst others brew their own beer, damson gin and wine. Cumberland honey has a wonderful, fruity taste and is a fine accompaniment to some of our Herdwick recipes. In some parts of the county hand-made raised pies are still produced together with homemade Cumberland sausage and smoked Herdwick.

Cumbrian cheeses are well to the fore and are used in many of our recipes. The local dry cured and air-dried ham with its unique traditional flavour and texture is a versatile product and can be used on a menu in many ways. The bacon produced in the region tastes like bacon used to taste! As for fish what better than that tasty Cumbrian delicacy, Arctic trout more commonly known as char, or a tasty piece of Borrowdale trout or salmon. Most of the products used in the recipes can be ordered by mail order and delivered any where in the British Isles. Some producers also mail order their products abroad.[1]

Historical Background of Cumbrian Cookery
CUMBRIAN cooking can best be described as simple, plain and wholesome. Mrs. Beeton praised the inhabitants of Cumberland and Westmorland for their pies and puddings. We live near the village of Lamplugh which boasts a very famous pudding namely Lamplugh Pudding.[2] This was specially made for farmers working all hours in the long, dark winters and particularly at lambing time. According to a rhyme it was also a traditional Christmas dish:

> *They feast on rost beef, and on raised guess pyes,*
> *And giblet, and mincepie and sweet,*
> *And many good things- Lamplugh puddin, for the bye,*
> *Smooks on a broad teable that neet*[3]

Another popular Cumbrian dish served traditionally on Good Friday was Fig Sue.[4] This was eaten before the main meal of fish. Carling peas were also served on Carling Sunday or the fifth Sunday of Lent. These were brown peas soaked overnight and then fried in butter. No doubt a welcome respite from the rigours of fasting!

The dishes of this area are filling and substantial, very necessary to satisfy a population working outdoors in the crisp, cold air of the high fells of northern England. For centuries Herdwick was the main source of meat for local people. In autumn, surplus stock was killed, salted and cured to provide food for the long winter ahead. Cumbria has many centuries old recipes for mutton hams (cured legs of mutton). A typical recipe would be, a stock made from water, salt, peppercorns, lemon rind, bay leaves, thyme, juniper berries and butter was put on to simmer for an hour. Meanwhile the mutton had brown sugar rubbed into it and was left for a minimum of twelve hours. The stock was cooked and left to become cold. Then the mutton was placed in the stock and left for at least three weeks. It was then removed, dried and often smoked. Alternatively

[1]See the food trail at the end of the book for details.

[2]*Lakeland Recipes Old and New,* Joan Poulson, see page 152

[3]from a verse referring to Christmas in Cumbria, *Memorandum of Old Times,* 1875.

[4]see page 102

it was wrapped in muslin and hung to dry until required.[1]

In *Rambles In The Lake Country,* 1861, Edwin Waugh mentions he was walking in the Duddon Valley area near Cockley Beck when he came upon a remote farmhouse. He was invited in and he describes how: "smoky rafters were hung with hams and shrunken legs of cured mutton; and on a long shelf near the ceiling there were little cheeses, dried herbs, staves, jars and a tattered book or two." He later experienced first-hand Cumbrian hospitality that has been handed down through the generations.

On returning from a walk to Hardknott Castle to the farmhouse where he was staying he describes homemade Cumbrian fare. On entering the house he found: "candles were burning inside; clouds were gathering gloomily; and it began to rain, a white cloth was on the table, and a bright wood fire filled the room with ruddy light. The good wife spread our board with ham and eggs, white bread and spice cakes; cheese preserves, strong tea and cream - such as cities seldom get to see."[2] Quite an advertisement for locally produced food, both then and now.

A late 19th century recipe for broth uses a sheep's head boiled in salted water, thyme, barley and vegetables and in 1888 Sir Henry Thompson wrote: "The Englishman loves the flavour of three to four year old mutton."[3]

More recently Herdwick mutton was served at the Coronation of Queen Elizabeth II in 1953. Beef was often roasted and the fat from it when set was known as "jelly dripping." The juices from the meat formed a jelly under the layer of fat. This was spread on bread and lightly seasoned with salt.

Large areas in the Lake District used to be deer parks including parts of Ennerdale and Ullswater and as such venison was highly prized. In 1542 Andrew Boorde wrote: "I am sure it is a lord's dish, and I am sure it is good for an Englishman for it doth animate him to be as he is, which is strong and hardy…"

Venison is a traditional Lakeland dish and always served with red cabbage. Like all wild meat, venison is very lean and needs barding, ie., thin slices of pork fat placed over the joint. It also requires marinading to make it tender and to add moisture.[4]

Being an island, fish has been a staple food for the British since prehistoric times. Religious customs have also played an important part in influencing our diet. During the middle ages there were many fast days so fish became an important part of the Englishman's diet. The 16th century book, *The Good House-wives Treasure* has a recipe for fish, which includes rosemary, parsley, mace and prunes simmered in a stock made from water, vinegar and crab apple juice. From the Elizabethan era fish and meat were preserved in jars and sealed with clarified butter to make them airtight.

Here in Cumbria, awash with lakes, rivers and tarns fresh fish such as salmon and brown trout have always been available, although surprisingly, it was not a main stay of the Cumbrian diet. However, a less well-known fish, related to the salmon family, the char has always been popular, though for many years it has been very rare, and

---

[1] For a Cumberland ham recipe please see page 131

[2] *Lakeland Recipes Old and New* by Joan Poulson

[3] For a modern take on Herdwick broth see our recipe on page 100

[4] See recipe on page 133

was found mainly in the lakes of Windermere and Coniston. Recipes for char pies date back to the 17th century. One such recipe, that is reminiscent of a paté, is to season the fish with salt, pepper, cloves nutmeg and mace. Place in a dish, cover and steam for two hours, then carefully remove the skin and bones. It can then be left whole in the pot and covered with clarified butter or mashed and beaten to almost a paste and covered with the butter.

With the advent of the tourist industry in the 18th century potted char became really popular. In 1738 the Duke of Montague wrote to a Mr Atkinson of Dalton near Ulverston: "I received ...the pot of char which you sent... It was the best I ever ate."

The char pots, with their hand-painted designs of fish on them, became collector's items. The demand for potted char went out of fashion for a while but is now making a comeback and can be found in some speciality shops in the area.

Perhaps the most famous food of the north west is the Cumberland sausage. Traditionally it is a long, meaty, rope coil, several feet long. It consists of minced pork strongly flavoured with herbs such as rosemary, thyme and sage and spices. Many butchers in the region boast their sausages are in excess of 90% meat. Sausages were made by the Romans and contained a variety of herbs and spices including parsley, savoury rue, peppercorns and cumin. A number of sausage recipes have been recorded in the *Roman Cookery Book of Apicius* where you can also find a recipe resembling the north west's famous black pudding and a reference to: "That blood sausage I sent you at mid–winter, arrived at my house before the seven days of Saturn."[1]

It is very probable that the Romans brought these meat dishes, among others, to England during their occupation. Nowadays, Herdwick sausages are being produced along the lines of the Cumberland sausage and are extremely tasty particularly when coated with a crunchy mustard and Cumberland honey. Excellent accompaniments are a fruity braised red cabbage, apple sauce or fritters.[2]

Easterledge or Spring Pudding was served during springtime. Before the 19th century there were few fresh vegetables in the diet and, until well into the 20th century, there was a shortage of fresh green vegetables during the winter. The winter diet of oatmeal, dried or smoked mutton and beef led to a lack of vitamins in the diet. With the advent of spring and the abundance of fresh, wild, green leaves in the hedgerows Cumbrian housewives would prepare a herb or Easterledge pudding. Easterledges were the leaves of the bistort, hence the fashion for savoury herb puddings in the north of England. Leaves traditionally used were nettles, dandelion, sorrel, and sweet dock leaves. In the days when the value of wild plants was recognised, it was believed to clear the blood.[3]

One of my grandmothers came from Yorkshire and I can remember her making a herb pudding that she would serve with a white sauce sometimes adding chopped bacon. Perhaps it originated from the Easterledge type pudding.

Cumberland Sweet pie is a traditional dish that used to be prepared in the Lakeland area, the

[1] Martial 14.72., *Apicius*, John Edwards

[2] For more ideas, see our recipes for Toad-in-the-Hole with mustard and honey, page 122; Braised Red Cabbage recipe, page 135; Cumberland Sausage recipe, page 133 and recipe for Herdwick sausage meat on page 112

[3] For recipes for Easterledge Pudding see page 143 (*In Search of Food* by Richard Mabey) and Nettle Haggis, see page 143 (*Lakeland Recipes Old and New* by Joan Poulson).

main ingredient being the sweet meat of the Herdwick. This dish is the original sweet mincemeat used at Christmas time. It can be made in two ways. If you want to store it you mince and mix all the ingredients namely, minced mutton, dried fruit, brown sugar, spices, mixed peel and lemon juice with rum, place into raised pie cases and bake. They will keep for several months. When times were hard only the fat of the meat was used. Nowadays, we still have suet in our sweet mincemeat, a remnant of the old recipe. For use straight away, you could use mutton chops instead of the minced meat. Place all the ingredients in a pie dish and cover with puff pastry and bake.[1]

Cumberland Tatie Pot is to the Cumbrians what Haggis is to the Scots! It has been popular in Cumbria for almost two hundred years, with both Westmorland and Cumberland laying claims to it. It is very similar to a Lancashire Hot Pot, but with the addition of black pudding and a variety of vegetables. The best meat to use is Herdwick because of its strong flavour. It requires long, slow cooking.[2]

Lowland Cumbria had reasonable conditions for producing grains. For centuries oatmeal was the mainstay of the diet in the north as wheat was too expensive to buy. Introduced into the north by the Romans, it was one of the few crops able to survive the cold, wet weather of the northern fells. Here it was made into clap or "Havver" bread. The word havver comes from the Old Norse "hafrar" meaning oats. Celia Fiennes visiting Kendal in 1698 watched the making of this bread and said: "they clap it round, ...till thin as paper... and still they clap it...the same size as their clap board...it will bake and be as crisp and pleasant as anything you can imagine." Clap bread was the basis of the Lakeland diet well into the 19th century.[3]

Oatmeal was often made into "poddish" or porridge made with water and served with treacle, milk and butter. Kendal "piggin" bottoms were made from oatmeal. These were snaps stamped out of the dough with the iron rim of the base of a "piggin" or small wooden tub. The main ingredient of the morning and evening meals was oatmeal. In 1852 William Dickinson wrote: "a great quantity of oats is ground into meal ...and constitutes the breakfast and supper of the chief part of farm households in this county."[4]

Yet another traditional bread roll of the area is known as a "whig." Hawkshead has a special association with them. A recipe for Hawkshead whigs dating back to 1710 gives the ingredients and method as: "a quarter peck of fine flour, 3lb of butter, rubbed in fine, $\frac{1}{2}$lb of sugar, half a nutmeg, half a race of ginger, three eggs. Beat well and put to half a pint of yeast and three spoonfuls of sack. Make a hole in the flour and pour in with as much milk, (just warm) as will make a light paste. Let it stand before the fire to rise for an half an hour. Then make into a dozen whigs and brush them over with egg. Put into a quick oven and bake for an hour."[5]

William Wordsworth went to school in Hawkshead and no doubt enjoyed Hawkshead Whigs whilst he was boarding in the village with Mrs Anne Tyson.[6]

Rum and spices have played an important role

[1] see page 134 for recipe

[2] You will find the recipe on page 127

[3] See recipe on page 159

[4] *Lake District Life and Traditions* by William Rollinson

[5] from an article on traditional Lakeland recipes, *Cumbria Magazine*.

[6] *Lakeland Recipes Old and New* by Joan Poulson, for recipe see page 162

throughout Cumberland in its dishes, folklore and customs. The port of Whitehaven is the reason why and today you can visit the excellent visitor attraction, "The Rum Story," to find out more about the connection. Suffice it to say that during the 18th century Whitehaven was one of the most important ports in the U.K.

With the increased demand for sugar and rum, traders were involved in the slave trade and returned home laden with rum, sugar and spices. A statement of harbour dues for Whitehaven in 1828 lists among other things, molasses, mace, mustard, nutmegs, coriander, pepper and turmeric. This perhaps explains why many of the old recipes of the area contain spices, for instance, Westmorland Pepper Cake. Allspice was originally used in this cake which has the combined flavour of clove, nutmeg and cinnamon.[1]

A recipe steeped in rum and Cumbrian tradition is Rum Dog served to both dog and man after an exciting hound trailing event with the hounds receiving the better recipe in my opinion! Hound trailing, not to be confused with fox hunting, is a very popular sport in Cumbria and rivals that of Cumberland wrestling in its popularity. A trail of aniseed is laid over fell, valley, mountain and scree.

We've watched hound trailing and the hounds are totally committed to the scent, ignoring all other distractions including other dogs and sheep. Trailing hounds are not fox hounds. They have been bred for speed rather than stamina and are lighter and faster than the fox hound. They can average speeds of up to 20 miles an hour over the rugged Cumbrian countryside. The success of these dogs is said to lie in their diet which is a closely guarded secret. However, tradition has it that after a race they are fed a pudding called "cock-loaf" consisting of raisins soaked in port and sherry, mixed with flour and eggs, which is then cooked like a pudding, sliced and toasted and served up to the dogs!

The owners have a similar, but less rich, fare of raisins soaked in rum mixed with flour, suet and water that is then steamed. This sounds very much like a pudding from childhood, spotted dog or spotted dick, named perhaps because the raisins resemble the coloured patches on a dog. Perhaps the origin of our favourite childhood pudding was Cumbrian.[2]

Rum turns up in another sweet recipe, Cumberland Rum Nicky an old sweet dish traditional to the area and sometimes known as Westmorland Sweetbake. These are similar to mince pies.[3]

As the trade between the West Cumbrian ports, especially Whitehaven and the West Indies, increased during the 18th century, commodities such as rum, Barbados sugar, ginger, pepper and treacle gradually became an intrinsic part of the culinary heritage of Cumberland and Westmorland. The main link seems to have been with the slave trade: the ships from Whitehaven running a triangular route first to the African coast picking up slaves to take to the Caribbean and the American Colonies and then returning to England laden with spices.

Ginger is a common ingredient in old Cumbrian recipes. The famous Grasmere Gingerbread recipe is a closely guarded family secret. In 1855

[1] We have used these spices in the recipe which you will find on page 155

[2] See recipe on page 153

[3] You will find a recipe on page 152

Sarah Nelson started baking ginger bread for the chef of a large house nearby. Soon her recipe was much in demand. Being a shrewd lady, and realising the business potential of her cooking skills she patented the recipe. After her death it was stored in the vaults of the local bank until the present owners bought it. Even they didn't know what they'd bought until they copied out the notes from that precious piece of scrap paper!

Sarah Nelson's Gingerbread seems to us to be more like a shortbread, but very tasty. Gingerbread was originally made using bread crumbs mixed with honey and spices including pepper, ginger and cinnamon. Saffron was often added for colouring. It was then moulded into shape and decorated with cloves. Gradually treacle gained precedence as the main sweetener in Gingerbread and on porridge.[1]

Rum butter is especially popular in Lakeland cooking and has an interesting social history. There is a story saying it was first made by smugglers hiding from excise men in caves at Parton (there are no caves there now). They hid in the caves for some weeks existing on the only food they had - rum, Barbados sugar and butter - which they mixed together to form a sweet buttery paste.

Whatever the origin rum has long played an important part at christening ceremonies. The new born baby's head would have been doused with rum, an effective antiseptic ready to hand in the Cumbrian household The local midwife, after attending to the birth of the new baby, would often prepare the christening feast. Spiced ale and "groaning" cheese, fingers of cheese,

aptly named after the pangs of childbirth, were handed round to all the unmarried women to place under their pillows! Then oat cakes and a large bowl of rum butter, made from butter, Barbados sugar, rum and nutmeg was passed round as a special treat, but especially for the new mother to speed her recovery. I wonder if she knew that nutmeg is said to be an aphrodisiac! The ingredients of rum butter were believed to represent life; sugar for its sweetness, butter for its goodness, nutmeg its spice and rum its richness. All the family and friends would partake of this delicacy. but the dish was never completely finished. Guests would then leave some money in the dish to ensure the baby had plenty for the future.[2]

Perhaps one of the oldest dishes served in Cumbria within living memory is Frumenty. In *Antient Mynstrals Sollem Song,* 1575, it is described as: "A boll of furmenty and in the midst of it sticking a dozen of horn spoons in a bunch as the instruments meetest to eat furmenty porage with."

Frumenty is basically a hot gruel made from new wheat. It was the breakfast or supper dish for the rural population for many centuries. The new wheat was shelled and then cooked very slowly in milk; then it was flavoured and sweetened. In Elizabethan times it was often served on Christmas Eve with the addition of egg yolks, spices and dried fruits.[3]

[1] See page 155 for our Gingerbread recipe based on ingredients used in the past.

[2] See recipe page 162

[3] For a typical Frumenty recipe, see page 162

Buttermere

BUTTERMERE VALLEY

Buttermere Valley is a glacial formation, its lowlands verdant green, as smooth as soft velvet encircled by majestic, rocky turrets. The valley is flanked on the west side by the imposing heights of High Crag, High Stile and Red Pike which wind their way onto Grey Knott and Wainwright's favourite, the craggy, magical buttresses of Haystacks; whilst Mellbreak, solitary and sphinx-like, towers out of the landscape at the north end on the west side of the valley. On the east, the grandeur of Robinson curves down onto High Snockrigg, and the lower sheep tracks of Buttermere Moss. Then, slowly they creep up to the narrow, rugged ridge of Whiteless Pike eventually snaking their way up on to the stately, broad summit of Grasmoor and Whiteside Pike. At the southern end stands Fleetwith Pike, with its giant-like arm sweeping down into the lake.

A white cross poses starkly on its lower inclines commemorating the memory of an eighteen-year-old servant girl, Fanny Mercer, who fell to her death on 8 September 1887. She was a servant of the master of Rugby School and accompanied the family to the Lakes for their summer vacation where they stayed at Wood House in Buttermere. Whilst out walking with the family she tripped whilst descending the steep slopes of Fleetwith and fell to her death.

Two passes guard the entrance to the Valley. Newlands Pass, with untamed, steep-sided fells and boisterous becks tumbling down to the narrow road which twists its way up, over and down into the tranquil Newlands valley. Honister Pass the wilder, more tortuous ascent slowly worms its way upwards between towering, grey slate pinnacles to the greeny-grey slate quarries. The descent is sheer, with vertical zig-zags down into the jaws of Borrowdale.

The area is blessed with three lakes. Buttermere, two and a quarter kilometres and about three quarters of a kilometre wide, which is almost oval in shape. This lake is believed to be named after the Norse warrior Boethar who fought with the English against the Normans at the Battle of Rannerdale: the name also means "dairy pasture lake." Trout and Arctic char can be found in the lake. It is bordered on one side by Burtness Wood, with a meandering footpath along the lake side giving stupendous views. Once through the gate you are out onto the open fell with the call of the wild beckoning you up the "yellow brick road" to Haystacks and over and beyond and down into the wild untamed beauty of Ennerdale. On a summer's day soft, fronded ferns, and the brilliant green foliage of bilberries fringe the roadside. In autumn a carpet of crisp, russet brown creeps up onto the pink and grey scree-scarred slopes often wreathed in soft, gentle mists.

The road curves its way past farms that go back to time immemorial. Gatesgarth farm, nestling at the foot of Fleetwith Pike, a couple of barns, dark and foreboding alongside the brilliantly white-washed farm house is on the site of what is believed to have been a mediaeval "vaccary" (dairy farm). The vaccary would have included all of the head of the valley, which is why there are no other farms or settlements here. Buttermere village lies between Buttermere and

Crummock Water. At one time the fields beyond the village were submerged. Over time rock and silt deposits from Sour Milk Gill and Sail Beck have created rich grazing pastures between the two lakes. Many assume that Buttermere and Crummock Water were at one time one lake. However, contrary to this belief, there have always been two separate lakes. They are separated by a rock bench that has deposits of boulder clay on it which is the reason for the rich fertile soil. If there had been one lake at some time there would be evidence of a higher shore line.

As you enter the village from Newlands Pass, a Celtic-looking church with a bell tower catches your eye. A diminutive building in pinky-brown stone, it perches impressively on a rocky outcrop at the entrance to the village. Churches built on rock had no graveyard so corpses had to be transported several miles to Loweswater or Lorton for burial. Corpse Roads came into existence for this purpose and can be found throughout the Lakes. One runs along the top of Loweswater and is incidentally a beautiful walk in all seasons. You can make it a circular walk to include Holme Wood.

The village boasts two hotels and four farms. The Fish Hotel, famous for its connection with Mary Robinson, the Beauty of Buttermere, stands at the end of the village. It is a white-washed, flower bedecked building which looks out onto the heights of Red Pike. The Bridge Hotel, once a corn mill, the original edifice impressive in dark, horizontal slabs of Lakeland slate, has now been extended to include self-catering facilities. A lively beck skips past the hotels and a pet Herdwick sheep, sporting a Mohican haircut after shearing, chomps away on the grass verges opposite the Croft House Farm Café.

Crummock Water, Crombocwater or, "crooked lake," derives its name from the river Cocker that flows from the lake; Cocker is from the Old Norse "krokr" meaning crooked. It is the largest of the three lakes in the area, four kilometres by one kilometre wide. From Wood House the Victorians used to take a boat trip across Crummock Water. Landing on the opposite shore near the remains of an old settlement of Norse/Irish farmers and fishermen, they would walk up past old iron mines to Scale Force, at 50m the highest waterfall in the district.

Guarding the entrance to Buttermere village from the north like some prehistoric monsters, are the knobbly protuberances of Rannerdale Knott. Rannerdale Farm is all that remains of the medieval hamlet of Rannerdale that once had its own chapel. By the 18th century the hamlet was uninhabited and today all that remains is a pile of stones in the secret valley. At Lanthwaite Green, below the craggy heights of Whin Ben, are the vestiges of a Romano-British settlement. Here a community made a living from the land.

Cinderdale, situated between Lanthwaite Green and Rannerdale, takes its name from the past industry of smelting iron ore, mined from the surrounding fells. The depressions in the ground are the remains of the pit steads (charcoal burners) and bloomeries (a furnace used for melting iron). The earth is black and covered with cinders, remnants of past industrial activity.

Wrynose Pass

The Secret Valley

SOME say the author Nicholas Size is the only person to be buried in Buttermere. His grave is marked by a small clump of wind swept trees on the fell side above the church. Nicholas Size was a writer and also owned the Bridge Hotel in the 1930's. He is best remembered for his work, *The Secret Valley*, which is the story of the Battle of Rannerdale fought between the local inhabitants and the Normans and the Saxons who wanted to take over the land. The Cumbrians asked the Norwegian commander, Olaf Tryggvesson, for his advice on how to defend their territory. On surveying the area from Great Gable, he could see the valley was a natural stronghold. The mountain passes were easy to defend in the event of any attack so he built stockades at the far end of Crummock Water. These were to be used as store houses in readiness for any assault.

A century later Earl Boethar was the Cumbrian leader and an experienced warrior well versed in warfare against the Normans. The Normans had little expertise in mountain warfare and were no match for the local farmers and shepherds brought up in the hills. The Norman leader, Ranulf Meschin, gained an overwhelming victory at Brackenthwaite, albeit at a price. Many Normans were slaughtered and five burial grounds were dug to bury the victims. This battle is remembered by the burial grounds in the area namely Palace How, Cornhow, Pickett How, Turner How and Brackenthwaite How.

Ranulf Meschin then made the fatal decision to continue the attack up into the valley of Rannerdale, but Boethar had anticipated his move and altered the route to the valley directing it up into the narrow pass of Rannerdale bordered on either side by high, rugged crags. Here the Cumbrians lay quietly in wait for their enemy. Once the Normans were well into the Secret Valley the Cumbrians struck and poured down the rocky heights and slaughtered the Normans. In springtime the Secret Valley is ablaze with bluebells said to be the result of all the Norman blue blood lost in the Battle of Rannerdale. Strangely enough bluebells do not grow anywhere else in this valley.

Boethar's brother Ackin was killed in the battle and his body was buried in the chapel of the Blessed Mary Magdalane in the old village of Rannerdale. His body was then moved to Newlands Valley and buried on what is now Aicken Knot.

A story with a different flavour is that of Mary Robinson, the Maid of Buttermere 1779-1837. She was the daughter of the landlord of the Fish Inn, Buttermere. Captain Joseph Budworth of London first saw her whilst he was staying at the Fish Inn. His first glimpse of her was seeing her spinning in the kitchen with her mother.

He was so impressed by the beauty of this fifteen-year-old that he wrote about her in his book, *A Fortnight's Ramble To The Lakes*. This quickly brought visitors to the area including the Lake Poets. Wordsworth who wrote of her story in *The Prelude, Book VII*, refers to her: "modest mien and carriage, marked by unexampled grace." Southey, Coleridge and de Quincey were also tempted to visit and subsequently wrote about her.

Mary's fame led her to become the victim of an unscrupulous fraudster and bigamist namely

John Hatfield. Under the false identity of Alexander Augustus Hope, brother of the Earl of Hopetoun, he booked into the Queen's Hotel in Keswick in July 1802 and then sought out Mary, courted her and eventually married her at Lorton Church on 2 October 1802. Little did anyone realise that, not only was he a bigamist, having a wife and two children in Tiverton and he had also promised to marry a lady in Keswick, but also he was a forger. Their wedding was publicised in newspapers country wide and his debtors were soon alerted as to his whereabouts. He was arrested and sentenced to death for forgery and was publicly hanged at Carlisle on Saturday, 3 September 1803.

By this time Mary was expecting a child by him; it is believed the child was either stillborn or died at birth as there is no record of it in local registers. She went back to live with her parents and is said to have eventually got over the tragic affair. Novels and melodramas were produced during the 19th century and in our own time Melvyn Bragg has written *The Maid of Buttermere*. As to what became of Mary; the story has a happy ending. At the age of 30 she met a local farmer Richard Harrison of some substantial means. They were married at Brigham in 1808 and went to Richard's family farm of Todcrofts, Caldbeck. They had seven children, although two died in childhood. Their descendants are scattered over Cumbria, Australia and New Zealand. In Caldbeck churchyard is a gravestone commemorating Richard, Mary, four of their children and one grandchild.

Loweswater, which means the leafy lake in Old Norse, is one and a half kilometres long and half a kilometre wide. It is strictly speaking not in the Buttermere Valley, but because of its proximity to the others it has been included. Take care when driving along this thickly wooded lake, as red squirrels can often be seen scampering nimbly along the tarmac, darting desperately into the hedgerows seeking refuge from the traffic. Incidentally, red squirrels don't hibernate, so be careful at all times of the year!

Loweswater is frequently swathed in gentle mists at lake level with the trees of Holme Wood floating mysteriously above like an Arthurian Camelot. Holme Wood is a rich woodland containing a variety of trees, a waterfall, Holme Force and a network of footpaths. The small building by the lake side used to be a fish hatchery and is now used as a bothy. When the wood was replanted in 1937 it was designed to resemble the shape of a pheasant. This can be best appreciated in autumn from Darling Fell on the opposite side of the lake when the trees are resplendent in golds and red-russets.

Farmers' Viewpoint

DAVID and Lana Norman are National Trust tenant farmers. David has worked on farms ever since he was a lad. He attended Newton Rigg College, then went to Mungrisedale as a shepherd. The Normans farmed at Cragg Farm, Buttermere for ten years and then moved to Kirkhouse farm at Isel, just outside Cockermouth, where they have been for three and a half years. On 23 April 2001 one of their cattle was found to have foot and mouth, possibly contracted from deer in the woodland nearby. Over 1000 ewes and more than 1000 lambs were slaughtered.

Crummock Water and inset, Shepherd's Pie

Langdale and Old Norwegian sheep inset

David and Lana are now looking ahead to the future and have plans for diversification. They are stocking with a diverse range of sheep including Herdwick which they intend to market. David and Lana see traceability of meat as a key issue in meat production as the public become more aware of the issues involved. They have earmarked some of their barns to be converted into affordable workshop space for local crafts people. Here the public will be able to visit and see craftsmen and women at work. One barn has already been allocated to an interior designer.

A Walk in the Buttermere Valley

Start and Finish: *Scale Hill, Lanthwaite Wood, National Trust car park*
Distance: *12 kms*
Time: *4-5 hours*
Grid ref: *149215*
Map: *OS Outdoor Leisure Sheet 4*

This walk takes you through picturesque woodlands, the lower fells alongside Crummock Water and through the Secret Valley of Rannerdale to the slopes of Whiteless Breast: returning with views across Crummock Water to Mellbreak, Red Pike and High Stile.

Leave the car park by the gate at the far end and follow the lower track, which leads to the lake shore. Pause for the views across the lake to the surrounding fells. Leave the lake shore by the path to the left and continue along the hard track above the lake to reach the boat-house on the right. Follow the lake path to a stile. Go over the stile and follow the path through a private wood. Continue on this path just above the lake.

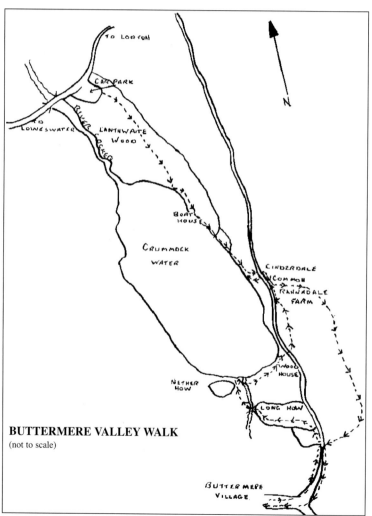

BUTTERMERE VALLEY WALK
(not to scale)

To your left you will see your first views of Grasmoor. Follow the path along the lake until you come to a stone wall. Follow the steps up the path to the kissing gate in the corner of the field. Cross the road and turn right. Walk towards the parking areas on the left side of the road to Cinderdale Common. Cross the beck by the road and turn left to follow the path up between the wall and the beck to meet a definite track going off to the right.

Pause and admire the grandeur of the surrounding fells and if you're lucky, the reflections on the lake. The track continues round the side of the fell and through a gate. Start to look for a wooden footbridge down to your right, the first on your OS map. Cross over the bridge and turn left to go through the gate in the wall. Turn left and follow the definite path that climbs steadily to the top of the valley. To your right are the craggy slopes of Low Bank dotted with grazing fell sheep, to your left the steep flanks of Whiteless Pike.

Take time to look back and admire the distant mountains of Dumfries and Galloway across the Solway. When you reach the top of the valley, it is an ideal spot to have a break and soak in the views of the three lakes. To the left you have your first impression of Buttermere backed by the surrounding fells of Haystacks and High Stile. Below, and nestling between Buttermere and Crummock water is Buttermere Village surrounded by a patchwork of green fields and hedgerows with Sourmilk Gill tumbling down from Bleabury Tarn below Red Pike.

To descend to Buttermere village, take one of the many grassy paths visible between the bracken. Take care, as the grass can be very slippery if damp under foot. When you reach the road, turn left to go into the village where refreshments are available at the hotels or the café.

Leave the village turning left at the Bridge Hotel and walk up the hill to the car park on your left. Enter the car park and turn right to the kissing gate in the corner. Go through the gate into Long How Wood. Follow the path through this ancient wood until you come to a footbridge over the beck. Cross the bridge, go over the stile and turn right. Follow the fence to the small woodland of Nether How. Continue down the path to the kissing gate on the right. Go through the kissing gate and follow the path across the field with views down the lake to the distant fells of Loweswater.

Go through the next kissing gate and turn left skirting Wood House on your right. Follow the path until you reach the road. Cross over the road and bearing left, follow the ascending path of Low Bank up onto the lower slopes of Rannerdale Knott. Take the descending path down to the road. Turn right when you reach the road and walk along the road past Rannerdale farm and Rannerdale Cottage to Cinderdale Common. Look for the kissing gate in the wall on the left and retrace your steps back to the car park.

Coniston

Borrowdale and, inset, traditional gate post.

BORROWDALE

Situated to the north of Derwentwater is the Skiddaw range of fells dominating the town of Keswick and regarded with affection by the locals. Southey referred to it as: "My neighbour Skiddaw." Its massive heights gaze far down into the narrow corridors of the Borrowdale valley. The town of Keswick, meaning cheese farm, has past memories as the mining centre for the Borrowdale and Newlands valleys. Today, its grey slate buildings and wide market place around the imposing Moot Hall, once the site of a 19th century jail, act as a base for walkers and climbers seeking the exhilarating challenges of the northern and western fells. The town is a popular tourist centre with a variety of interesting shops including a number specialising in outdoor pursuits. Tourism came to the town with the growth of the railways in the 1860s and many of the hotels date from that era.

This is the gateway to the "U" shaped Borrowdale valley carved out millions of years ago during the ice age. From its length, other valleys spiral outwards, including the gentle, peaceful pastures of Troutdale where you can still see the remnants of a 19th century trout hatchery. Langstrath, is as it sounds a long but beautiful walk alongside a burbling beck. However, Borrowdale's, "Jewel in the Crown," must be the hanging valley of Watendlath. Reached by a narrow, single, track road forking off to the left of the main road, the route climbs steeply to the picturesque, packhorse bridge at Ashness. The beck in full spate after heavy rain is a sight to see as the white waters of the beck tumble down furiously over the jagged stones and boulders. From there the road twists and turns on its switchback route up through the wooded inclines and then out into the steep-sided, rugged valley immortalised in Hugh Walpole's *Rogue Herries*: "Through this vale twisted the mountain torrent, fighting with the stones."

As you travel down the valley, the jagged rocks on either side seem to become higher, the road narrower and the stone walls closer. On a wild and windy day the landscape is ominously, threatening. Finally, you reach your journey's end, the idyllic hamlet of Watendlath. The origin of the name is somewhat obscure, but two possibilities are, "lane to the end of the lake" or "barn at the end of the lake." Watendlath Tarn is well stocked with trout and the pack-horse bridge over the beck is on the ancient pack-horse route to Rosthwaite. Around the tarn and the tea-room you will find a variety of resident ducks, geese, fell ponies and a pet pig, whilst higher up on the fells is an ideal place to see Herdwick sheep grazing.

Another unique feature of this area are the ancient oak woodlands of Ashness, Johnny's Wood, Great Wood, Stonethwaite Woods and Seatoller Woods. These are the last remnants of some of the temperate rain forests that existed all along the west coast of the British Isles. As such they are a unique habitat for rare liverworts, ferns and mosses that bestrew the boulders and undergrowth. Here you can see wood anemone and dog mercury always signs of antiquity, oxlip and bluebells. These woods are rich in insect life and birds such as chiff chaffs and pied fly catchers. Bats, foxes red squirrels and roe deer live in these magnificent woods.

To the south of Keswick is Derwent Water. It stretches for approximately four and half kilometres along the Borrowdale Valley and is roughly two kilometres wide. Derwent Water and Bassenthwaite Lake were once joined, but gradually separated as rock and silt deposits from the River Greta built up. Bassenthwaite Lake is the only one of the lakes to have the word lake in its name; all the others have mere or water.

Taking one of the pleasure launches that operate on Derwent Water is an ideal way to relax and admire the breathtaking scenery surrounding the lake. The forested heights of Great Wood, Walla Crag and the rocky buttress of Falcon Crag border the east, the latter being the remnants of a former volcano. The range continues with the slopes of Shepherd's Crag and High Lodore. These fells are composed of the rough and rugged Borrowdale volcanic rock whilst, in contrast, on the west side, are the smooth, undulating heights of Cat Bells, Maiden Moor and Narrow Moor consisting of Skiddaw slate the oldest rock formation in the lakes' geological structure.

At the south end of the lake are the hamlets of Manesty, snuggling up peacefully below Cat Bells and Grange-in-Borrowdale lying at the foot of Maiden Moor. Grange is reached by a double arched bridge from the main road. The area used to be owned by the monks from Furness Abbey and was the site of the Grange hence the name today.

Castle Crag is one of the Jaws of Borrowdale and was an Iron Age fort and later a Romano-British fort, ideally situated for defence purposes with its views up and down the valley. The valley itself is a lush green carpet of fields neatly carved up into geometric patterns by the traditional, hand-built stone-walls. The valley is watered by the meandering River Derwent that flows through Derwent Water and Bassenthwaite Lake and then joins the sea at Workington.

Further down the valley are the hamlets of Rosthwaite and Stonethwaite, "thwaite" being the old Norse word for clearing. Rosthwaite, "the clearing with the heap of stones," is by the How, a small hill. This is the area to find Herdwick sheep in the fields and on the fells. Stonethwaite, " the stony clearing," is the end of the road before entering the Langstrath valley.

After leaving Rosthwaite you come to the hamlet of Seatoller, "summer dwelling by the alder trees," where picturesque cottages sit by the roadside. They once housed the workers in the Honister slate mines at the top of Little Gatesgarthdale. An old barn has been converted into a craft centre for local crafts people including a spinner, weaver and wood carver. It is an interesting place to visit, though you must check with the National Park as to the open days. In a side valley to the south west is the last dwelling place in Borrowdale, the tiny hamlet of Seathwaite, " the clearing among the sedges." This is a popular starting point for walkers making for the heights of Great Gable, Scafell and Scafell Pike. This hamlet has the reputation for being the wettest place in Britain.

In the past Borrowdale was mined for graphite that was discovered at Seathwaite and was the beginning of the Keswick Pencil Factory. Here

Ennerdale with, inset, Herdwick rugs, hand woven and gun tufted by Chris Crofts, the Wool Clip.

the famous Cumberland pencils are produced. The oak woods that once bordered both sides of the valley were felled and used for charcoal. Whilst the Honister Slate mine, opened in 1643, and still in business, produces a wonderful green slate so evocative of the Lake District scenery. There is a wonderful range of products to be had including, garden and kitchen-ware, and a range of attractive ornaments. It is well worth a visit to look for a present that is different or unusual and it boasts a tea-room.

Legend has it that the slate miners of the past would knit stockings and other items from the wool spun by their wives as they climbed up to the mines. These were then sold at the local markets. An old resident of Borrowdale told us this story. Not such a strange thing for men to do when you realise that in Elizabethan times only men were allowed into the Guild of Knitters.

A local attraction in the valley is the famous Bowder stone. This is a massive single rock with an estimated weight of 2,000 tons. It is approximately ten metres high, (30 feet) and some 12.000 years old. If two people lie down one on either side of the stone, you can shake hands through the gap at the bottom!

Borrowdale has had its share of characters, one being a modern hermit, Millican Dalton. He was born in Alston, Cumbria in 1867 and worked for a shipping company in London. He gave up his secure employment in favour of the outdoor life. Millican became a tour guide at home and abroad. When he was in England he lived in a cave on Castle Crag and spent his time passing on his outdoor skills to others. He was often seen on a homemade raft on the River Derwent and wandering through the streets of Keswick. He died at the age of eighty in 1947.

Another anecdotal tale of Borrowdale folk is the story of the Borrowdale cuckoo. The people of Borrowdale enjoyed the sound of the cuckoo at spring-time. It heralded the warmer, brighter weather of spring. They believed that if they could keep the cuckoo in the valley, they would have spring all the year round. So they decided to build a wall across the valley at Grange. Alas the cuckoo never stayed. Why? According to the valley folk the wall, should have had just one more layer on that would have kept him in and ensured the valley of an eternal spring.

Another account refers to the wall at the end of Watendlath valley as being the "end of the world." But why build a wall to keep sheep in when they are heafed? Some believe this was the wall built to keep the cuckoo in. Needless to say, when a typical spring day does arrive in the valley it is a heavenly place to be.

Farming Viewpoint

HAZEL and Joe Relph have been farming at Yew Tree Farm for some eighteen years. They are both Cumbrian born and bred. Joe comes from a farming family at Ashness Bridge and Hazel originates from Keswick. Their daughter has recently completed a dissertation on Herdwicks that has merited an award from the Worshipful Company of Woolmen.

Yew Tree Farm is situated in the heart of Herdwick country in Borrowdale. The Relphs run a Herdwick farm that has bed and breakfast accommodation. Some years ago they diversified and opened the Flock In Tea Rooms. Here Hazel oversees a very successful venture. Local ladies provide a variety of homemade specialities including Herdwick sausage rolls, Herdwick stew and a delicious sticky toffee pudding. But perhaps the Relph's "piece de resistance" is their superb Herdwick paté, in our opinion the best commercial paté we have ever tasted. Hugh has devised a recipe using the paté namely, Herdwick Cutlets Rosthwaite based on the classical beef dish Tornedos Rossini.

For the past few years they have been marketing their own Herdwick meat. Joe told us it has been a steep learning curve for him to produce meat in prime condition to meet the specifications of his butcher in Keswick. This means a new approach to the husbandry of the sheep to ensure the fat content is the correct ratio to meat when it is ready for the market. He holds similar views regarding the slaughter of animals to other farmers we have interviewed. Their Herdwick meat is sold in the Flock In and can be purchased by mail order.

The garden adjacent to the tea rooms has a long terrace overlooking the Relph's fields of Herdwick sheep. Here customers can sit in idyllic surroundings savouring not only the view of the magnificent Borrowdale scenery but also the tasty Herdwick sausage rolls and stew. Hazel told us that occasionally a customer will comment that it seems wrong to be watching the lambs in the field whilst eating them. She is very quick to point out that, if Herdwicks were not marketed for the table, the breed would become extinct.

Herdwick is an unique breed of sheep in many ways. It is born black and it changes colour as it grows older. It is a slow growing sheep and does not mature until it is a year old, unlike other sheep breeds that are ready for the table at three months. By the time it is a year old the flavour is far superior to that of other breeds resembling venison in its sweet, gamey taste. The fat of Herdwick is unlike that of other sheep. Research by Bristol University has shown that fat from Herdwick meat is of the omega 3 unsaturated type. It is more akin to olive oil and consequently far more healthy to eat.

The Relphs are firm believers in the traceability of meat and indeed of all food. They believe a section of the public is becoming more discerning. They want to know where and how their food has been produced. Here at Yew Tree Farm you can see the production at first hand and be assured it is of the very best quality. Hazel informed us that the UK imports and exports the same quantity of meat. The difference being that we export meat produced under strict EC regulations that the UK farmers adhere to. This makes our meat a more expensive commodity to produce. Meat imported from countries such as Argentina, America, New Zealand, China and Brazil do not have to abide by EC rules so they can produce meat more cheaply. In addition there are other reasons such as economies of very large scale production, lower labour costs and cheaper imports.

The Relphs believe the time is right for an innovative type of supermarket that will give the public the opportunity of choice. They would like to see farmers' supermarkets developed across the

UK where locally produced food can be sold. The public can then be assured of the traceability of their food. They envisage these new type shopping malls including an educational area providing information about locally produced food and an outlet for locally produced crafts. They feel such ventures would be financially viable even if only 10% of the community shopped there.

Shepherd's Walk, Borrowdale

Start and finish: National Trust car park, Rosthwaite

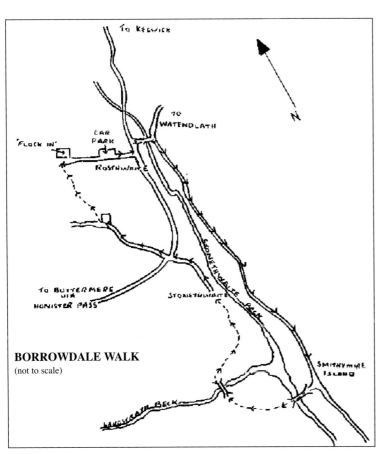

BORROWDALE WALK
(not to scale)

Distance: 6 kms.
Time: 2-3 hours
Grid Ref: 257148
Map: Outdoor leisure 4, English Lakes, north western area

At certain times of the year, this low level walk brings you face to face with Herdwicks in their natural environment on the fells. Whatever the weather, you can admire the stunning scenery on either side of this delightful part of Borrowdale valley.

On leaving the car park, turn left and walk down the main road. Turn left at the main road and walk for approximately 50 metres. Cross the road and go down the track in front of you. Turn right and go over the bridge leading onto the bridle way. The bridle way follows the dry stonewall as it snakes its way through the valley.

Ahead of you the ridge of Greenup Edge dominates the skyline. The cornerstone of Eagle Crag rises above the junction where Langstrath Beck meets Stonethwaite Beck at Smithy-mire Island. Continue along the bridle way with the wooded fellside on your left. Take note of the dry stone walls on your right dividing the neat enclosures. Soon the wooded fell side gives way to the open fells where you can often see Herdwicks grazing away minding their own business.

Continue on the bridle way until you reach a large footbridge on your right that crosses Stonethwaite beck. Walk down to the bridge and cross over and follow the path. Ahead of you is the narrow steep sided valley of Langstrath. Walk along and look for the gated footbridge on your right. Cross over and turn right. Take time to admire the surrounding fells. Continue along the track to the quaint hamlet of Stonethwaite with its grey slate and whitewashed cottages.

Once through the hamlet continue to the main road. Cross over and go down the road ahead of you. Where the road turns left note the footpath sign in the wall on the right and go through the gate between the two houses. Follow the footpath across the fields to Rosthwaite and the car park. The Flock In at Yew Tree Farm, Rosthwaite, is an ideal place to relax and have some refreshments. On a fine day you can sit in the garden and soak in the stunning scenery of Borrowdale. You can also buy Herdwick meat and sausages from the tea-room.

ENNERDALE

To the west of the Lake District National Park lies the remote, unspoilt valley of Ennerdale. The lake stands at its entrance leading the eye down the valley, along the wooded slopes and up onto the majestic heights of such giants as Pillar and Steeple. This is a lake of extreme moods wrought by the changes of atmosphere. The fells sometimes ethereally bathed in soft, peachy tones tinged with gold and turquoise rising to meet sky and clouds of the same delicate, iridescent colours, and below the waters calm and blue. On such a day the heights seem benign and godlike so near yet so far away.

On other days the fells glitter with sun-bright rocks and the lake appears a steely grey, an ominous fore-warning of a changing mood. At times it is a dark, forbidding place, the crags glowering down as wind and rain sweep through the valley whipping up the surface of the lake into scudding white horses that crash over the lake shore onto the side; all views obscured as a storm gusts down the valley.

The origins of the name are obscure. One suggestion is that it is related to the Welsh name "Iain" meaning cold, thus River Ehen meaning cold river. In 1135 it was known as Anenderdale and in 1321 as Eghnerdale. The name of the valley itself probably means, "valley of a man called Anunder."

You reach the valley by a narrow, hedge-lined road that twists and turns. In February the route sparkles with snowdrops, heralding spring. With the advent of March, the hedgerows are ablaze with daffodils. The road through the village of Kirkland gives panoramic views reaching right down the valley and across the lake to the splendid back cloth of fells rising and falling along the skyline.

The route takes you past spoil heaps, and railway embankments. These are the landmarks of the iron ore mining industry of the past. The Murton and Kelton Fells to the north of Ennerdale had veins of hematite, a valuable iron ore. In 1877 the mining of this mineral started and a railway line from Rowrah was constructed. The spoil heaps and the old bridges remain to tell the tale of past activities in these now quiet and secluded fells.

From the village of Ennerdale the roads meet at Croasdale. This was once a thriving hamlet of industry including hatters, joiners and a tea shop. Nowadays, the stone buildings have been converted into holiday accommodation. The road ends at Bowness Knott, a Forestry Commission car park. Between the scree line of Herdus and the tumbling Rake beck is an unusual structure of the past, a goose bield. These were built as traps for foxes. A pit was dug and lined with stones and a plank was balanced over the edge of the pit. One end of the plank was attached to the ground with a short rope. At the other end of the plank, bait was placed - a dead goose or chicken. The fox walked the plank to get to the lure, the plank tilted and the fox fell into the pit and was unable to climb out The other point of access to this spectacular valley, is from the car park on the edge of Broadmoor Wood at Bleach Green.

Ennerdale is approximately twelve kilometres long and runs eastwards, with Green Gable, Great Gable and Brandreth at its head. The north side is bordered by Herdus, Starling Dodd, Red Pike, High Stile, High Crag and the rocky, turrets of Haystacks. On the southern boundary of this glacial valley stand Crag Fell, The Side, Ennerdale Fell, Steeple, Pillar, Pillar Rock and Looking Stead. These fells are composed of Skiddaw slate with deposits of granophyre which is similar to granite but of a smoother texture. The only way out of the valley is on foot over Scarth Gap into the Buttermere valley or via Black Sail pass into Mosedale and Wasdale.

In the 1920s the Forestry Commission carried out extensive planting of conifers and created Ennerdale forest, changing the face of this once wild and remote valley. This was the start of the decline of farming in the valley, particularly at High and Low Gillerthwaite which were renowned for their prize Herdwick sheep. Nowadays, there is a Youth Hostel and an Activity Centre in this area At the head of the valley, is Black Sail shepherds' hut which had fallen into disrepair as a result of the decline of sheep farming in the area. Fortunately, the Youth Hostelling Association took it over and carried out extensive renovations. It now provides a haven for walkers and climbers in this wild, isolated and secluded valley.

Ennerdale Water is about four kilometres long and approximately one and a half kilometres at its widest point. The lake is fed by the River Liza which rises high upon Great Gable and Green Gable. A myriad of sparkling becks cascade off the surrounding fells into the river and zig-zag their way through the tree lined valley. The crystal clear waters tumble over pebbles and stones. A shimmering colour wheel of ochres, green greys and browns, ideal camouflage for the Arctic char re-introduced to these waters by Sir Chris Bonnington in 2000. The river continues its way through the wooded valley towards the Irish Bridge.

The local farmers use the fields at High and Low Gillerthwaite for grazing Herdwicks. The River Ehen flows out of the lake, through the village of Ennerdale Bridge and on to Egremont and finally into the sea at Braystones on Cumbria's west coast.

Evidence in the valley suggests it has been inhabited for thousands of years. The ruins of centuries old enclosures and settlements are still obvious. Remains can be found at the clearing by Smithy Beck, Gillerthwaite and Dodsgill beck. At the head of the lake the ground is dotted with hillocks. This is an important site of an ancient settlement. The remains of the outer walls of the dwellings can still be seen. The walk passes this site. These signs indicate the valley was widely used for agricultural and industrial purposes.

The dale and surrounding fells have been mined for iron ore and slate. The forests of oak, birch, alder and hazel were felled for making charcoal. The charcoal platforms can still be seen. One of these platforms has the substantial ruins of a stone charcoal burners' hut complete with a fireplace. Charcoal was used for heating the bloomeries, kiln-like structures fashioned out of the local stone, to smelt the iron ore. Bleach Green at Broad Wood car park, was once the site of a bleach works.

The enclosure known as The Side and Side Wood was Ennerdale Park, a deer forest. Many times we've been fortunate to see deer up on the heights of this valley.

In 1855 The Angler's Inn was built on a site below How Hall Farm. The inn was demolished in 1968 when the water company had ideas of raising the level of the lake to increase the domestic water supply. This never materialised so the inn was in effect demolished for nothing. The area is known as Anglers car park and is reached by a very rough track.

How Hall has also been known as The How and How Hall Farm. The original hall was built in the 16th century and the large barns were part of the hall. The Patricksons, a powerful family, known locally as the Kings of Ennerdale owned the property. Anthony Patrickson was Lord of the Manors of Loweswater, Thackthwaite and Dean. He married the daughter of one of the privy councillors to Henry VIII. Patricksons' tenants had their rents reduced in return for being prepared to fight in the border wars. This was an advantage to the king in the time when the border regions were being fought over by the kings of Scotland and England.

With the Union of the Crowns at the turn of the 17th century, this threat decreased, so Patrickson increased the rents without informing the tenants or the king. This illegal act caused fury among the tenants and they took Patrickson to the High Court and won their case. In the 17th century the estate changed hands though the Patrickson family continued to reside in the district. In 1681 a Thomas Patrickson was buried with his body wrapped in wool. To promote the woollen industry an Act of Parliament in 1667 stated everyone had to be buried wrapped in wool.

On the south side of the lake above the fells is the wild and remote Kinniside Common, grazed by Herdwicks and other fell breeds. This vast expanse of open moorland has remains of ancient homesteads, settlements and field systems.

Further south on this bleak, open fell is Stockdale Moor with a huge mound approximately two metres wide and thirty metres long. This is possibly an ancient burial site from the Neolithic Period and is known as Sampson's Bratful. Legend has it that it was built by the devil, who carried the stones in his apron and dumped them. The old name for an apron was a brat.

The most famous legend concerning Ennerdale is about the escapades of the "Girt Dog of Ennerdale" It is said to have killed over three hundred sheep and lambs in four months between May and September 1810. The dog was believed to have been a cross between a bull mastiff and a greyhound. It was extremely large and strong and was a brindle colour. The animal was hunted by local hounds, but to no avail. Local men spent hours keeping a watch for this predator that was causing so much havoc amongst farm-stock. On one occasion it was chased over to Loweswater, but soon returned. Eventually it was shot and was reputed to have weighed 56 kilos.

This lake is easily explored using the numerous forest tracks and the lake side path from either of the car parks. The views at any time of the year are dramatic, each season having its own special atmosphere. At certain times the reflections of the fells in the lake are quite stunning and worth recording on camera.

Farmer's Viewpoint

William Rawling's family have farmed at Hollins Farm, Ennerdale, for centuries. They can trace their family history back to the 1500s. The present house was built in 1717 and the oldest date stone is the late 1680s. William was one of five family members operating the farm that included his father, two uncles and himself. Now only he and his son manage what were once five farms.

He believes farmers are now working harder. Gathering sheep from the fells used to be a communal activity involving four or five farmers. Nowadays, one or two men gather large numbers of sheep. He thinks today's farmer is even more skilled in these traditional activities as there is less manpower and more sheep. Because of lack of manpower, they now have to use contracted labour for some tasks such as shearing.

William feels farming is now in a period of transition. Just after the war the emphasis was on food production geared to feeding everybody. Now the emphasis is on environmental issues. He understands the public's right to have a say in the way food is produced and their belief in having access to the environment. However, he points out that the Herdwick sheep grazing the fells and recent farming methods have created the Lakeland environment the public love so much.

William is concerned there is no scientific basis for the current changes recommended by the government. He feels no-one knows for certain the consequences of the changes and is worried farmers are being used as guinea pigs. In his opinion, government policy towards farming has been short-sighted.

Traditionally, Herdwick sheep have been bred on the fells and kept there until they are too old to graze the fells. Then they were sent to lowland areas for cross breeding, e.g. with Texel. Now, under ESA (environmentally sensitive area) regulations they have to be removed from the fells during the winter and wintered away in lowland areas. This is one reason why farmers in the Lake District lost their breeding stocks in the foot and mouth disease epidemic of 2001.

He is fortunate in having a hill farm and a marginal farm. This means he can winter his own home-bred stock. He has Herdwick ewes of thirteen and fourteen years of age! Longevity is another attribute of this unique breed.

Despite being a very busy farmer, William makes an important contribution to the local community. He is secretary of the Ennerdale Agricultural Show. He believes passionately that these shows should continue in their entirety. Because of restrictions still in place because of foot and mouth there was no livestock at the show in 2002. These shows embody the history of the farming community. To water them down or lose them would deprive the community of their cultural traditions, and visitors of an enjoyable day out, and their contact with the farming community.

William is also chairman of the Kinniside Graziers' Association, an organisation which looks after the local community's right to graze their animals on common land. These rights are a legacy from before the Enclosure Acts. Common lands exist across the country and include, Clapham Common, Hampstead Heath, the New Forest and Epping Forest. Forty five per cent of England's common grazing land is in Cumbria and seventy per cent is in the north of England including Lancashire and Yorkshire.

One of William's major concerns is that very few youngsters are coming into farming and the rural industries. This is mainly because of low pay and the high cost of housing in rural areas. Youngsters in farming cannot afford to buy property. In William's youth Ennerdale Bridge was a typical farming village. It was virtually self-sufficient. There were three shops, a pub, a blacksmith's and a clog maker. Now, there is one shop and two pubs and it has become a residential dormitory for middle class management working in the surrounding towns of the West Coast of Cumbria.

A Walk Around Ennerdale Water
Start & Finish: *Bowness Knott car park*
Distance: *12 kilometres*
Time: *4-5 hours*
Grid Ref: *110154*
Map: *OS Outdoor leisure sheet 4, the English Lakes, north west area.*

This walk takes you round the lake. There is a degree of difficulty in getting round the rocky section of Anglers Crag. You may prefer to go up and over the Crag, a steep climb, but it avoids the scramble over the rocks with the sheer drop into the lake about 75 feet beneath you! At certain times you can see Herdwick sheep at the far end of the lake going towards Black Sail. If you're there at the right time of the year on the right day, you can see all the farmers in the area with their dogs gathering the sheep off the fells and bringing them down to the sorting pens. On occasions the sheep are driven along the lake side track.

Turn left as you leave the car park and walk along the wide forest road down the hill to the lake-shore. Keep on this track, following the lake-shore until you come to the concrete bridge on your right (the Irish Bridge) which crosses the River Liza. Turning right, cross over the bridge and follow this track with the wall on your right.

This is where you will possibly see Herdwicks.

At the end of the wall, go through the kissing gate on your right. Continue through the field keeping close to the wall to reach a gate with a stile on your left. Go over the stile and follow the path across the field to the lake shore. The well-defined path now follows the shore-line. Take care along this section, the path is rocky and uneven and can be slippery. Look out for Herdwicks in the woods.

After you leave the last bridle gate on the fell, look for the track on your left if you are going to follow the steep path over the top of Anglers Crag. The views are stunning from the top of the

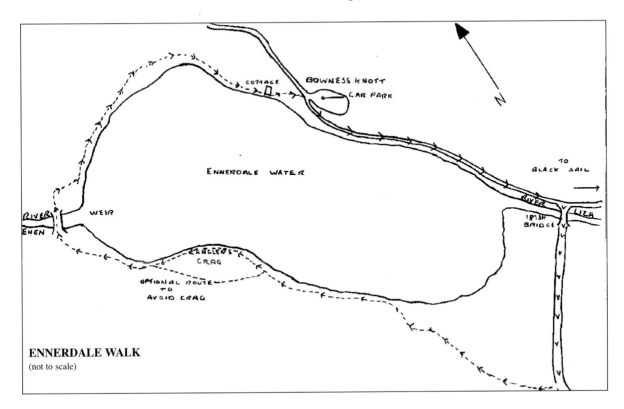

ENNERDALE WALK
(not to scale)

crag. Descend and join the main lake path.

If you decide to tackle the scramble round the edge of the lake, take care as you may encounter a line of Herdwicks coming in the opposite direction! So, if you have dogs with you be careful! Once over this tricky bit the path is easy to follow. Go through the bridle gate and continue to the bridge ahead and slightly to your right, crossing the River Ehen, and follow the path to the gate and turn right to the lake shore. Turn left and continue along this path by the lake side through the gorse. This path can be very wet and muddy.

When you reach the iron gate go through and continue following the path beside the lake. You will come to a clearing on the left hand side, where the Angler's Hotel stood. The track continues along the lake shore, climbing gently with gorse bushes on either side. Go over the stile and turn immediately right and down to rejoin the lake path.

Continue along the path with the fields on your left - many of them have Herdwicks in at certain times of the year. Go through the bridle gate, over the beck and take the path off to the left that goes uphill for a short distance. On the left in front of you is a cottage. Follow the track past a picnic bench, cross over the main lake track to arrive back in the car park.

ULLSWATER

The valley of Ullswater is in the north east of the Lake District National Park and is accessible from the A66. At the foot of the valley is Pooley Bridge, in the north, and at the head of the valley, in the south, are Glenridding and Patterdale. The open field patterns of the lowlands around Pooley Bridge suddenly give way to sensational views of the rugged high fells on both sides of the valley.

The lower fells with the smoother grassy peaks are of the older less rugged Skiddaw slate. Towards the head of the valley, the higher more rugged fells are of Borrowdale volcanic rock. The name of the lake is Old Norse meaning Ulfr's lake.

At the head of the valley is the Kirkstone Pass which leads down to Troutbeck and Windermere. Ullswater is unique in that the lake dominates the valley. The second largest lake, Ullswater is about eleven kilometres in length and approximately one kilometre at its widest part. The view up or down the lake is deceiving. The long, serpentine shape of the lake with two bends creates three distinct sections preventing you from seeing from one end to the other.

At Pooley Bridge the River Eamont drains the lake. Becks from the surrounding fells swell the waters of Ullswater including Goldrill beck from Brothers' Water. To the east is the almost horizontal ridge of High Street an old Roman Road. It used to connect Brocavum (Brougham) with Galavi (Troutbeck) and still stands guard on this side of the valley. The Helvellyn range rises high to the west overshadowing the lower fells at the head of the valley.

The ideal way to absorb the atmosphere of Wordsworth's favourite lake is to take a relaxing cruise on the steamer from either Pooley Bridge or Glenridding. As you glide along, each reach gradually unfolds with its own special, magical charm. The lake is alive with yachts darting swiftly across the glistening waters their colourful sails billowing in the breeze. Traditionally built boat-houses dot the shoreline, their architecture a memory of Victorian days.

Picturesque dales lead up to the surrounding fells bearing the scars of their mining and quarrying past. Glenridding and Greenside mines were worked until the early 1960's. The village, once dependent on the mining industry, is now a tourist spot and a starting point for fell walkers tackling Helvelyn and other surrounding peaks. Grisedale, "the valley of the pigs," leads up to Grisedale Tarn, a wild place where you will find, "The Parting Stone," immortalised in Wordsworth's poem of the same name. It was here that Wordsworth unknowingly said a last farewell to his much-loved brother John who returned to his ship the *Earl of Abergavenney* never to return again. John drowned when his ship was wrecked off Weymouth. Wordsworth composed the poem here, as it was the last time and place he saw his brother.

Glencoyn and Glenridding are the only dales having their origins in the Welsh language, the former meaning "the reedy glen" and the latter "the glen over grown with bracken". Other dales in the area have their origins in old Norse or old English; Fusedale - "valley with the cattle byre" Boaredale - "the valley with the herdsman's hut" and Hartsop - "the valley of the harts" (male deer).

The rocky expanse of Gowbarrow Park rises up from the lake. The time and effort spent climbing this fell is well rewarded, particularly in the autumn when the rich golds, browns and reds on a bright sunny day are stunning. On reaching the top the vistas around the head of the valley are breathtaking and to be cherished for a long time.

Whatever the weather, the varying moods and changing atmosphere of the valley lend their own special beauty to this magical lake. Far below the heights of Gowbarrow, nestling in the trees surrounded by verdant green pastures is Lyulph's Tower. Built in 1780 by the tenth Duke of Norfolk as a shooting lodge, possibly on the site of an old pele tower, it is a building associated with the legend of Aira Force and recounted in Wordsworth's poem *The Somnambulist:*

> *List ye who pass by Lyulph's Tower*
> *At eve; how softly then*
> *Doth Aira Force, that torrent hoarse….*

These pele towers were built from the 14th century onwards as a means of defence and protection for livestock from the Scots border raids. Constructed of stone, these towers had three levels. The ground floor was used to shelter animals. The middle floor was the main living area and the top quarter was the ladies' accommodation. Battlements were sometimes added around the top. A good example of a pele tower can be seen in the hamlet of Dacre between Ullswater and the A66.

In Roman times both Gowbarrow Park and Glencoyne Park were deer forests. Aira Beck, "the stream with the gravel banks," (old Norse) flows through a cleavage in the rocks dividing the two parks and tumbling some 25 metres through a steep-sided chasm to a deep pool below. Clinging to its rocky sides are a variety of ferns and foliage of different shades of green, the droplets of water on the leaves sparkling in the diffused sunlight. This is Aira Force, a name derived from the Norse "foss," meaning water-fall, and Gaelic, "airdh." There are footpaths on either side of the water fall leading up to the arched, stone bridge spanning the turbulent, boiling waters cascading down to the pools below. After heavy rain the falls are at their most spectacular, making a thunderous roar that can be heard some distance away. Extreme care is required because the paths can be very slippery.

William Wordsworth, among countless others, considered Ullswater to be the finest of the lakes. Here, below Gowbarrow, he and Dorothy first set eyes on a myriad of wild, golden daffodils. Dorothy wrote: "When we were in the woods beyond Gowbarrow Park, we saw a few daffodils close to the water-side. We fancied the lake had floated the seeds ashore, and that the little colony had so sprung up. But as we went along there were more and yet more; and at last under the boughs of the trees we saw there was a long belt of them along the shore... I never saw daffodils so beautiful."[1] This vision prompted Wordsworth to write his most famous poem:

I wandered lonely as a cloud
That floats on high o'er dales and hills,
When all at once I saw a crowd,

[1] From an entry in Dorothy's *Lakeland Journal,* Thursday, April 15.

A host of golden daffodils;
Beside the lake beneath the trees,
Fluttering and dancing in the breeze.

On leaving Glenridding, the road makes its way into Patterdale with its quaint slate buildings. In the 13th century Patterdale was known as Patricdale and was possibly named after the owner of the land. A more romantic origin is that St Patrick preached and baptised in the area on his pilgrimage. The church is dedicated to St. Patrick.

Before the road makes its tortuous ascent of Kirkstone Pass, you come to the hamlet of Hartsop, once a mining centre, with its traditional Lakeland architecture. Some of the cottages have classic examples of spinning galleries. These were built on the north side of the cottages with space underneath. In the summer, this space was used for shearing and clipping Herdwicks. Being on the north side, it was a cool area to carry out this activity. Once sheared, the fleeces were stored in a room or space behind the gallery. After being washed, the fleeces were dried and spun in the gallery. The walk starts from this hamlet giving you an opportunity to see at close quarters the old galleries.

At the foot of Kirkstone Pass is the small lake of Brothers' Water. Two brothers were drowned in the lake, hence the name. In 1777 it was known as Broad Water.

Kirkstone Pass links the Ullswater valley with Troutbeck and Ambleside. At the head of the pass is the Kirkstone Inn. The pass takes its name from the large rock that resembles a church. This rock stands high above Brothers' Water. Panoramic views over this delightful valley are

Ullswater

visible from the head of the pass. Throughout the valley Herdwicks graze on the fell-sides, the open moorland and in the fields. Karel Capek once said of this breed of sheep: "They graze on silken lawns and remind one of the blessed in heaven. Nobody watches them, and they spend their lives in feeding, sleeping and divine pondering."

A well-known legend in the area is based around Lyulph's Tower and Aira Force. The lady of the House of Greystoke, Emma Howard, owned the estate. She was married to a gallant knight, Sir Eglamore. Although married, Sir Eglamore didn't stop gallivanting around the countryside in search of amorous adventures. One account of the time reports him as: "making children fatherless, and their mothers widows." He was so successful in his escapades that his name was known far and wide for his ardent exploits.

Word eventually reached the remote area of Ullswater. Emma's heart was broken whilst her wayward husband roamed the rural provinces. Doubting her husband's devotion to her she began to sleep walk. Her nocturnal wanderings always led her to the place where they had courted - Aira beck. Eventually Sir Eglamore returned home. Arriving in sight of Lyulph's tower late at night, he decided to rest by the beck where he had spent his courting days, rather than disturb the household. Falling asleep, Sir Eglamore was awakened suddenly by an apparition dressed in white. Reaching out he grasped at the figure with all his strength; the "ghost" rudely awakened from her sleep lost her footing, stumbled and fell head first into the beck.

[1] William Wordsworth, *The Somnambulist*

Sir Eglamore immediately jumped into the fast flowing beck to retrieve a lifeless and bruised body that once he laid on the bank he recognised as his beloved Emma. Inconsolable at his loss, he became a hermit, tormented for the rest of his life by his unfaithful escapades and the drowning of his adorable Emma.

Within the dell he built a cell
And there was Sorrow's guest
In hermit's weeds repose he found
From vain temptations free[1]

The sequel to this legend takes place in the 1830s. The writer Thomas de Quincey lived at Grasmere and recorded the experiences of Miss Elizabeth Smith, a visitor to Aira Force. In the 19th century visitors to Aira Force did not have the sign posted footpath of today. It was such a perilous ascent that the 1859 guide recommended: "A stranger... will take a guide at Lyulph's Tower and be conducted along the brow of the ravine to the bridges." Thinking she knew the area well enough, as she lived not far away, Miss Smith did not stop at the Duke of Norfolk's hunting lodge for a guide. Usually one of the gamekeeper's family would guide the tourists up the steep footpath to see the spectacular 60 foot plunging waterfall of Aira Force.

Being something of an amateur artist Miss Smith wanted to be alone to do some sketching. Very soon, however, she lost all trace of the footpath but, being sure footed, she carried on clambering over and around rocks as she continued ascending the rocky gorge. Reaching the brim of the ravine she realised she could go no further, turning round she could see no trace of the route down.

Surrounded by towering vertical rocks she began to panic, but suddenly a young woman appeared and waved to her and appeared to be pointing out the route down. With a sense of relief Miss Smith began the slow descent. All the time following the woman in white who guided her away from the dangerous edge of the ravine. Soon she was close enough to see the young woman was her sister and the path was now clearly marked. Turning to thank her sister she was surprised to see she had disappeared.

Miss Smith continued her way down somewhat surprised that her sister had not waited for her. Some hours later a weary Miss Smith arrived home to discover her sister sitting waiting for her and to learn she had not left the house all afternoon.

Farmer's Viewpoint

MARY Bell has been farming at Crookabeck for 26 years. She began with dairy goats and then bought Angoras when they came into this country. She diversified by sending their mohair away to be processed into knitting yarn. Living on a footpath she decided to open a farm shop. Mary invested in a couple of older Herdwick ewes. They were two show sheep from Dick Wilson, two of his favourite "old girls" as he called them. Dick was a famous local Herdwick breeder. From them Mary has bred up a flock of 50 ewes from the original two using a different top quality ram each year.

Mary was fortunate to be one of the Millennium Award holders in 2000, enabling her to do research into adding value to fell bred wool. She visited a Wool Board auction to see the wool sold and watched the grading process. The next stop was to visit a large wool scouring plant where tons of wool are processed each hour. A visit to the carpet spinners was the next port of call, where the Herdwick wool is also dyed.

Mary became fascinated with dyeing the light Herdwick into subtle shades and rainbow effects, and this is used in her knitted Herdwick hats. A range of hand-knitted garments, a jumper, tunic, cardigan, waistcoat and a jacket using the two natural Herdwick colours have been designed and these are available either as a hand knit kit or hand knitted to order.

As members of the Wool Clip Co-operative at Priest's Mill, Caldbeck, she and Pam Hall of Fornside Farm, St John's in the Vale, applied for an exemption from the rule which requires farmers with more than four sheep to send all their wool to the British Wool Marketing Board. The four sheep rule means a farmer is only allowed to keep back four fleeces a year for his use, whether he has 40 or 4000 sheep.

All the rest has to be sent to the Wool Marketing Board where it is all processed together with tons of other wool. This means farmers are unable to use the wool bred on their own farms to produce and sell unique products specific to their farm. Mary and Pam have successfully gained a two year exemption from the Wool Board to keep all their Herdwick fleeces and send them to be processed separately. This has enabled them to sort their wool into light Herdwick from older ewes, dark Herdwick, the hogg wool, from young sheep, and the white wool from Pam's Cheviot and Swaledale sheep.

Ullswater and inset, a selection of items made from Herdwick wool.

Ullswater and inset Herdwick sheep

The wool is washed, spun and dyed in various colours evocative of the glorious Cumbrian landscape throughout the seasons of the year - deep lake blue, heather pink, mossy green and winter bracken. From there it is sent to a top designer/weaver and woven into beautiful rugs and throws known as the Helvellyn range. These include a large wall hanging depicting the head of a Herdwick tup, along with floor rugs all made from the wool.

These items are available from the Wool Clip Priest's Mill or by mail order from www.herdwick.com or from Mary's shop at Crookabeck.[1]

Shepherd's Walk

Start and finish: Hartsop car park at the end of the hamlet
Distance: 11 kms
Time: 4-5 hours
Grid Ref: 409130
Map: Outdoor Leisure No 5, The English Lakes, north east area

Walk down through the hamlet and look out for the two spinning galleries on the left, one on the roadside and one set back behind it. At the Adventure Centre turn right and walk down the metalled road. Continue along the track between the stone walls and the rugged fells of Borrowdale volcanic rock, a skyline of turreted rocks. At Hartsop Fold take the track to the left. Continue with the fields of the valley on your left behind the dry stone wall. Now the track becomes rough in places.

Soon you will hear the sound of rushing water as it cascades down the waterfall from Angle Tarn. Cross over the footbridge, and continue along the path. Go through the farm and walk towards the hamlet of Crookabeck. This is a delightful little place, with its

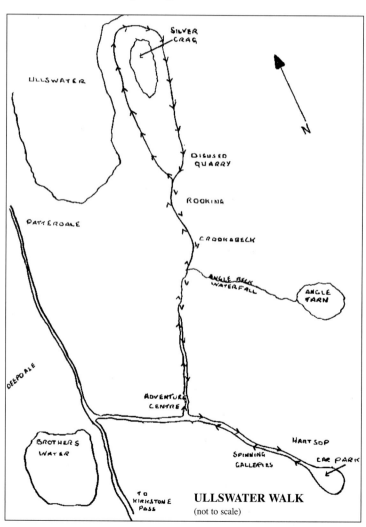

ULLSWATER WALK
(not to scale)

[1] Being a busy farmer, a phone call will ensure she is there to open the shop 017684 82742.

slate and whitewashed cottages. Here you may see Angora goats in the fields together with free ranging ducks and chickens giving an altogether "olde worlde" atmosphere. On the left you will see a fine example of a slate gate stoop. The holes were used to insert poles through to form a gate at the entrance to the fields. At the entrance you should see Herdwicks in a variety of colours. The lambs are black to dark brown. As they get older they turn to dark grey and become lighter with age. If you see an almost white Herdwick she's probably quite old!

Keep your eyes open and scan the heights - you may be lucky enough to see deer on the fells below Boredale Hause between Crookabeck and the hamlet of Rookin. Once leaving Crookabeck, the path becomes a metalled single track road leading into Rookin with its quaint, traditional buildings. Follow the road round to the right and up the hill. Go through the gate sign posted Side Farm. (this part of the walk is popular, as walkers take the steamer to How Town and walk back to Glenridding. The latter part of the walk behind Silver Crag is not so well used.) Continue on this wide track. You will have views of the head of Ullswater and Glenridding with its landing stage for the steamers which ply up and down the lake.

The fell to your right is Place Fell and the fell ahead is Silver Crag. Continue past the campsite. The fell that dominates the skyline is the Helvellyn range. When you reach the highest point of the path, the lake widens as the middle reach comes into view. Follow the path carefully, as it descends steeply down a rocky incline towards the lake shore. Continue along the perimeter of the lake. The path starts to ascend again and to bear round behind Silver Crag. In the distance you can see the path worming its way through a forested area towards How Town. Look for a path to your right climbing steeply up behind Silver Crag.

You will come to a rock fall that marks the start of this steep ascent going back towards Crookabeck. The path climbs sharply upwards between Juniper bushes. Juniper was used to make gunpowder in centuries gone by and the berries are used to make gin today. Take care here, as the path is very rocky and uneven. Occasionally, stop, turn round, and take in the sights and sounds below you: the yachts skimming along the surface of the lake, the sails flapping in the breeze and the sea gulls' cries as they circle and wheel above the waters of Ullswater.

When you reach the top of the path the views towards Kirkstone Pass dominate the skyline with Red Screes and Stony Cove Pike on the left and the gleaming waters of Brothers' Water at the foot of the pass. Now the path is easier and well defined. There are good views over Glenridding and up Greenside where you can see the old lead mine workings. The terraced houses running in a straight line up towards the mine workings were the old miners' cottages, once owned by the mining company. The walk continues past old mines and quarries, evidence of the areas industrial past.

Keep dogs and children under close control as the shafts are large and look deep. You are now above the track taken on your outward journey. The path descends to meet the track to Side Farm. Turn left and retrace your steps back to

Langdale and, inset, landscape picture felted in Herdwick wool by Therese.

Eskdale

Hartsop with views up Deepdale, the farmsteads nestling in the trees at the entrance to this valley. The witch-like hat of Cofa Pike is high on the skyline to your right.

On passing through Crookabeck, you may wish to browse in the shop owned by Mary Bell which sells a wide range of wool products grown from her own flocks of Angora goats and Herdwicks. Ring first to ensure Mary is there as she is a farmer and won't be sitting in the shop waiting for visitors, but is always happy to open on request.

THE LANGDALES AND CONISTON

The Langdales

Hidden away in the south of the Lake District is perhaps the most visited of the valleys despite the fact that it does not have a lake and there is no sign of commercialisation. Great Langdale, old English for "the long valley," is a "U" shaped valley carved out during the Ice Age. Around that time the valley floor was covered with water forming a lake. Nowadays, Herdwick sheep graze the rich green fields when they are not on the fells where they are heafed. Great Langdale Beck threads its way through the fields like a silver ribbon weaving its way alongside the dry stonewalls. Ash, oak and beech used to grow on the lower slopes of the fells. These were felled for charcoal and the area made over to intake fields.

The valley is surrounded by Borrowdale volcanic rock dominated by the famous Langdale Pikes at the head of the valley. From here the dales of Oxendale and Mickleden give access to the higher fells beyond the pikes. Dotted along the valley floor are whitewashed farmsteads snuggling into the foot of the fells.

Wordsworth said of Great Langdale that it: "should on no account be missed by him who has a true enjoyment of grand separate forms, composing of sublime unity, austere but reconciled and rendered attractive to the affections by its deep serenity that is spread over everything"

The valley is accessed by Skelwith Bridge over the River Brathay with its cascading falls of

Skelwith Force. Slate dressing is now the main industry, a far cry from the days of the bobbin mills. The road switchbacks between wooded banks and open fells to the hamlet of Elterwater. The lake of Elterwater, old Norse and old English for, "the lake of the swans" has become silted up over the years and is now much smaller than it used to be. Great Langdale Beck and the River Brathay, which rises above Little Langdale Tarn in the valley, feed the lake. The Brathay also drains Elterwater and flows into Lake Windermere.

In the 19th century Elterwater was a thriving hive of industry with gunpowder works and slate quarries. Today tourism is the main industry of this small hamlet of whitewashed cottages and slate buildings stretched out along the road. The centre of the village revolves round the sparkling white Britannia Inn.

The grey-green slate church of Chapel Stile set into the fell side was built in 1875. It towers above the other styles of architecture in the village. Many of the buildings are of slate, a memento of the village's industrial past.

Guarding the valley are the Langdale Pikes; a sight once seen, never forgotten. Their distinctive peaks silhouetted against the skyline - Pike o' Stickle, old Norse, "peak with a sharp summit"; Loft Crag with its more rounded summit; Thorn Crag, the baby of the group has the flatter ridge; Harrison Stickle, Harrison is a personal name whilst Stickle is old Norse for, "steep place" and is the tallest of the group. The fan shaped rock face of Pavey Ark that includes Jack's Rake, has challenged many generations of rock climbers.

Pavey may have been derived from "Pavia" a personal female name and Ark could be derived from old Norse," Erg" meaning shieling or shelter.

Pike o' Stickle was the site of a Neolithic Stone Age axe factory. The axe heads were sent further afield to be polished and finished. When Ehen Tarn, near Beckermet, in the west of the county was drained, a number of stone axes were found.

Dropping sharply between Loft Crag and Thorn Crag is Dungeon Ghyll, middle English for "donjon," meaning a dark place below ground. Here the main ghyll draining the Pikes cascades over rocks with sheer sheets of water plummeting down through a deep gorge known as "the dungeon," hence the name. Wordsworth refers to Dungeon Ghyll in his poem, *The Idle Shepherd Boys:*

> *If ever you to Langdale go;*
> *Into a chasm a mighty block*
> *Hath fallen and made a bridge of rock;*
> *The gulf is deep below;*
> *And, in a basin black and small,*
> *Receives a mighty waterfall.*

Stickle Tarn was dammed during the 19th century to provide water for the gunpowder works at Chapel Stile and Elterwater.

At the end of Great Langdale the road climbs out of the valley into the hanging valley of Little Langdale. At the top of the climb is the blue water of Blea Tarn below the craggy Rake Rigg. This tarn is known as a corrie tarn. Corrie tarns usually have a sheer rock face as a backdrop. They were formed in the Ice Age by rocks and boulders grinding away the surface rock to form

Wrynose Pass and inset, Borrowdale teabread

large pools. Further up the valley is Little Langdale Tarn, a sparkling surface of light, with the silver strand of the beck threading its way through the tarn. Little Langdale is much quieter than its neighbour, in contrast to its previous history, when it was the main packhorse route from Ambleside to Ravenglass. Imagine negotiating Hardknott and Wrynose Pass with laden pack horses on an unmade road!

Before climbing out of the valley by way of Wrynose Pass, which is old English for twisting, is the very old farm of Fell Foot. Behind this building is a rough, rectangular mound with a flat top. Archaeologists have found no evidence as to what or why this man made mound was constructed or used. Lake District historian, W. G. Collingwood, believes it to be a "thingmound." This was a meeting place of the Viking council for the two Langdale valleys.

The Three Shires stone on Wrynose Pass marks the spot where the old counties of Lancashire, Cumberland and Westmorland used to meet. The enchanting landscape of the Langdale valleys has changed very little over the years and traditional farming methods are much in evidence, with small fields enclosed by stone walls.

Between the vales of Eskdale and Langdale is Wrynose Bottom the source of the River Duddon. The Duddon gently meanders its way through Dunnerdale to enter the sea at Duddon Sands near the market town of Broughton-in-Furness. This river was the natural boundary between Cumberland and Lancashire. The valley is sparsely populated, containing scattered farmhouses and two hamlets - Ulpha and Seathwaite.

The River Duddon threads its peaceful way through thickly wooded slopes with gently rising fell sides and fern-lined gorges. Its clear water ripples over a colourful, stone strewn bed, reflecting the ever changing colour of the sky, as it flows through the cultivated plain.

Black Hall farm at the head of Dunnerdale is one of the great Herdwick farms in the Lake District. Further down the valley is the old pack-horse bridge at Birks. The bridge spans the river across a miniature gorge with sparkling crystal water below and is the most photographed bridge in Dunnerdale. The old pack-horse route from Coniston follows the Walna Scar road over the fells to Seathwaite.

Wordsworth made the River Duddon the most famous of Lakeland rivers in his 24 Duddon Sonnets. He was very fond of the upper reaches of the river:

Pure flow the veins, pure, vigorous, free and bright
For Duddon, long-loved Duddon is my theme.

Coniston Valley

JUST south of the Langdales is Coniston Valley running north to south, approximately eleven kilometres long. The head of the valley has rugged fells and mountains of Borrowdale volcanic rock. At the southern end, towards the foot of the valley, the landscape gives way to lower, gentler fells. The roads from Ambleside and Hawkshead enter the valley at the north end through picturesque scenery of wooded hillsides and rocky slopes.

Coming from Ambleside you travel through

Yewdale and High Yewdale, past an old farmstead with a spinning gallery. The area around Coniston belonged to the monks of Furness Abbey who farmed the earliest "herd wykes" or sheep farms. Today it is still predominantly Herdwick country.

The village of Coniston, old Norse, "konungr" and old English, "tun" meaning "the king's farm," is not a chocolate box village, but it has a rugged, charm of its own. Slate buildings abound, giving a somewhat drab appearance to the streets on dull overcast days, but transformed in the sunshine after a shower to a glinting, shiny grey. The slate is a memento of the town's mining past when its economy relied heavily on quarrying the local resources. In the main street is the Ruskin Museum, which houses many of the writer's personal artifacts. The Black Bull is one of the older buildings in the village and is the oldest public house.

Borrowdale volcanic rock forms the high Coniston fells of Dow Crag and the Old Man of Coniston range whilst the rounder fells are of Silurian rock and contribute to the wooded landscape of the valley. Both of these rock formations have deposits of good quality blue slate. This has been extensively quarried. Coniston limestone can be seen just below Copper Mine Valley. A gorge has been cut through it by Church Beck and a small bridge known as the Miners' Bridge crosses it.

Coniston Water, "Thorstein's Weater," an early Scandinavian personal name, is a long, straight and narrow expanse of water some seven and a half kilometres long and 800 metres wide. At the north end it is fed by Yewdale Beck and Church Beck that drains Levers Water. Coniston Water is drained by the river Crake meaning "rocky river," which weaves its way through the valley. Peel Island was made famous by Arthur Ransome in his novel, *Swallows and Amazons*.

Of all the lakes Coniston was the most industrialised. Where the becks draining the fells entered the lake, there were furnaces or bloomeries for smelting iron. The woods were felled for making charcoal to feed the furnaces. For 75 years the lake was a busy waterway with iron ore being brought in to the furnaces for smelting. Slate from the mines of Coniston and Tilberthwaite were shipped out via the lake until the 1890s when the slate mines stopped production.

Coniston Water with its long straight course was ideal for attempts on water speed records. Sir Malcolm Campbell's water speed record of 141 miles per hour was made in 1939, ten years before his death. His son Donald, bitten by the speed bug of his father, achieved 260 miles per hour on the lake. On 4 January 1967 he reached 300 miles per hour, when his boat, *Bluebird*, suddenly shot into the air and sank without trace. His body and *Bluebird* were not located until 2001 when his remains and the wreck of *Bluebird* were recovered from the depths of the lake. Donald Campbell was given a family burial in Coniston.

The lake today is a pleasure waterway with vessels and crafts gliding and skimming across the glittering surface. Close to the shore is the cruck framed building of Coniston Hall, built in the late mediaeval period. This is a fine example of a mediaeval hall with enormous round chimneys. Unfortunately, the hall was neglected and fell into disrepair. In 1971 the National Trust acquired the property and extensive renovations were carried out to restore it to its original condition.

Standing surrounded by trees on the east side of the lake is the imposing house of Brantwood. This was the home of John Ruskin which he purchased in 1871, without even seeing it. He took up residence on the 13 September. After he saw the house for the first time he wrote to C. E. Norton: "I've had a lovely day. The view from the house is finer than I had expected, the house itself is dilapidated and rather dismal. A small place here, with fine views of rock and moor, a streamlet, and I think on the whole the finest view I know in Cumberland and Lancashire with the sunset visible. Here I have rocks, streams, fresh air, and, for the first time in my life, the rest of the purposed home."[1]

John Ruskin was an artist, writer, critic and philosopher. He died at Brantwood and is buried in St Andrew's Churchyard, Coniston. His grave is marked by an elaborately carved Anglo Saxon cross made from local slate.

Rising above the village is the Old Man of Coniston - "man," is a local word for the large cairn at the summit. He has stood guard over the village for centuries, though his flanks show scars of wear and tear from quarrying and mineral mining. Copper Mines Valley, enclosed by the surrounding fells has been worked for 300 years. Mining for copper began in the 1500s with miners brought over from Germany by Elizabeth I. Production of copper was at its peak from the late 1700s to the end of the 1800s when production ceased.

Scattered around the valley are old relics from the mine workings - rusting machinery, water courses and spoil heaps. Old mine shafts and tunnels have penetrated the fells to make a honeycomb of passages that can be dangerous if entered. The old mine buildings have been converted into holiday cottages and a Youth Hostel. Levers Water was dammed to supply water to the mine workings and the water course can still be seen. The Walna Scar road skirts the fell below the Old Man and Dow Crag. This was the old pack horse route into Dunnerdale.

Goats Water snuggling between the Old Man and Dow Crag is another corrie tarn. Dow Crag could have been Dove Crag, Doe Crag or the Welsh "Dhu," meaning black. Dow Crag is a haven for rock climbers who can be seen in their brightly coloured gear clinging to the rock face and inching their way to the top. Occasionally, a shout or a word of encouragement can be heard coming from the cliff face.

The steam yacht *Gondola* is the only steam powered vessel sailing on the lake. This luxury boat was built in 1859 for the Furness Railway Company and it was in service until 1937. The National Trust rescued *Gondola* and started work to restore her to her former glory. In 1980 *S. Y. Gondola* was back in service running trips on the lake. Being steam powered, there is very little noise from the precision machinery. To take this Victorian steam boat trip is an excellent way to

[1] *The Wider Sea* by J. Dixon Hunt

see the lake and the Old Man, keeping his watchful eye over Coniston. The *Gondola* glides over the water silently with only the sound of the gulls overhead and the water gently lapping the sides of the boat, making you feel completely relaxed.

Marie Corelli was probably the best selling romantic novelist of the Edwardian period. Her forté was romantic, melodramatic, novels which were immensely popular. A lady with a vivid imagination, she wrote 28 novels and invented a personal family history to rival that of any *Mills & Boon* heroine. She claimed her father was Italian and her mother of Venetian royal blood, although in truth her real origins were more down to earth. She was born in London in 1855 of Cockney parentage, her family name being Mackay. She lived in Stratford-upon-Avon and enlivened the neighbourhood by driving through the streets in a chaise drawn by two Shetland ponies and gliding along the Avon in a gondola piloted by a true-blooded Venetian gondolier. Being a best selling author, there was nothing money couldn't buy - that is until she visited Coniston.

On the east shore of Coniston was Brantwood, the former home of Ruskin. The old house now belonged to Arthur and Joan Severn. Arthur's father Joseph was an artist who had lived in Italy and had a talented circle of friends including Keats, Turner and Ruskin. Arthur had inherited his father's artistic gifts and as a young man had accompanied Ruskin on a tour of Italy. Joan or Joanna Agnew was a cousin of Ruskin's and had lived with Ruskin and his mother from the age of seventeen taking on the daily running of Brantwood. On her marriage to Arthur, they continued to care for Ruskin during his frequent bouts of ill health. On his death, Ruskin bequeathed Brantwood to the Severns.

In 1906 Marie was staying at the Waterhead Hotel, Coniston, and decided she wanted to visit Ruskin's old home. Her request was granted and this small, plump, golden-haired 51-year-old embarked on what nowadays would be a holiday romance. Arthur Severn was by now a distinguished looking man in his mid-60s. With the stature of a guardsman and the air of a classical artist, he was very attractive to ladies of all ages. Having toured the house with her companion Bertha Vyver, Marie's thoughts were racing ahead - the very able artist and the accomplished writer... a meeting of artistic spirits... a romance on a higher plane than mere earthly mortals - this was the very substance of one of her romantic novels.

Arthur was obviously captivated and flattered by the attentions of this well-known, youthful woman and invited her to dinner. Marie was her usual theatrical self at dinner and initially impressed her hosts with her vital enthusiasm. The relationship blossomed over the next few years with Severn visiting her in Stratford and Marie staying for weeks at a time at Brantwood.

Eventually Arthur began to tire of Marie and her theatricals and his interest began to wane. Her visits were now becoming tiresome, so much so, that on her last visit he left his wife to entertain the guest whilst he painted in his studio. After this there were no more visits to Brantwood and poor Marie's dream romance was never fulfiled.

The Newfield Inn in the hamlet of Seathwaite,

Dunnerdale, was the scene of a siege in 1904. Around this time the demand for water to supply the towns put pressure on resources in the Lake District. Seathwaite Tarn was surveyed to supply water to Barrow. A work force was taken on and excavations began. As is often the case with large numbers of imported manual labour, relaxation was taken in the local inns, where large quantities of the local brew was consumed. On one particular occasion a group of labourers worked their way up the valley visiting the various hostelries imbibing large quantities of alcohol at every stop.

By the time they arrived at Seathwaite they were very much the worse for wear and the licensee of the Newfield Inn refused to serve them. The siege began. The drunkards attacked the inn hurling anything they could lay their hands on. The local policeman was out of the hamlet at the time. The licensee took the law into his own hands, armed himself and his daughter with a shotgun, and started to fire at the rioters. One was killed and two were injured. The licensee appeared in court for the murder but was acquitted.

In country areas the inn was the meeting point for the community and in some cases housed the local post office. This was the case in Seathwaite and the acquittal was on the grounds of defending Crown property, namely the post office

Farmer's Viewpoint

ERIC Taylforth has farmed Herdwicks at Millbeck Farm, a National Trust farm in the Langdale Valley, for nearly twenty years. His wife runs bed and breakfast in the farmhouse and they also have holiday cottages. Eric also operates a cattle farm in Hawkshead. At present he has developed a mail order business for selling Herdwick meat bred on his farm. He has customers nationwide and has even sold mail order overseas. Eric believes the way forward is for farmers to become actively involved in the process of marketing their products. He envisages production geared to twelve months a year.

This will entail co-operation amongst interested Herdwick producers and careful husbandry to ensure each producer has his stock in prime condition on a rotation system that will allow all year round availability.

Eric believes good meat starts on the farm. Farmers have to become more aware of the needs of the butcher and the consumer. He has developed his skills to enable him to control the fat growth of his stock to suit the needs of the meat market. One aspect of improving quality is to prevent stress in the animals through live transportation over long distances to slaughter houses. If an animal is slaughtered when it is stressed, it produces chemicals in the meat that results in poor quality meat i.e. tough.

Eric is fortunate in having an abbatoir very close to his farm. He believes there should be more slaughter houses closer to farms and that there should be a cutting room and butchery adjacent to them. Such an arrangement would mean that for a few days a week there would be very busy periods. Staffing could be a problem, but not necessarily so. Local farmers could be trained to develop butchery skills to assist at busy periods, thereby giving them an insight into the

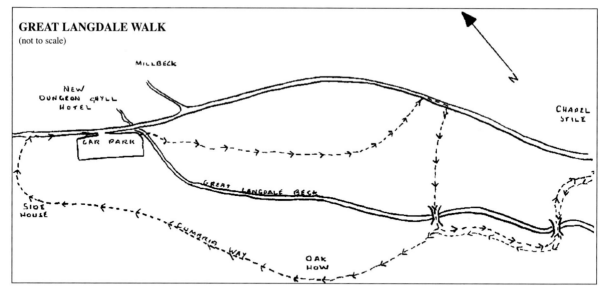

GREAT LANGDALE WALK
(not to scale)

MILLBECK

NEW DUNGEON GHYLL HOTEL

CAR PARK

GREAT LANGDALE BECK

SIDE HOUSE

CUMBRIA WAY

OAK HOW

CHAPEL STILE

quality required by the meat market and providing an additional source of income.

He believes the public are becoming far more discerning in relation to their children's well being. He says his guests care strongly about two things - their children's education and what they eat. Both these aspects will have long term effects on the child's life. He believes the public want to know how its food is produced.

Eric runs an open farm and would like to see more such initiatives where the public can see the meat growing in the field and the excellent conditions the animals are reared in. In the Lake District as a whole, where Herdwicks are bred, the majority of farms are open to view because of public rights of way. Eric sees the way forward as planning development for grant assisted projects towards farming co-operatives and farmers' markets.

Langdale Walk

Start & Finish: National Park car park, opposite New Dungeon Ghyll Hotel
Distance: 6.5 kms
Time: 2¹/₂-3 hours
Grid Ref: 295 063
Map: Outdoor Leisure 6, the English Lakes, south west area.

If you are touring the valley by car, and would like to get closer to the scenery and see some Herdwicks either in the fields, or on the fells depending on the time of year, this is a suitable short walk for the morning or afternoon. The walk allows for a refreshment stop at Brambles Café above the Langdale Co-op, in Chapel Stile. Light refreshments are available including morning coffee, light snacks and afternoon teas. The Co-operative also sells local Herdwick lamb (frozen), reared on Millbeck Farm at the head of the valley.

Leave the car park by the track in the left hand corner. Verdant green fields border the path. In May they are full of Herdwick ewes grazing whilst keeping a watchful eye on their lambs as they sunbathe in the warm spring sunshine or play " king of the castle" with their playmates on a hilly tussock. The stone walls and fields on the fell-side are a jigsaw pattern of greys, greens and browns.

As you walk to the foot of the valley, the fells on either side slope down to the entrance of the valley. Follow the track until it reaches the road. Turn right and continue for approximately 100 metres and then go through the first gate on the right. The track is very well defined with a wall of large slate slabs on your left in front of the hawthorn bushes. Continue on this track and cross over the Great Langdale Beck Once over the bridge turn left and follow the track with the beck on your left. Here, at certain times of the year, the fields are full of Herdwicks.

The fell side on your right has traces of past mining activities in the form of quarries and spoil heaps now surrounded by trees. The lower slopes of the fells on the left are lined with white-washed terraced houses, once cottages for the miners.

The many trees in the valley are a mixture of conifers and broad leaved trees. Soon you will see a single arched, stone bridge crossing the beck; its structure reflected in the crystal, clear waters. Cross over the bridge and continue along the track with views of the old quarry. When you reach the road, turn right and continue into the village of Chapel Stile. Here there are many attractive slate buildings. The blue grey slate of the church tower contrasting against a back cloth of greens, browns and greys of the fells. Continue into the village past the post office and you will see the Langdale Co-operative and Brambles Café on your left.

To continue your walk, retrace your steps over the bridge with the beck on your right. Ignore the second bridge and follow the path off to the left which climbs up to Oak How. You are now walking on a section of the Cumbrian Way. From here on, the walk is an uneven, rocky footpath with some quite steep climbs. The views towards the head of the valley are magnificent and the sky-line is dominated by the famous Langdale Pikes. To your left, Pike of Stickle, and to your right Harrison Stickle and far right the ragged fan shape of Pavey Ark and below this Stickle Tarn.

The fields become smaller towards the head of the valley and eventually disappear as the steep, rocky fells take over the landscape. Once through the last gate, the green fields of the valley floor open up before you. Take care on this section of the footpath as the pitched path descends to Side Farm. Go right over the bridge and through the farm yard to join the main road. Here turn right and make your way back to the car park.

WASDALE AND ESKDALE

In the south west of the Lake District National Park about fourteen kilometres from the Cumbrian coast are two secluded and unspoilt valleys. Wasdale gets its name from old Norse and means, "valley with the lake." Eskdale means, "valley of the river Esk," from the Welsh "esk" meaning water and the old Norse "dair" meaning dale. Another interpretation is from the old Norse " valley of the ash trees." Wastwater is approximately four and a half kilometres in length, 750 metres wide and the depth is in the region of 70 metres.

The lake is fed by Lingmell beck, Mosedale Beck and Lingmell Gill which drain the fells at the head of the valley, whilst Nether Beck and Over Beck tumble down from Haycock and Yewbarrow. The River Irt, from the Welsh "Ir" meaning fresh or green river, flows out of Wastwater and gently meanders its way through the undulating plains to enter the sea at Ravenglass.

Wasdale is remote and can sometimes seem to be the most foreboding valley in the Lake District. Surrounded by harsh, oppressive mountains, its dark, mysterious lake has a sinister tale to tell. Locals say that every year the lake claims a life. Yet on a cloudless day with the sunlight on the screes it has a soft, majestic beauty which lulls you into serenity.

The approach to Wasdale is by beautiful switchback lanes that curve their way between dry stone walls and hedgerows. Suddenly the scenery changes, opening out into green, spacious, common land with small hummocks of green hills, crowned with glorious pink heather and rocky outcrops sweeping down to the lake.

The valley boasts it has the smallest and deepest lake, the highest mountain, the smallest chapel and the biggest liar! Wasdale is about six kilometres long and is bounded by some of the highest and most rugged fells in the Lake District. At its head is the rounded peak of Great Gable with the steep ridge of Yewbarrow descending sharply from the north west. From the south east Lingmell reaches down to the edge of the valley floor.

This view has been used as the model for the Lake District National Park logo. Here are England's highest mountains with their rough, rugged fell sides, crags, buttresses and walls of vertical rock towering above Lingmell. These are Scafell and Scafell Pike, old Norse for, "bare fell" with their summits at over 1070m and 1054m respectively, and rarely free from cloud.

Illgill Head on the south east is also referred to as the Screes. Here the lake shore is strewn with boulders where the loose rock and scree above has fallen from the perpendicular sides of the fells in sweeping phalanges running down towards the lake edge. The colours of the screes at different times of the year has to be seen to be believed - in summer soft pinks and peaches, in autumn red, russets and golds.

The fells are mainly Borrowdale volcanic rock giving that rugged, impenetrable appearance. The only road in the valley runs down the north side of the lake to the hamlet of Wasdale Head and is a dead end.

The Wasdale Head Hotel has many photos of

early climbers and mountaineers and is still a haven for dedicated walkers and climbers. The landlord of the hotel in the mid 1850s was a Will Ritson who had the reputation of being the greatest teller of tall stories. He was also renowned for his abilities as a wrestler. This Cumbrian character has been immortalised by having a little waterfall named after him. Ritson's Force is in Mosedale beck about 800 metres behind the hotel.

The hamlet of Nether Wasdale is situated at the entrance of the valley with its picturesque church snuggling up to the neighbouring farmstead. The church is over 500-years-old and is built of Wasdale stone and, it is said, the roof beams were salvaged from wrecked Viking ships. The church is surrounded by 32 yew trees. This dark mysterious ever green tree has associations with church yards dating from the first Christian missionaries. They would preach under the year round protection of these ancient trees. The yew tree is said to be the symbol for eternal life.

Further down the lane is the neat, dry stone walled cemetery surrounded by green pastures where Herdwicks quietly graze. To the west of Nether Wasdale the valley opens out to the undulating pastures of the Cumbrian coastal plain where the verdant fields are bordered by thickly wooded hedges.

From Wasdale Head the only exits are up over the old packhorse routes or the old corpse road. These are only accessible on foot and are rocky and uneven and very steep in places. Behind the hotel is a single arch bridge with low walls. This is a pack horse bridge. There are many dotted all over Cumbria and the neighbouring counties. The low sides were designed to prevent the horses falling off while at the same time allowing the panniers to pass across the bridge without obstruction. From Wasdale Head one pack horse route went up through Mosedale then climbed its way up onto Black Sail Pass, descended down into Ennerdale, then climbed sharply up to Scarth Gap and finally dropped down into Buttermere. The other route out of Wasdale was through Burnthwaite to Styehead Pass, and then on to Borrowdale.

In the mediaeval period, parishes in the Lake District were very large and small chapels of ease were built, where people could easily worship. However these chapels had neither burial sites nor were they licensed for burials. This meant that corpses had to be carried to the nearest parish church for burial. On some of the old corpse roads you can still see the resting stones used to place the coffins on whilst the bearers rested or changed over. One of these old coffin routes runs from the chapel at Wasdale across Burnmoor to St Catherine's Church in Eskdale, a distance of some eleven kilometres.

In the days before St. Olaf's was licensed for burials, the corpses were carried along the corpse road over Burnmoor to St Catherine's. One story tells of how the corpse of a young man was being taken for burial to St Catherine's. The body, strapped to a horse and followed by the mourning procession, was crossing Burnmoor when a sudden mist descended over the funeral party and they became dis-orientated. The horse with the body disappeared. Once the mist had cleared a search party was set up to look for the horse and the corpse but without success. The funeral party returned to Wasdale. The dead man's mother was very distressed over the loss of her son and some time later she died of grief.

Again a funeral party set off to Eskdale retracing the route taken by her son. Yet again a thick mist came down and the party were once more lost. Once the mist cleared, a horse carrying a coffin was seen - but it was the coffin of the young dead man not his elderly mother. The coffin of the old lady was never found. So if you are out walking in the mist near Burnmoor Tarn and you hear the sound of horse's hoofs...!

Eskdale is an "U" shaped valley formed during the Ice Age and is unspoilt. The hamlet of Eskdale is at the start of the valley with white-washed houses and cottages on both sides of the main street. It is a valley without a lake though in the glacial times there were three; one at Eskdale Green, one in an area behind Brotherilkeld and one high up in Upper Eskdale at Great Moss. The fells on both sides of the valley reach down to the sea at Ravenglass.

The higher rugged fells are of Borrowdale volcanic rock whereas the lower approaches are of Eskdale granite. In the past the granite was widely used as a building stone. The outcrops of granite are rugged in places, but on the whole give a softer feel to the landscape in contrast to the Borrowdale volcanic rock.

The valley is divided into three main areas - Upper Eskdale, High Eskdale and Low Eskdale. Upper Eskdale at the head of the valley extends from Brotherilkeld to the Scafell range. This is an area of peace and tranquillity unchanged for centuries, where the landscape stretches out into loneliness. High Eskdale is from Brotherilkeld to where the railway runs parallel to the road. Low Eskdale continues from this point to Eskdale Green. The valley's length from Eskdale Green to the foot of Hardknott Pass is approximately eight kilometres.

The hamlet of Boot is in Eskdale. An old corn mill stands beside Whillan beck, its crystal, clear waters flowing over stones rounded by time. Small clusters of stone buildings lie grouped around the old pack horse bridge. The slate roofs glisten in the sunshine after a shower of rain, bringing a sparkle to this sparsely populated spot.

It is thought the name Boot derives from "boot" old English meaning bend or turn in the valley. Further up the valley is the old Woolpack Inn, its stone washed façade contrasting with the countless shades of green on the surrounding fells, fields and foliage. Wool merchants used this inn on their journeys with the pack horse trains between Kendal and Whitehaven.

Above Boot, on the desolate Burnmoor, is one of the largest tarns in the Lake District. An old hunting lodge stands nearby, adding to the sense of solitude. Dotted over the moor are numerous stone circles and cairns believed to be Bronze Age burial sites. It is thought that these burial cairns or "borrans" could be the origin of the name of Burnmoor. The tarn is the source of the Whillan Beck and a little way to the south of the tarn is the source of the River Mite. The River Mite flows through the little known wooded valley of Mitterdale to the sea at Ravenglass.

At the head of the valley is the notorious

Hardknott Pass with sharp, almost vertical, elbow bends zig-zagging up at breathtaking gradients to the summit. The descent, as it plummets down to Wrynose bottom from this, the highest pass in the Lake District, can be hair raising to newcomers to the area. However, the views from the top of Hardknott down the Eskdale valley are breathtaking and make the ascent or descent worthwhile. A panoramic vista opens up with Birk Fell and Harter Fell to the south, to the north Great Crag and Hare Crag, with the fells on both sides of the valley rolling down in giant tidal waves to the verdant green pastures below. The medley of fields crossed by hand-built stone walls, and isolated white washed farmsteads lend a touch of civilisation to the valley. Further down the valley the buildings become grouped together in small communities at Boot and Eskdale Green.

At the foot of Hardknott Pass, old Norse for "rough craggy fell" is Brotherilkeld, also known as "Butterilket," which is old Norse for "the booths of Ulfkil" - booths meaning hut or temporary shelter. In the 10th century Norse settlers possibly established the first sheep farm here. By 1242 the farm belonged to the monks of Furness Abbey and extended the full length of Upper Eskdale to Throstle Garth. Throstle is the old Norse for "song thrush".

By the old pack horse bridge over Lingrove Beck is an excellent example of a dry stone walled sheep pen which is thought to have been built by the monks. Brotherilkeld is the largest Herdwick sheep farm in the Lake District. The low, white washed farmstead was built in the 17th century.

Above Brotherilkeld are the ruins of Hardknott Fort built by Hadrian around the 1st century A.D. Some of the walls and the parade ground are still visible today. Hardknott (Medeobogdum), was on a Roman road to Ravenglass, (Glannoventa), to the west, Ambleside, (Galava) to the east and Brougham, (Brocavum), to the north.

At the head of the lonely valley of Upper Eskdale lies a semi-circle of craggy slopes forming an almost sheer wall of rock. The ridges of these heights cut into the skyline in dramatic shapes highlighting their structure of Borrowdale volcanic rock. The two summits of Scafell and Scafell Pike with their massive buttressed slopes drop down to Great Moss. In the centre is the pimpled summit and deep gullies of Esk Pike. To the east lie the rough slopes of Crinkle Crags with their serrated dog, tooth ridges. The towering craggy, rock face of Bowfell forms a pyramidal summit completing the arc of rock.

The River Esk rises above Great Moss in the shadows of these giants, fed by the gills and becks draining off the high fells. Meandering through Great Moss, the Esk then crashes down a series of ravines as cascading waterfalls into deep, blue-green pools below Green Crag. The waters of Lingcove Beck join the Esk just below the packhorse bridge. It continues its course through the valley in a series of rock pools, cascades and shallows, the coloured stones forming a mosaic pattern in the river bed. Sections of this delightful watercourse have picturesque walks along its banks as it flows to its estuary at Ravenglass.

St Catherine's, the parish church of Eskdale, is

in an idyllic riverside setting. The church is built of local granite. It has a small bell tower, a font and a graveyard, enabling the rites of baptism, marriage and burial to be performed in the church. The bell is mediaeval and believed to be the original. In the years prior to 1400, the residents of Eskdale had a long journey to St Bees to be baptised, married or buried. In 1445 the people of Eskdale petitioned the Pope to allow them to carry out these rites in their own parish. The Abbot of Calder granted their request on behalf of the Pope and the church of St Catherine was built. It is named after St Catherine of Alexandria who was martyred in the 4th century for her Christian beliefs. She was condemned to die by being lashed to a giant wheel but this collapsed so she was beheaded. Catherine is the patron saint of craftsmen, particularly spinners, wheelwrights and millers.

The Ravenglass and Eskdale Railway, affectionately known, as "La'al Ratty," is a narrow gauge line running from Ravenglass to Dalegarth, a distance of approximately ten and a half kilometres. This little railway was built as a 90 centimetre (three foot) gauge mineral line to carry iron ore from Nab Gill Mine, just above Boot, to Ravenglass. Nab Gill Mine was worked during the 1870s when the line was built. The track was extended to Gill Foss Mine but this was closed in 1877 when the mining company collapsed. Nab Gill Mine was worked until 1912 when the line was closed.

Bassett Lowke, a model railway engineer, bought the line in 1915 and converted it to a 37.5 centimetre (fifteen inch) gauge. It was then used to carry granite, but the quarry closed in 1953 and the railway closed once again. It fell into disrepair over a period of seven years until 1960 when it was sold by auction and saved. This gem of a railway now has a future as a passenger service and tourist attraction with real live steam engines. The Eskdale Valley scenery, which you can see from this little train, is of outstanding natural beauty and not to be missed.

Just adjacent to Eskdale is the little known valley of Miterdale. A story from the valley tells of how a farmer set off for market one morning. He told his young wife, who had recently had a baby, that he might not be back till the following day and to take care and lock up at night. It was October and the young woman busied herself during the day collecting rushes for candle making. In the evening, she duly followed her husband's instructions and locked up and then sat down for the evening near the window making tallow candles. A large pot of mutton fat bubbled quietly on the stove nearby, ready for the rushes to be dipped. Now and then she would look up to see if her husband was coming up the dale.

In the darkening gloom she saw a figure coming towards the farm house, but it wasn't her husband - it was a woman wearing a scarf over her head. The woman knocked at the door and asked if she could stay the night as she had lost her way. The farmer's wife didn't like the look of this uninvited guest, but as the woman looked very weary, she invited her in and showed her to a chair beside the fire. After a while the farmer's wife stopped what she was doing and went to feed the baby. Meanwhile the stranger had fallen asleep by the fire.

When the young woman returned she saw, to her horror, that the head scarf had slipped off the "woman's" head to reveal a very evil looking man with an unshaven face, head thrown back, his mouth wide open, snoring away. The young woman's mind raced - what would he do if he woke and realised she knew he was an impostor; he would surely kill her and her young baby? He was obviously up to no good, going round the countryside dressed as a woman. Tiptoeing to the stove she picked up a ladle of scalding sheep fat and tipped it down the man's throat, followed by another and another...

The following morning the farmer returned to find his wife hysterical and a dead man dressed as a woman on his kitchen floor. Calming his wife down, the farmer disposed of the body and told his wife not to tell any one what had happened. It was not until 1960 that the mystery of the dead man was explained. The Cumbrian writer Dudley Hoys found an old newspaper with an article about a murder in Whitehaven. Two seamen had had a quarrel in the town and one had been stabbed to death whilst the other had disappeared without trace. However, a lonely farm house had been burgled and a quantity of women's clothing had been stolen...

Farmers' Viewpoint

THE Harrison family run Brotherilkeld farm. It is one of the oldest farms in the Lake District dating back to the time when the monks of Furness Abbey owned the land. It is the largest Herdwick farm in the lakes dedicated to primarily farming Herdwicks in the traditional way and has some 1,500 breeding ewes. The Harrisons see the way forward for them in the development of the home market for Herdwick meat and the farm supplies a local butcher. The Eskdale Show has, in the last few years, been held on Brotherilkeld land and is one of the most important Herdwick shows in Cumbria, organised by the Fell-Dales Association for the improvement of Herdwick sheep.

Another local family are the Hartleys who have been in farming for generations and the present generation is at least the fourth to be employed in farming. Anthony Hartley told us of family farms in Eskdale and up on Birker Moor. Turner Hall Farm in Seathwaite, Dunnerdale, is at present run by Anthony, and his parents Tyson and Joyce. They employ a young man, Andrew Birkett, who has trained at Newton Rigg College and is from a farming family in the Langdales. He has to travel every day over Wrynose Pass to get to work!

The day we visited, Anthony and Andrew were busy shearing Herdwicks. The farm has in the region of 2,800 head of sheep of which 2,000 are Herdwicks the remaining being Swaledale, so they have quite a task on their hands with only two of them! Anthony also has 30 suckler cows for the beef market. The fells above the farm are common land and there are 23 farmers with grazing rights with the Hartleys being one of them.

With the advent of changes in farming policy the numbers of stock on the fells have had to be reduced. Anthony sees this as something of a challenge as with 23 graziers they have to come to an agreement as to how many sheep each farmer has to reduce by. One of the advantages may be that the quality and size of the meat produced may well improve. He stressed how the Herdwick destined for the meat market spends much of its first year grazing on the fells. It is this that gives Herdwick meat that individual flavour. He also believes animals should only travel short distances to an abbatoir. He uses Ulverston just a short distance away.

Anthony feels the way forward for him as a farmer is in supplying butchers with a specialist, top quality meat product. He is a member of the Farm Assured British Beef and Lamb scheme. This means his farm is regularly inspected to ensure he is maintaining high standards of care and production.

He is a regular exhibitor at all the agricultural shows in the area and showed us one of his tups which had won over twenty rosettes in one year.

Eskdale Walk

Start & Finish: Grassy verge before ascent of Hardknott Pass
Distance: Approximately 6 kms
Time: 3 hours
Grid Ref: 200 011
Map: OS Outdoor Leisure 6, English Lakes, south western area

This is a linear walk and takes in the beauty of the upper Eskdale fells. Here you will see Herdwicks (at certain times of the year with their lambs) in the inbye fields and on the surrounding fells.

Park on the grass verge on the right side of the road about 150 metres from the start of the ascent of Hardknott Pass. Walk towards the bottom of the pass and go left through the entrance gate to Brotherilkeld farm. There is a National Trust emblem to the right of the gate. Follow the track to the farm and turn left at the farm entrance with the fence on

THROSTLE GARTH

WATERFALLS

LINGCOVE BECK

LINGCOVE PACKHORSE BRIDGE

N

TONGUE POT

SHEEPFOLD

HERON CRAG

HERON STONES

RIVER ESK

BROTHERILKELD FARM

ESKDALE WALK
(not to scale)

HARDKNOTT PASS

PARKING

the right and the River Esk on your left. Continue along the riverside path, ignore the footbridge on your left. Continue following the path with the river on your left and go through the gate and follow the track across boulder-strewn fields. The rugged fells of Borrowdale volcanic rock tower above on both sides of the valley. Continue following the well-defined track across the field to reach a ladder stile. Once over the stile you are out on the open fell.

The path is still easy to follow. It snakes across the fell ahead of you. The two large rocks on the opposite side of the river are known as the Heron Stones that fell from Heron Crag towering above. The wide river soon starts to narrow and becomes deep-sided and ravine like with a variety of trees clinging to its rocky sides. Now the river cascades over falls into deep bluey-green, still, pools. The valley narrows considerably and the landscape is becoming wilder. Continue up the valley to Lingcove Bridge, an old packhorse bridge, over the Lingcove Beck. Just before the bridge is Tongue Pot.

Just across the bridge is Throstle Garth, the fell between Lingcove Beck and the river Esk. At this point the River Esk tumbles down a series of vertical waterfalls. Now ahead of you is a steep climb, which is worth the effort for the views of the Scafell range, and the views back down the valley. The path is very steep up to the top of Throstle Garth, and it is not recommended to go further than this point unless you are fully equipped for fell walking and are an experienced fell walker. Likewise it is not advisable and is not recommended to continue up Lingcove Beck. The stone sheepfold by the beck is very old. A

relic from the days when the farm was part of Furness Abbey.

Take time at the old packhorse bridge to admire the view back down the valley of Upper Eskdale. Above Throstle Garth is the Scafell range, to the right is Crinkle Crags and Bowfell. Retrace your steps back to the car park. The lower path on the OS map is not recommended, as it is often very wet and boggy.

SPINNING, WEAVING, DYEING AND FELTING

Wool has a colourful and exciting history and evidence of woollen cloth production goes back to prehistoric times. In 1994, *Discover* magazine published an article showing amazing pictures of ancient mummies clothed in brightly coloured, felted, woollen clothing dating back to 1,000 B.C. Even more surprising was that these mummies had Caucasian features, but that is another story.[1]

One theory as to why the colours had been so well preserved was that the soil had a high content of salt. Salt is used in dyeing to brighten colours. The clothes were actually what we would call felt. One of the mummies had coloured fibres of unspun wool wrapped round his legs obviously to protect him from the extreme cold. With constant wear, the wool would have become matted and turned into a felt-like material.

To felt wool you need three conditions - warmth, moisture and friction. It is possible that the making of felt was discovered quite by accident. If you place some fleece in the heel of your shoe and walk around all day, by the end of the day you should have a piece of felt. The verb "walk"[2] originally meant to felt, because walking meant to stamp up and down on wool in a tub of water to make it felt. If you bear the surname Walker you probably come from a line of felters!

Felt has been produced worldwide for thousands of years and is believed to have been the first textile produced by man. For centuries it has been used in many different ways, including saddles for horses, for roofing and housing material. Pliny[3] states that felt compressed and well soaked invinegar was capable of resisting iron and fire.[4]

Nowadays, more is known about the felting procedure. Wool from different breeds has different felting qualities, the Merino being the best felter. Herdwick is one of the most difficult to felt, although I have found that by combining two felting techniques you can persuade Herdwick to felt. A wool fibre has scales down the side of it. Some breeds of sheep have more of these scales or barbs than others. Merino fibres have numerous scales very close together while Herdwick fibres have far fewer.

When the wool fibres are subjected to heat, moisture and friction these barbs open up and then close together, thus forming felt. The more barbs there are, the quicker and better, the wool will felt. It is also helped by slightly alkaline conditions, so nowadays soap is used. Before the advent of soap, plants with a soap-like substance in their roots were used, for instance, soapwort.

During excavations in Turkey at Catal Huyuk, minute remnants of a hand spun fibre was unearthed. It is believed to be the earliest sample of woven material. It has been dated as 8,000-years-old. Similar fibres were found on the Venus Lespugue, an ivory carving of a woman, dating back to 2,500 BC.

References to spinning abound throughout literature. The bible has two:

Proverbs 31:19: "She layeth her hands to the spindle and her hands hold the distaff."

Exodus 35 25-26: "She takes the spindle in her right hand, by twisting which she twists the thread:

[1] See the *Mummies of Urumchi* by Elizabeth Wayland Barber

[2] OE wealcan meaning to toss or roll; ME walcun meaning to full/felt

[3] viii. 73

[4] *The Art of The Felt Maker* M. E. Burkett

while she holds the distaff on which the wool or flax is rolled in the guard of her left arm and draws down the thread with the fingers of her left hand."

Plato talks of spinning in *The Republic* in preparation for reincarnation. He says everyone has a daemon or deity that accompanies people through life as a guiding force. This daemon eventually leads you to the spinning wheel of the Greek god Necessity. The spinning wheel sits in the lap of Necessity. Plato then relates this wheel to the outer wheel of the Zodiac. There are seven inner wheels, the sun the moon and the five planets.

The goddess of Necessity had three daughters - Lachesis, meaning she who allots, was the measurer of the thread; Clotho, meaning weaver was the spinner of the thread of fate and Atropos, meaning unyielding, was the cutter of the thread. Every soul had to visit the three sisters who then determined his eternal destiny. Perhaps this is where the expression: "As you cut your cloth so you must wear it," comes from.[1]

The crafts of spinning and weaving have played an important part in many cultures. In mythology spinners and weavers have been revered as goddesses. Arachne was a beautiful maiden highly skilled in the arts of spinning and weaving. So skilled was she that no God could match her. The patron of spinners and weavers was Athena who was no match for Arachne.

In her capacity as goddess of war Athena threw down the gauntlet to Arachne to compete against her in the skills of spinning and weaving. Arachne accepted and wove a tapestry of thread depicting the desires of the gods, namely an amorous god pursuing a mortal woman. Athena's response was a picture of a man flying with wings made from feathers. He flew too near the sun and the feathers were set alight. This was to illustrate human arrogance. Athena was angry about the topic of Arachne's work and punished her for her insolence and arrogance by turning her into a spider. The rest of her short life was spent spinning thread from her own body and weaving it into a web; and was to be the fate of all her descendants.

Fairy stories abound with references to spinning, for instance, *Rumpelstilskin* and *Sleeping Beauty*. I am often asked how did Sleeping Beauty prick her finger on a spinning wheel? As people can see, the modern wheel does not have any sharp pins. The origin of the English fairy story is French and is based on the story of a Neapolitan Princess who pricked her finger on a piece of flax. Most continental stories say the fibre being spun was flax. It is unlikely that she could have pricked her finger on the wheels that we know today. One explanation is that a sharp piece of flax became wedged under her nail and she went into a coma and was brought out of the coma by her child sucking her thumb and dislodging the splinter. Another version is that, as the French word for spindle and distaff, is Fuseau, she may have pricked her finger on the distaff which does have a sharp piece; alternatively in those days spindles did wear down and become very sharp.

Cumbria's most famous poet, William Wordsworth also made frequent references to the craft of spinning. The beautiful lilting *Song For The Spinning Wheel*, is evocative of the calming, rhythmic motion of spinning fleece:

[1] *The Republic*, Plato, Book 10, section 620

Ply the pleasant labour ply
For the spindle while they sleep.

In the famous Lucy poems, which some scholars believe to be about Dorothy, he says: "She I cherished as a friend turning her wheel by an English fire."[1] Two of Wordsworth's most famous poems make reference to the spinner, spinning wheels, the spindle and carding brushes. In *Michael, A Pastoral Poem*, he writes:

Two wheels had she of antique form;
This large, for spinning wool;
That small, for flax;[2]

While in *The Brothers*, he writes:

His wife sate near him teasing matted wool,
While from the twin cards toothed with glittering wire
He fed the spindle...[3]

In 2001 when Cumbria faced the worst outbreak of foot-and-mouth disease, Wordsworth's *Last of The Flock*, said it all. This poem tells of the grief of a shepherd who has had to watch his animals die:

Sir! 'Twas a precious flock to me,
As dear as my own children be;'

And every week and every day,
My flock it seemed to melt away,
They dwindled, Sir, sad sight to see
From ten to five, from five to three
A lamb, a wether, and a ewe,
And then at last from three to two;

Of my fifty, yesterday
I had but only one;
Here it lies upon my arm,
Alas! and I have none:

Spinning

SPINNING wool using spindles is an ancient craft. The activity of spinning fibres to create threads probably dates back some 10,000 years. If we believe the rhyme: "When Adam delved and Eve span, Who was then the gentleman?" then spinning goes back to the dawn of mankind.

Archaeological evidence suggests the activity was around in Neolithic times. Whorls from hand spindles have been found dating back to 5,000 BC. Basically all that was needed was a stick and a weight known as a whorl. The word, "spin," means to draw out whilst, "whorl" means to whirl round. Different cultures have developed different types of spindles, the commonest being the drop spindle and the thigh spindle.

Spinning Wheels

SOME experts believe the wheel was invented around 3,500 BC.[4] India is often thought to be the country of origin of the wheel, though Sanskrit doesn't have a word for wheel; they use the Persian word "Charka." The oldest illustration of the spinning wheel is believed to be a painting by Chien Hsuan in 1270. The Chinese may well have had a spinning wheel for their silk production long before this, ie a date of 500-1000 AD has been suggested.

In Europe the first wheels recorded in use are in the 13th century and in England in the 14th century, while the flyer wheel is first recorded in Southern Germany in 1475.[5] As to the types of spinning wheels, they are too numerous to mention here. An in depth account worth reading on this subject can be found in Patricia Baines' book *Spinning Wheels, Spinners and Spinning*.

---

[1] 1.12, *Lucy* Poem, IX

[2] Michael, L 82-84

[3] L 21–23

[1] See *Spindles* by Bette Hochberg

[2] *Spinning Wheels, Spinners and Spinning* by Patricia Baines

Early Spinning, Weaving and Dyeing in the British Isles

SPINNING and weaving in the Anglo Saxon and Viking periods in Great Britain was a thriving industry. Women were very adept at making cloth. Wheels had not been invented at this time so the fibres were spun using a drop spindle. Both wool from the local sheep of the area and flax were spun. Flax comes form a blue flowering plant, a member of the hemp family, and was grown in the south of Cumbria. When spun it produces a linen which is a much softer fabric than wool. There have been times in Cumbria's history, right up to the early 20th century, when the spinning and weaving of linen has been a flourishing industry.

The local wool would have been first washed and then combed or carded and made into rolags or rolls and then placed on a distaff, a forked stick. The rolls of wool would have been wound onto the distaff and then leant against the shoulder of the spinner so that she or he could have both hands free to manipulate the spindle. The spindle would have been made out of wood or bone and weighted at the bottom with a "whorl," a circular piece of wood, stone or metal.

Dyeing was done either before or after spinning. Dyeing is a very ancient craft; one of the earliest written records of the use of dye stuffs is in China in 2600 BC. Dye stuffs from the surrounding countryside would have been used. Since the 15th and 16th centuries a small shrub like plant called, "dyers weed" has been found in the Kendal area around Kentmere, Troutbeck and Windermere. Seventy per cent of plants found in the British Isles will give you a yellow dye; while oak galls will give a black colour and lichens scarlet, so there was no shortage of dye stuffs. To help the dye "stick" to the wool, the wool would have been mordanted using oxalic acid obtained from wood sorrel, or using an alkaline solution from stale urine.

The yarn was then woven into cloth using a warp weighted loom. This was leant up against a wall. The warp threads hung down and were pulled tight and weighted by rows of clay weights. The two layers of warp threads were kept apart by means of a shaft. This could be moved up and down to create a shed, i.e. the space between the warp threads, for the weaver to pass the weft. Two shafts create a basic pattern known as a tabby. By introducing more shafts more complex patterns can be woven, for instance, twills and herring bone patterns.

After weaving the cloth would have been "fulled," that is washed with fullers earth to thicken the cloth to make the threads of wool bind together more. The cloth would then have been tentered; stretched out tightly over a series of hooks to dry. There are areas in Kendal that tell of this former industry namely High Tenterfell and Tenterfields. On Prickly Fell the former tentering areas are still visible and appear as stepped ridges on the side of the fells. An expression still in modern usage which comes from the woollen industry is: "I'm on tenterhooks," when our nerves are stretched to the limit rather like the wool fibres when they are drying!

The county of Cumbria has a history woven closely with wool. An Iron Age burial urn containing a charred piece of wood, which had an imprint of a finely woven piece of cloth on it, has been found in the Lakeland area. This suggests that wool has been produced in Cumbria for over 3,000 years.

In mediaeval Britain the processing of raw materials was a growth industry and an important source of income, not only for the country's coffers, but also for smugglers! Smuggling wool out of Cumbria by land and sea was a profitable enterprise because of the high duty imposed, even the monks were not above dabbling in this trade! In 1423 Robert, Abbot of Furness was accused of smuggling wool across to Zealand in his own ship! Because of its high quality, English wool was much sought after on the continent, so much so that in 1190 AD, Richard the Lionheart's ransome was paid for in wool, Kendal supplying two sacks.

In Cumbria, wool was a major source of income for the peasant farmer. The 1220s saw the monasteries of the south of Cumbria, namely Holm Cultram and Furness, dominating the trade with their vast flocks of sheep. In 1290 Furness Abbey had fourteen granges including Dunnerdale, Eskdale and Borrowdale. Records show some 15,000 sheep belonging to them were wintered on Walney Island.

The monks needed to market their wool to pay for the churches they were building. At the same time the wool was used to make heavy woollen habits to keep out the wet and the cold. Cumbrian wool was also being exported to the continent at this time. Italian wool buyers were the only continental wool buyers allowed to travel throughout England buying wool, and Cumbrian monastic houses appear on an Italian wool buyer's list for 1315. Holm Cultram sent 40 sacks of wool each year to Italy.

The Cistercians were the only producers of wool at that time to grade the wool into top, medium and poor quality. Prices paid ranged from 26-28 marks per sack to five marks. The price paid for wool from Cumbria was 18 marks per sack, so it was obviously not regarded as the lowest quality. Records suggest large quantities were sold for use by the region's local woollen industry. In the 1260s a flock of over a thousand sheep from St. Bees was sold to Richard Thornborough, a Westmorland wool factor.

Other evidence for the importance of the wool trade is in the high number of fulling mills in the area. These mills were built near water-courses as water power was necessary to drive the machinery, namely powerful hammers which beat the cloth to shrink and full it up. Wool is the only cloth that has to be fulled. Fulling mills were first recorded in Cumbria in the 12th century. By the 13th and 14th centuries the number of fulling mills in Cumbria had risen considerably. Three major towns, Cockermouth, Kendal and Carlisle, had fulling mills in 1200. The industry then spread rapidly into the surrounding area and by the mid 1400s there were fulling mills at Staveley, Whinfell, Brundholme, Embleton and Brackenthwaite, near Loweswater. Land near Mosedale beck in Loweswater was also set aside for a further two mills. In the 16th century the number of mills in Grasmere mills trebled from six to eighteen, whilst in Lorton the corn mill of the priory belonging to Carlisle, was converted to a fulling mill. All this suggests a thriving industry based on wool.

Kendal was the major wool town and its history is deeply rooted in the woollen industry. Kendal's motto: "Cloth is my Bread" and the various pub names, "The Woolpack," "The Fleece" and "The Rainbow," are testimony to this. The rainbow, incidentally, is the symbol for dyers. The town's coat of arms has teasels and wool hooks. The Company of Shearmen-Dyers has a coat of arms bearing a swag of cloth, teasel bats and cropping shears, which can be seen over the entrance to Sandes Hospital.

In 1695 out of 275 households, 133 of them were engaged in the wool trade. There were 1040 tradesmen in a guild procession of 1794, of these 80 were shear men, 100 were wool combers, 300 weavers and 150 were tailors. In the 17th century Kendal was producing hosiery, worsteds and coarse woollen cloth. Thomas Pennant remarked in 1774: "Ambleside is much employed in knitting stockings for the Kendal market and in spinning woollen yarn to weave their linseys." Linseys were a coarse cloth woven from linen and wool.

Records also show Hawkshead had a spinning industry. During the hard winter of 1785 there is a record of John Ireland, the manager of Stramongate Mill, having the yarn spun in Hawkshead, then transported to Kendal on sledges to keep his weavers employed. Cloth made in Kendal achieved a certain notoriety when Catherine Parr, whose family owned Kendal Castle, gave a coat of Kendal cloth to King Henry VIII.

In the 15th century Cockermouth was the next most important wool town in Cumbria, after Kendal. A plentiful supply of water power in the Cockermouth area contributed to the development of the town's woollen and leather industries. With the advent of the Reformation, and the subsequent dissolution of the monasteries, between 1536 and 1540, towns such as Cockermouth benefited because the buying and selling of wool passed to local people and they experienced a new prosperity. Between 1640 and 1700 the main industries of Cockermouth were woollen weaving, the manufacture of shalloons, a type of hat, and leather goods.

In the early 1700s the town experienced an increase in the number of spinners. By 1790 woollen products were making an annual profit of some £6,000 for the town. In 1847 records show 300 people were employed in the production of, "coarse woollen cloth." Cockermouth has a number of old mills and weavers' cottages. The house in Sand Lane, where Fearon Fuller was born, was once a weaver's cottage. There was also a weaving settlement in Sullart Street and Teetotal Lane.

Transportation of wool throughout the United Kingdom was done by pack horse. The tools of the trade can still be seen in a stained glass window in St Martin's Church, Bowness, where a panel of 15th century glass shows a hook, a rope and a set of skewers. The wool was wrapped in sheets, held together by the skewers. The pack was then hoisted onto the horse using the hooks and the rope secured the bale to the horse. Cumbrian wool was dispatched via the ancient pack horse routes for export from Southampton. Each horse carried a pack of 240 pounds. A ship would carry a maximum of six packs of wool. On the return journey the horses were loaded up with raisins, figs, madder, woad and alum, the latter being used for dyeing.

Kendal was the most important town in England for dyeing. The reason for this was because the area was able to produce large quantities of potash soap. Potash soap is obtained by burning green bracken of which Cumbria has an abundance. It was necessary for the dyeing process, as wool has to be thoroughly cleaned before it can be dyed successfully. Records show there was a dye house in Kendal in 1310. Celia Fiennes records seeing: "several fatts they were a dyeing in of black, yellow, blew and green—which the last coullours are dipped in the same fatt that which makes it differ is what they were dipped in before which makes them either green or blew." A certain William de Ros owned a dye house in 1310, perhaps it was the one Celia visited: "The colours in use there are listed as: "browne, blew, greene, red and black." During the 1670s Sarah Fell, a member of the famous Quaker family, of Swarthmoor Hall, sent material for dying to John Fell in Kendal.

By the 16th century there was foreign competition and in 1666 parliament passed an act to protect the home woollen market, namely that all burials had to be in woollen cloth. In the archives of Hawkshead Church there are some 200 certificates stating that the: "corps...was wrapt or wound.... in sheeps wooll onely."

Right up until industrialisation in the period from 1790-1825 the wool industry was a major part of life in Cumbria. In 1790 Sir Frederick Eden commented that clothes worn in Cumberland were all produced in the cottages. Evidence of this is supported by inventories of numerous farmers. On their death possessions listed included items of spinning and weaving. For instance, in the 17th century, a John Birkett had two wheels and carders; in 1706 George Asburner of Grasmere left: "cards, and wheels and weaver's loom," while John Addison of Hutton Park left: "a pair of weaving looms" - to name but a few. All this points to the use of and the importance of local wool in the everyday life of Cumbrian people.

With the advent of industrialisation, spinning and weaving passed into the mills, and a way of life all but died:

> Grief thou hast lost an ever ready friend
> Now that the cottage spinning wheel is mute;[1]

He added a note to this saying: "I could write a treatise of lamentation...on the changes brought about by the silence of the spinning wheel."

Yet Herdwick wool continued to be spun in the factories. In the 1830s there were over 80 woollen mills producing large quantities of hand-woven Herdwick tweed, rugs and blankets. Gradually the home market lost interest in this hand spun cloth and in the 20th century much of the raw material was exported to America for the manufacture of carpets.[2]

The future for Herdwick wool products: wool and meat by Geoff Brown

Like many leading breeders of Herdwick sheep in the second half of the 19th century, Edward Nelson of Buttermere and John Wilson of Newlands, put great store on wool. In 1879, in one of the "Essays on Herdwicks" in the *Shepherds' Guide* of that year, they began by writing: "It is above all things necessary that a Herdwick should have a good coat... a good coat

[1] Wordsworth, *Miscellaneous Sonnets, XIV*
[2] R. H. Lamb

is the first and most important point in judging a Herdwick." Not only did a good coat enable the sheep to withstand the winter weather, "a good crop of wool" also added "much to the receipts of the flockmaster." There is little doubt that over the next generation or so this advice was widely followed.

Anyone comparing a Herdwick of the 1920s or 1930s with one from the present time will immediately be struck by the considerably greater amount of wool they had in the past. Old pictures show that just before clipping their fleeces nearly touched the ground. Today the staple on a Herdwick fleece is considerably shorter. There is very little doubt that what this shows is the changing relationship between the value of a sheep's wool to the value of its meat. For many years now the value of wool produced by Herdwick sheep has declined as against the value of its meat - and at the present time Herdwick wool is at an all-time low with a minimal value.

Sheep historically, as the previous section has shown, were kept largely for their wool producing qualities - and Herdwicks will have been no different.[1] The Herdwick is now a meat animal - even perhaps a conservation grazing animal. Herdwick wool was at one time of better quality than the white wools of the black-faced breeds - but on balance now this is not the case. The wool of the Herdwick has almost certainly got shorter and harder to the touch - there being a pronounced trend in favour of these "harder" coated sheep amongst breeders.

F. W. Garnett in his book *Westmorland Agriculture*, written just before the First World War records that a speaker at an agricultural

dinner in 1862 estimated the amount of Herdwick wool grown in Cumberland, Westmorland and Lancashire at a staggering 2,000,000lbs. Given that fleece weights seem to have averaged about 3.5lbs[1] this means that there were probably more than 500,000 Herdwick sheep in the Lake counties - which seems a very large number indeed. There was a similar amount of black-faced wool, though the Herdwick made $\frac{1}{2}$d to 1d more per pound. Prices however fluctuated wildly.

Garnett reports that, at the time he was writing, Herdwick wool was "principally used at Keswick, Cockermouth and Kendal for the manufacture of linsey woolseys, blankets and scouring flannels but is not used for felting purposes and in the low tweed trade." When the Herdwick Sheep Breeders' Association first issued a list of breed points and a scale for the allocation of points for judging in the 1920s, the fleece was joint equal in importance with the characteristic stocky body shape - and great store was put on the value of the wool clip. Very little wool was wasted - diggings (dirty wool), broken wool and even wool from dead sheep was collected and cashed in.

During the great depression of the inter-war years, however, the price of Herdwick wool plummeted. As R. H. Lamb, the secretary of the Herdwick Sheep Breeders' Association put it, there was an almost "unprecedented slump in the value of both sheep and wool." It was an era of private sales with wool buyers having their regular customers on the farms. Many breeders refused to sell their wool at the very low prices offered and kept it over hoping for a better trade the next year. One of the biggest Herdwick flockmasters, Isaac Thompson of West Head, Thirlmere, famously

[1] Tallow was also an important product from sheep.

Eskdale and shearing inset

kept his clip for three years only to sell it for less than he had originally been offered.

Lamb took action to "promote some demand for wool" and approached the two woollen mills remaining in Cumberland to create new products, especially a Herdwick tweed suitable for clothing. Both mills successfully produced Herdwick tweed, one of them doing well with London buyers if the Herdwick was mixed with some Cheviot wool. A retired army officer in Herefordshire also enjoyed a modest success with a Herdwick tweed produced on a handloom. On top of this there were various local efforts within the Lake District. Women in Eskdale set up the Lake District Herdwick Wool Industries Association and, according to Lamb, in Borrowdale some handlooms were set up. In the 1931-32 *Herdwick Flock Book* he expressed his gratitude "to all those enterprising people in the dales who are developing sidelines and producing useful goods from Herdwick wool."

Reflecting on all these efforts and developments a few years later, Lamb wrote: "And what, it might be asked, is the result of this venture in the light of cold fact?" He remained steadfastly realistic suggesting that it would have been absurd to suggest that all the efforts had made any serious difference to the price of Herdwick wool to the primary producers. The efforts had shown that it was possible to make good products, especially tweed. It had been his objective to show that Herdwick wool was fit for more than carpets and horse blankets and this had been achieved, but he continued: "in order to absorb anything like the bulk of the output of Herdwick wool a large sale other than local must be gained and this can only be attained by the process of building or the lucky turn of fashion."

What made the real difference and what restored wool (at least for a few years) to its place as a serious contributor to the economies of the Herdwick farms, was the arrival of war - creating as it did demands for home produced raw materials - even relatively low quality ones such as Herdwick wool. Also there was the beginning of the serious provision of state support to hill farming - something which continued after the war and was strongly marked by the 1947 Hill Farming Act. This Act was especially welcome and established a pattern of support which lasted for about 50 years with its emphasis on "food from our own resources." The major development as far as wool was concerned was the establishment in 1950 (under the Agricultural Marketing Acts) of the British Wool Marketing Board. The Board was created to organise the orderly marketing of the entire clip of all wool growers, achieving this partly by requiring all owners of more than four sheep to register with the Board and to sell their wool to the Board at whatever is the annual price for that grade or type of wool. It also aspired to remove the wild fluctuations in price which occurred before its creation, achieving this to some extent by cross-subsidising the low value wools such as Herdwick with the proceeds from the sales of higher value wools.

For most of the years from the 1950s to the 1980s the Wool Board system worked fairly advantageously for Herdwick breeders. To be sure, Herdwick wool was either the lowest or one of the lowest value wools in the BWMB's wool price schedule, but there was a "guaranteed" price which paid for clipping (whether by farm or brought in labour) and often a lot more. The late Scott Naylor of Wasdale Head told me that when he started farming on his own account in the early 1960s, the wool cheque for his clip paid the farm rent and a man's wage for the year. There have even been exceptionally good years recently: for example, Herdwick wool on one occasion topped the market at the Bradford wool auction in the 1980s when there was a sudden unexplained demand for it from Japan. Needless to say this was not repeated and Herdwick wool has in more recent years remained stubbornly at the bottom of the pile, the cross-subsidy "guaranteed" price has gone and the Board can only pay the producers of Herdwick wool what the market says it is worth.

Since the early 1990s, the market has been saying remarkably consistently that Herdwick wool is surplus to requirements. There is a world over-supply of wool, Herdwick is a coloured wool (which is allegedly less versatile than white wool), there are currency conversion problems, there is the inexorable rise of synthetic fibre: elements of a familiar story. But in the meantime the sheep need clipping and fleeces need to be disposed of. The price of Herdwick wool, in its two shades of light and dark, has been for a number of years now, worth just a handful of pence per kilo. The 2002 price for Herdwick wool is 1p per kilo with the prospect of a further 1p in 2003. Although three or four years ago, when this desperately weak price for Herdwick wool began, farmers felt very uncomfortable about burning their wool, many of them are now getting used to it. Wool burns well straight off the sheep on the day of clipping; there are no fleeces to roll; no wool sheets to pack and to lift and to store - and no bills to pay to transport the wool to the warehouse. A good and interesting commodity has essentially become a waste product, requiring a disposal rather than a marketing solution. The Wool Board legislation, designed to correct market failure, has itself failed with regard to low value wools. A system, designed by the state (and retained by the state when all the other marketing boards have been closed down) to intervene on behalf of the producer in an uncertain market does not correct market failure: it merely creates an environmental cost which wool burning must surely be.

The Wool Board is very aware of the Herdwick wool price situation and deploys a great (and probably disproportionate to its significance in the wool industry as a whole) amount of time trying to interest wool users in Herdwick wool and to work on new product development. These efforts are clearly based on a belief in the "trickle down" theory on which the Board works: the more Herdwick product there is the more demand there will be in the wool auctions for Herdwick.

Regrettably however, this has yet to work in the crisis of Herdwick wool prices over recent years. Within the last ten or so years, for example, there have been three new Herdwick carpets put on to the market (admittedly of greatly differing quality). All three have been launched to all the right noises invoking the fells, the Lake District, the National Trust, with Beatrix Potter getting her obligatory (and usually exaggerated) mention. Given that carpet manufacturing has more potential than most other products to consume high volumes of wool, this should have worked - but the fact remains that Herdwick stays at the bottom of the pile - and now the issue is not so much one of

Shearing and inset Therese felt making

Main picture Therese spinning, top felt making and below a shoulder bag made from felted Herdwick wool.

demand but more one of supply.

The manufacturer of the most recent carpet, and arguably the best, produced by a Cumbrian firm in the historical centre of the Cumbrian wool trade, Kendal, may find it difficult to source wool unless the producers of the wool can be given sufficient incentive to send it in to the Board: a price of a least 50p per kilogram is widely seen to be the lowest acceptable price and nobody currently is expecting that the Wool Board's price for Herdwick wool will reach these dizzy heights.[1] Not that there is any money to be made at this price, but at least there is no loss, given that the sheep have to be clipped anyway for health and welfare reasons. Herdwick breeders as a group are proud to see their product turned into something useful and/or beautiful: but they have wondered over the past few years as to why they, the primary producers, fail to benefit whilst everyone else involved in the fibre chain seems to.

Farmers are very conscious now of the injunction of the Curry Commission on *Farming and Food* to add value to their products, to lift the above the level of commodities and, if possible, to use the qualities of the place of production and of the nature of production to market their product. A good number of Herdwick farmers are now successfully doing that with their meat - and, appropriately, some are also trying to do the same with Herdwick and other fell wools, though it must be pointed out that they do so against the background of the statutory instrument which established the British Wool Marketing Board.

The deteriorating situation in the price of Herdwick wool in the mid-1990s lead a number of women involved in the Farming Women project run by Voluntary Action Cumbria, the rural community council, to set up a Women's Wool Group to explore the issues and to seek solutions. One result was the formation of a co-operative called the Wool Clip which does educational work on wool and wool products and runs a retail area at Priest's Mill in Caldbeck in the northern fells.

Members of the Co-operative market a number of different products and are interested in wools other than Herdwick. Two of the members have developed a range of well designed products under the label "Helvellyn Herdwick." Their products use wool dyed to reflect colours evocative of the Cumbrian landscape alongside the natural colours of Herdwick sheep.

Also emanating from the original work of the Women's Wool Group have been a number of iniatives taken by farmers (both men and women) in the Duddon valley - again developing a range of high design-value new products but using other fell wools alongside Herdwick and trading under the name of Cumbrian Wool and Original Cumbrian Wool. All these farmers are clearly doing the right thing: they are being enterprising, they have understood the adding value message, they are transforming an effectively worthless commodity into valuable products expressive of the environmental qualities of Herdwick country.

Above all they are using their own wool, produced from their own farms and the area's fells. In order to be able to do so legally they have received temporary exemption from the Wool Board legislation and are allowed to retain their own wool in order to get it transformed into high value products. What arrangements will prevail in the future are not yet clear and one hopes that the farmers involved will be able to develop the enterprises further.

[1] It is pleasing to report that in the summer of 2003 the National Trust has devised a scheme to guarantee a price of 50p per kg. for Herdwick wool in order to supply the wool for the carpet scheme.

There probably is not much scope for many other breeders to follow the same course. The market in throws and rugs can soon become overcrowded and it is from bulk uses that the solution must come: possibly through the hoped-for success of the definitive Herdwick carpet or through its widespread use along with other low-value wools in environmentally-friendly insulation materials. This latter will probably only be readily achieved if the environmental value of wool in these applications becomes more recognised and the environmental costs of other products are more understood. Another interesting set of uses will almost certainly come from the creation of felted products and from the use of wool as stuffing and filling for pillows, mattresses and duvets.

Herdwick meat is a much shorter and more promising story. It has long had a very high reputation for eating quality. It was reputedly the mutton eaten at the Coronation Dinner in 1953 and has always been the favourite amongst local farmers and butchers for their own consumption. In 1997 a scientific study of meat quality carried out by the Animal Food Science division of Bristol University's Veterinary School established that the reputation of Herdwick was, indeed, well founded. As well as some intrinsic qualities which derive from the tight-grained structure of the meat, it was also felt by an expert tasting panel to have 'superior flavours' and better eating quality than the other sheep meats to which it was compared. Even older Herdwicks came out better than younger standard commercial lowland lambs.

Some producers have started in the last few years to realise the potential of the meat. For instance, the group developed by Eric Taylforth of Millbeck, Great Langdale and the enterprise of the Relph family at Yew Tree, Rosthwaite which won the Farming Today national prize for 2002 at BBC Radio 4's *Food Programme's* awards. Expert butcher Andrew Sharp, trading as Farmer Sharp, has also secured national recognition particularly among leading chefs and in 'foodie' circles with his weekly sales of Herdwick meat at Borough Market in London and his efforts to promote Herdwick lamb and mutton. He is very involved in the UK section of the Slow Food Movement and participated in the prestigious Italian Food Festival, Salone del Gusto (supported by the Fells and Dales LEADER + Programme) at the end of 2002. Other breeders have developed or are developing their direct marketing efforts - though there is still a long way to go before every Herdwick lamb or shearling is sold at a premium as Herdwick meat and not just subsumed in the anonymity of the food chain.

There is obvious potential for Herdwick to be branded: it is a highly specific, locally adapted and traditional breed which comes from a very special landscape full of associations with high landscape quality and environmental value. The associations of the breed with the Lake District and its links with the National Trust reinforce these attributes, as the Trust acknowledged after the foot and mouth outbreak with the appointment of a Herdwick promotion officer. There is also potential for Herdwicks to seek the European Union local food protection status, the PDO (Product of Designated Origin) as perhaps Lakeland Herdwick that might have the same resonance as Parma ham, the food product around which the PDO system was originally designed. The need to find a more profitable future for Herdwick sheep is great, but the possibility of doing so may well be within the grasp of the community of breeders.

STARTERS AND SOUPS

This section contains a selection of starters and soups that could be selected for a three/four course meal where a Herdwick main course is being served, or used as a light lunch/snack meal.

SAVOURY PARCELS

120 g (4 oz) smoked Herdwick
120 g (4 oz) Cumberland ham
60 g (2 oz) sliced mushrooms
360 g (12 oz) puff paste
30 g (1 oz) butter
30 g (1 oz) flour
30 g (1 oz) grated Cumberland farmhouse cheese
250 ml (¹/₂pt) milk
small bay leaf
seasoning

1. Melt the butter in a saucepan, add the flour and make a roux. Cook out on a low heat to a sandy texture do not colour. Allow to cool.
2. Add the cold milk slowly over a low heat and mix well to make a smooth sauce. Bring to the boil add the bay leaf and seasoning.
3. Simmer over a low heat for 20 minutes. Remove the bay leaf add the cheese and allow to melt. Place into a basin, brush the top with melted butter to prevent a skin from forming and allow to become cold.
4. The sauce should be thick enough to bind the other ingredients together.
5. Cut the meat into 1cms (¹/₂") squares. Slice the mushrooms. Add to the cold sauce and mix carefully.

To Finish:
1. Roll out the puff paste to 30 cm by 30 cm (12" by 12"), 3 mm (¹/₈") thick and cut into four 15 cm (6") squares.
2. Place a quarter of the mixture in the centre of each square. Bring the opposite corners to meet in the centre moisten the edges and carefully seal.
3. Place on a greased tray and put in the refrigerator to relax for one hour. Brush with beaten egg. Place in a preheated oven 200C for fifteen to twenty minutes.
4. Serve with a small side salad of lettuce, red pepper and grapes dressed with a lemon and garlic dressing.

LEMON AND GARLIC DRESSING

Place one small finely chopped clove of garlic in a basin with juice of ¹/₂ lemon, 1 teaspoon Cumberland Honey Mustard, 4 tablespoons olive oil, salt and milled pepper. Mix well together and serve with the salad.

CHICK PEA, HAZELNUT AND MUSHROOM PARCELS

This is a vegetarian variation on the previous recipe for Savoury Parcels.

45 g (1¹/₂ oz) chick peas, tinned

45 g (1¹/₂ oz) hazelnuts

60 g (2 oz) mushrooms
250 ml cheese sauce

Follow the recipe above for the sauce and making the parcels.

Filling:
1. Roast the hazel nuts in the oven or in a frying pan. When lightly roasted, turn out onto a rough cloth, eg. a clean oven cloth and rub to remove the skins.

Pictured previous pages, top left Melon and Tomato Cocktail with Apple and Mint Dressing. Bottom left - Patterdale Paté.

Pictured previous page right top Chilled Damson Soup and bottom right, Carrot and Apricot Soup.

2. Place the drained chick peas in a basin. Add the mushrooms cut in slices or quarters depending on size.

3. Add the nuts when cold. Bind all the ingredients together with the cheese sauce.

Helpful tip:

Both these recipes could be used as a main course. You would need to increase the ingredients appropriately. The chick pea one is popular with vegetarians.

PATTERDALE PATÉ

240 g (¹/₂ lb) Herdwick meat[1] (raw)

30 g (1 oz) finely diced onion
210 g (7 oz) unsalted butter
75 ml port, brandy or whisky
4 twists pepper mill
¹/₄ teaspoon salt
¹/₂ teaspoon thyme

olive oil for frying
6 crushed juniper berries
2 crushed cloves garlic
1 bay leaf
¹/₄ teaspoon mace

1. Cut the meat into small dice removing any skin and sinews. Place in a non-metallic dish.

2. Add the crushed garlic, juniper berries, thyme, bay leaf, mace, onions, salt and pepper. Pour the port, brandy or whisky over all the ingredients.

3. Cover and place in the refrigerator for twelve hours to marinade, turning occasionally.

4. Drain the meat and keep the marinade juices. Heat the olive oil in a frying pan.

5. Fry off the drained meat and other ingredients until the meat and the onions are cooked. Remove the bay leaf. Place the cooked ingredients into a liquidiser.

6. Add the marinade juices to the frying pan and bring to the boil and pour into the liquidiser with the other ingredients.

7. Liquidise slowly and carefully until you have a paste. Slowly add 150 g (5 oz) butter to the liquidised meat and mix in well.

8. Check the seasoning. Pass through a sieve. Place the paté into suitable dishes. Allow to get cold.

9. Melt the remaining 60 g (2 oz) of butter and pour over the paté. Allow to become cold.

10. Cover with cling film. Keep in the refrigerator for immediate use or freeze

11. Serve as a starter with oat cakes[2]

DAMSON FRUIT ICE

250 ml (¹/₂ pint) water
390 g (13 oz) damson puree
180 g (6 oz) caster sugar
1 egg white
¹/₄ teaspoon ground cinnamon

juice of ¹/₂ lemon

1. Make a stock syrup with the water and sugar. (Dissolve the sugar in the water and bring to the boil)

2. Make a damson puree (stoned damsons and cinnamon placed in a pan and brought to the boil and simmer for a few minutes then pass through a sieve).

3. Break up the egg white with a whisk. Mix all the ingredients together and add the lemon juice and chill.

4. Either use an ice cream maker and follow maker's instructions or place in the freezer and stir frequently until frozen.

[1] Use the loin or best end for pate having removed the bone.
[2] Home made Haver Bread see page 159 or toast and Cumberland sauce see page 130

Cumberland Curry

MELON AND TOMATO COCKTAIL WITH APPLE AND MINT DRESSING[1]

1 ripe melon, not honeydew
4 large ripe on the vine tomatoes
2 tablespoon mint (finely chopped with a little demerara sugar)
1 piece of ginger in syrup finely chopped

For the dressing:
1/2 teaspoon mustard powder

salt and milled pepper to taste
1 tablespoon finely chopped parsley
1 tablespoon finely chopped chives
4 tablespoons olive oil
1 teaspoon apple juice

1. Cut the melon in half and remove the seeds. Cut into 1 cm (1/2") cubes and place in a large basin.

2. Blanch the tomatoes to remove the skins. (Remove the eye of the tomato and plunge into boiling water for 10 seconds. Remove from the boiling water and plunge into cold water. The skin should now be easy to remove.)

3. Cut the tomatoes in half and remove the seeds. Cut the tomatoes into 1/2 cm (1/4") strips and add to the melon.

4. Add the finely chopped ginger and chopped mint leaves and carefully mix together.

The dressing:
1. Mix the mustard with the apple juice. Add the olive oil. Place in a jam jar.
2. Add the chopped chives and parsley. Add salt and pepper to taste.
3. Just before serving shake well and pour over the cocktail.

BEETROOT WITH A CHEESE AND CASHEW NUT TOPPING

4 small cooked beetroot
180 g (6 oz) sliced Crofton cheese (or a blue cheese)
60 g (2 oz) dried bread crumbs
30 g (1 oz) roasted cashew nuts

1. Slice the skinned beetroot and place in an oven proof dish. Cover the beetroot with the sliced cheese and sprinkle with the cashew nuts and bread crumbs.
2. Place in a pre-heated oven at 180C until the cheese has melted over the beetroot and is a light golden colour. Approximately 15-20 minutes.
3. Serve on hot plates with a tomato and cucumber side salad.

Note:
The beetroot for this dish are best plain boiled without any vinegar

PINEAPPLE, ORANGE & MINT COCKTAIL

2 large juicy oranges
4 slices of fresh pineapple
1 dessert spoon mint leaves
1 teaspoon demerara sugar

1. Remove the outer casing and centre core from the pineapple. Cut into rings and cut each ring into eight pieces.
2. Place in a basin and add the prepared orange segments. Chop the washed mint leaves with the sugar and sprinkle over the fruit.
3. Serve chilled in individual dishes.

---

[1] This recipe is adapted from a recipe from Colin Boocock of Gruline Home Farm, Isle of Mull.

HERDWICK SAUSAGE ROLLS

360 g (12 oz) Herdwick sausage meat
480 g (1 lb) puff pastry ready made[1]
1 egg

1. Roll out the puff pastry to form an oblong approximately 25 cm, (10") long by 18 cms (7") wide and 3 mm (1/8") thick. Even up the top and two sides.
2. Divide the sausage meat in half and roll into two lengths of 25 cm. Lay the sausage meat approximately 1 cm (1/2") from the top of the pastry, moisten the top edge with water and fold the pastry over and seal.
3. Cut off the long sausage roll from the remaining pastry. Repeat the process. You should now have two long sausage rolls.
4. Cut each of these lengths into six small rolls of equal length. Brush with the beaten egg. Lightly score the top of the pastry on each roll.
5. Place in a refrigerator for at least one hour to relax.
6. Place onto a greased baking tray and into a preheated oven mark 200C for 10-15 minutes or until golden brown and risen.
7. Serve hot with pickled damsons, chutneys, apple mint sauce or Cumberland sauce.

CROFTON CHEESE ECLAIRS

Pastry:
75 g (2½ oz) strong white flour
60 g (2 oz) margarine
125 ml (¼ pint) water
pinch of salt
2 beaten eggs

Filling:
500 ml (1 pint) milk
60 g (2 oz) butter or margarine
60 g (2 oz) flour
90 g (3 oz) Crofton cheese
small bay leaf

1. Sift the flour onto grease-proof paper.
2. Place the water, salt and margarine into a saucepan, place over a low heat until the margarine has melted.
3. Bring to the boil. Remove from the heat and add the sifted flour and stir in quickly with a wooden spoon until well mixed in.
4. Then beat vigorously until smooth and the mixture leaves the side of the pan clean.
5. Allow to cool slightly. Beat in the eggs a little at a time. The mixture should be shiny and should hold its shape.
6. Fill a piping bag fitted with a ½ cm (¼") plain tube. Pipe the mixture into 5 cm, (2") lengths onto a greased tray.
7. Brush with beaten egg and mark with a fork down the length of each éclair.
8. Cook in a preheated oven 200C for approximately ten minutes. When cooked the éclairs should be dry and sound hollow when you tap the bottoms.
9. Cool on a wire rack. These can be prepared and kept in an airtight tin/container.

For serving:
When cold split length ways and fill with the cheese filling.

Cheese filling:
1. Make a white sauce with the ingredients. When cooked, add the cheese and allow it to melt. The sauce should be thick and smooth.

[1] or see recipe page 153

2. Check the seasoning and allow to get cold. To prevent a skin from forming place a little melted butter or margarine on the surface.

3. Pipe the filling into the éclairs. Place on a tray and heat as required in a hot oven.

Variation:

Another suitable filling would be smoked Herdwick and Cumberland Ham[1]

CARROT AND APRICOT SOUP

480g (1 lb) carrots
60 g (2 oz) onions
1 stick celery
60 g (2 oz) butter or margarine
60 g (2 oz) flour
120 g (4 oz) dried apricots
1 lt (2 pint) vegetable stock
1 teaspoon tomato puree
1/2 teaspoon basil

1 bay leaf
salt and milled pepper

1. Soak apricots in cold water for at least one hour. Put aside two apricots for the garnish.

2. Wash the celery, wash and peel the carrots. Peel the onions. Put aside 1/2 carrot for the garnish.

3. Roughly chop all the vegetables. Melt the butter in a thick-bottomed saucepan; add the vegetables and fry without colouring.

4. Add the flour and mix well and cook over a low heat for two or three minutes.

5. Add the tomato puree and mix well. Add the stock a little at a time, mix well and stir until boiling.

6. Add the chopped apricots, basil, bay leaf and seasoning.

7. Allow to simmer until the carrots are cooked, approximately 30-45 minutes.

[1] See recipe page 131
[2] See recipe page 159

8. Cool slightly, liquidise and pass through a fine sieve. Check the consistency and the seasoning; add the garnish and finish with a little plain yogurt or cream.

To prepare the garnish:

1. Cut the apricots and carrot you have put aside into 2½ cm (1") long by 2 mm wide strips.

2. Cook the carrots and apricots in a little lightly salted water until tender. Drain and add to the soup.

CHILLED DAMSON SOUP

720 g (1½ lb) damsons
120 g (4 oz) demerara sugar
1 cinnamon stick
6 cloves
1 lt (2 pints) water
1 dessert spoon corn flour
optional ½ glass dry white wine
plain yoghurt or cream

1. Stone the damsons, place the fruit in a saucepan.

2. Place the stones in a saucepan and just cover with cold water. Bring the stones to the boil and simmer for 5-10 minutes.

3. Add the sugar, cinnamon and cloves to the fruit.

4. Strain the juice from the stones and make up to 1 litre with the water; add to the fruit.

5. Bring to the boil and simmer 10-15 minutes or until cooked.

6. Cool slightly and liquidise. Strain into a clean saucepan and bring back to the boil.

7. Thicken with corn flour mixed with a little cold water. Simmer for 5 minutes.

8. Do not thicken too much as the soup is served chilled and will thicken as it cools.

9. Mix in a little dry white wine just before serving and pour a little plain yogurt or cream in the centre. Serve with plain oat cakes.[2]

HERDWICK BROTH

480 g (1 lb) neck of Herdwick
120 g (4 oz) potatoes
120 g (4 oz) onions
120 g (4 oz) leek
120 g (4 oz) swede
120 g (4 oz) carrots
60 g (2 oz) green cabbage
60 g (2 oz) celery
45 g (1½ oz) pearl barley
1½ lt (3 pints) water
4 sprigs parsley
salt & milled pepper

1. Wash and drain the pearl barley. Place the neck of Herdwick in a saucepan and bring to the boil.
2. Remove the meat rinse under cold water to remove any scum. Place the meat back into the saucepan. Cover with 1 litres (3pints) cold water and bring to the boil.
3. Add the pearl barley and allow to simmer until the meat and barley is cooked, about 1½ hours.

4. Wash and prepare all the vegetables. Cut the potatoes into 6 mm (¼") dice and place in cold water.

5. Cut the cabbage and leek into 6 mm (¼") squares.

6. Cut the remainder of the vegetables into 6 mm (¼") dice.

7. When the meat is cooked, remove from the stock and allow to cool. Add all the vegetables to the stock except the potatoes and bring to the boil.
8. Add the seasoning. Allow to simmer until cooked. Add the diced potatoes 5 minutes after adding the vegetables.
9. Remove the meat from the bones and discard the bones. Cut the meat into 6 mm (¼") dice. Add to the soup and finish cooking.
10. Check seasoning. Serve sprinkled with plenty of fresh chopped parsley.

Notes:
This dish should be a thick broth of vegetables and meat and can be served as a lunch dish with buttered rolls, oat cakes or home baked bread. The selection of vegetables used can be varied according to personal taste and availability. The cutting of the vegetables can be done using a food processor.

POTATO AND WATERCRESS SOUP

480 g (1 lb) peeled potatoes chopped 1 cm (½") dice
1 bunch watercress, washed & rough chopped;keep back some leaves for garnish
60 g (2 oz) chopped onion
60 g (2 oz) chopped leek
1 stick of celery chopped
60 g (2 oz) butter or margarine
1 lt (2 pints) chicken or vegetable stock
½ teaspoon thyme
salt and milled pepper
yogurt or cream to finish

1. Melt the butter or margarine in a thick-bottomed saucepan. Add the celery, leek and onion and cook over a low heat without colouring with the lid on.
2. Add the potatoes and mix with the vegetables. Add the stock and bring to the boil; add the salt, pepper, thyme and the rough chopped watercress.
3. Simmer until the potatoes are cooked, approximately 30 minutes.
4. Allow to cool slightly and liquidise. Pass through a sieve, ensure that the potatoes and watercress are sieved through as these are the thickening and flavouring to the soup.
5. Check the seasoning and consistency; reheat and finish with a little yogurt or cream and the blanched watercress leaves.

To blanch the watercress leaves:
Place the leaves into boiling water for one minute; remove and place into a basin of cold water. Add to soup just before serving.

POTATO, WATERCRESS AND PEAR SOUP

This is a variation of the potato and watercress soup. A surprisingly, delicately flavoured soup - make as the above soup adding 480 g (1 lb) cooking pears (conference pears) to the ingredients.

1. Wash and cut the pears into quarters and remove the core. Keep back two quarters for garnishing the soup.
2. Add the remainder to the soup with the watercress and 1 level teaspoon of ground cinnamon. Cook and finish as above.

To prepare the garnish:
1. Thinly slice the remaining two quarters of pear and place in basin. Make a syrup with one level dessert spoon of brown sugar and 125 ml boiling water. Stir until the sugar has dissolved.
2. Pour over the sliced pears and leave to cool. This is sufficient to cook the pears for the garnish.
3. Lift the sliced pears out of the syrup and place in the soup just before serving.
4. Finish with the yogurt or cream and the blanched watercress leaves.

PARSNIP & PAPRIKA SOUP

360 g (12 oz) diced parsnips
90 g (3 oz) chopped white leek
90 g (3 oz) chopped onion
1 stick chopped celery
30 g (1 oz) margarine
30 g (1 oz) flour
1 lt (2 pints) chicken or vegetable stock
salt and milled pepper
1 level teaspoon paprika pepper
yogurt or cream
squeeze of lemon juice

1. Melt the margarine in a saucepan. Add the chopped onion, leek and celery.
2. Cook over a low heat for 5 minutes. Do not allow to colour.
3. Add the parsnips and cook for two to three minutes. Add the flour and mix well.
4. Stir in the stock and bring to the boil. Add the seasonings and paprika.
5. Simmer until cooked, 30-45 minutes.
6. Liquidise and pass through a sieve, add the lemon juice and check the seasonings.
7. Finish with yogurt or cream and sprinkle with a little paprika pepper.

SWEDE AND CINNAMON SOUP

This is a variation on the previous recipe. The ingredients and method are the same as the above soup but replace the parsnip with the swede and the paprika with ground cinnamon and add one tablespoon of toasted flaked almonds.
Finish the soup with yogurt or cream and sprinkle with ground cinnamon and the toasted, flaked almonds.

LENTIL SOUP WITH TAHINI

240 g (8 oz) red lentils
90 g (3 oz) sliced onion
90 g (3 oz) sliced carrot
1 dessert spoon tahini
1 celery stick sliced
1 lt (2 pints) chicken, vegetable or bacon stock
1 teaspoon tomato puree
salt and milled pepper
1 bay leaf
1 teaspoon marmite
$\frac{1}{2}$ teaspoon thyme

1. Soak the lentils for one hour in cold water. Rinse and drain.
2. Place in a saucepan and cover with the stock. Bring to the boil and skim.
3. Add the remaining ingredients except the tahini. Allow to simmer until cooked, stir occasionally.
4. Remove the bay leaf and liquidise and pass through a sieve. Add the tahini and mix well.
5. Finish with a little yogurt or cream.

Note:
Tahini is a puree of sesame seeds and is obtainable from health food shops and some supermarkets.

FIG SUE[1]

This dish was served traditionally on Good Friday and was eaten before the main meal of fish.

240 g (8 oz) dried figs soaked in enough beer to cover them
500 ml (1 pint) beer
4 tablespoons muscavado sugar
30 g (1 oz) butter
1 thick slice of bread
1 tablespoon black treacle
grated nutmeg

1. Soak the figs over night in the beer. Simmer until cooked.
2. Add the 500 ml beer, sugar and bread cut into quarters.
3. Bring to the boil then simmer for two minutes.
4. Just before serving stir in the treacle and grated nutmeg to taste. Serve hot.

[1] *The Lake District Life and Traditions* by William Rollinson

MAIN COURSE DISHES

CUMBERLAND CURRY

The fruity flavours of this particular curry recipe enhance the gamey taste of the Herdwick. The addition of French fried onions adds a satisfying, juicy crunchiness whilst the fresh fruit cleanses the palate.

1 kilo (2 lb) shoulder of Herdwick
240 g (8 oz) onion
50 ml (2 fl. oz) olive oil
60 g (2 oz) flour
30 g (1 oz or to suit your taste) curry powder
2 large cloves garlic
360 g (12 oz or 1 tin) tomatoes
750 ml (1½ pint) lamb stock /lamb stock cube
60 g (2 oz) stem ginger
2 teaspoons mango chutney
2 teaspoons lemon juice
180 g (6 oz) sultanas
480 g (1 lb) patna rice
salt and milled pepper
1 litre (2 pints) water
½ teaspoon salt
30 g (1 oz) butter

1. Cut the meat into 2½ cm (1") cubes and fry off in the olive oil. Add the finely diced onion and fry until lightly brown.
2. Add the flour and curry powder to the meat, and allow to cook for a few minutes, stirring occasionally.
3. Add the roughly chopped tomatoes stirring in well. (If the tomatoes are fresh, skin them, place into boiling water for ten seconds, remove, place into cold water and remove the skins.) If you are using tinned tomatoes, drain off the excess juice and add to the stock, then roughly chop the tomatoes.)
4. Add the lamb stock (or 2 lamb stock cubes and water)
5. Add the remaining ingredients, the crushed garlic, the finely diced ginger, sultanas, mango chutney, lemon juice, salt and pepper.
6. Place in a preheated slow cook pot on high for about 4 hours, (check with maker's instructions) or in a casserole dish and into a preheated oven 140C for 2 hours or until tender.

To cook the rice:
1. Bring to the boil 1 litre (2 pints) of salted water and put to one side.
2. Melt the butter in a thick-bottomed saucepan. Add the rice and cook off in the fat until the grains have a chalky appearance. This is important. The chalky appearance means that the outer case of starch has burst open and the starch is beginning to cook, you need to stir the rice every minute or so.
3. Add the boiling water and stir just once, no more. Cover with a tight fitting lid. Cook on the lowest possible heat and gently simmer for exactly 15 minutes. Do not touch it or remove the lid. If you do either, you will spoil the finished product!
4. After 15 minutes your rice should be cooked with no trace of liquid left and you should have a wonderfully, light, fluffy rice for your curry.

Accompanying dishes for Cumberland Curry:
FRENCH FRIED ONIONS

These are delicious with a curry and well worth the little extra preparation time.

1. Allow 60 g (2 oz) onions per person. Peel and finely slice into rings.
2. Separate the rings out into a basin and cover with milk. Allow to soak for two hours.
3. Just before cooking, remove the onion rings from

the milk and allow to drain well.

4. Prepare some flour by adding salt and milled pepper. Place onto a flat plate.

5. Coat the onion rings thoroughly with the flour. Shake in a sieve to remove the surplus.

6. Have ready a deep fat fryer with oil at very hot (follow your maker's instructions)

7. Fry until a light golden brown. Remove and place on kitchen paper to absorb any excess fat.

8. Lightly sprinkle with salt. Keep warm, serve on top of the curry.

Note:

Be careful when cooking this dish. The combination of the flour and the wetness of the onions causes the fat to froth up to the top of the fryer very quickly. The secret is to cook a few rings at a time. And do not leave the fryer unattended.

Also you can prepare individual dishes of the following enough for four people:

  ❦ **Fresh orange segments:**
  Allow at least ¹/₂ an orange per person.

  ❦ **Sliced fresh cucumber:**
  Serve with a yogurt dressing.

  ❦ **Sliced banana:**
  prepare this at the last minute to prevent discolouration (allow ¹/₂ banana per person)

  ❦ **Sliced apple:** allow ¹/₂ per person

  ❦ **Side dish of mango chutney**

  ❦ **Poppadoms**:
  You can buy these at a good super market. Follow instructions for preparation.

CRUMMOCK CUTLETS

The egg and breadcrumb coating locks in the succulent juices of the meat. Once cooked, the crispness of the outer crust is beautifully complemented by spaghetti and ham in a tangy, tomato sauce.

8 prepared Herdwick cutlets
1 beaten egg
fresh or dried bread crumbs
plain flour
cooking oil
salt and milled pepper

1. Lightly season the cutlets and coat with flour, shake off the surplus.

2. Pass the floured cutlets through the beaten egg and the bread crumbs. Patting the bread crumbs firmly in place.

3. Heat the oil in a frying pan and when hot carefully place in the bread-crumbed cutlets.

4. Cook gently turning when necessary until golden brown on both sides and cooked (should feel firm to touch). They may be finished off in the oven if they colour too quickly.

TOMATO SAUCE FOR SPAGHETTI

Ingredients for 500 ml (1 pint)
30 g (1 oz) margarine
30 g (1 oz) bacon scraps
1 small clove garlic
120 g (4 oz) onions
30 g (1 oz) flour
120g (4 oz) carrot
750 ml (1¹/₂ pints) stock
small bay leaf
60 g (2 oz) tomato puree
pinch thyme
salt and milled pepper
small stick celery

1. Peel and chop the onion, wash the celery and wash and peel the carrot and cut into approximately ¹/₂-1cm (¹/₄-¹/₂") lengths.

2. Cut bacon into small pieces. Melt margarine in a saucepan. Add the chopped vegetables and bacon. Gently fry until lightly browned.

3. Mix in the flour and cook to a sandy texture and allow to cool. Add the tomato puree and mix well. Cook for one or two minutes.

4. Stir in the cold stock, gradually mixing until smooth. Bring to the boil.

5. Add the thyme, bay leaf, crushed garlic and salt and milled pepper.

6. Allow to simmer for one hour, stirring occasionally to prevent burning.

7. Check the seasoning and pass through a fine sieve. Use as required.

SPAGHETTI IN TOMATO SAUCE

60 g (2 oz) cooked spaghetti
60 g (2 oz) Cumberland air dried ham cut into strips
30 g (1 oz) sliced mushrooms
250 ml (¹/₂ pint) tomato sauce

Grated mature stumpy cheese (or Parmesan)

1. Heat the tomato sauce and add the cooked drained spaghetti, ham and mushrooms and lightly mix together.

2. Serve as a garnish beside the cutlets. Sprinkle the cheese over the spaghetti just before serving.

Helpful tip:
Add herbs to sauces once you have added the stock and brought to the boil. If you add them before, the flavour will be lost.

DERWENT ROAST SHOULDER

An unusual medley of flavours, the Herdwick is enriched by the raspberry vinegar and the gravy is delicious. A Sunday roast with that "je ne sais quoi" about it.

1 shoulder Herdwick boned and rolled

250 ml (¹/₂ pint) Cumberland raspberry vinegar

125 ml (¹/₄ pint) olive oil

30 g (1 oz) sliced carrot

30 g (1 oz) sliced onion

1 clove crushed garlic

1 teaspoon rosemary

1 teaspoon thyme

1 small bay leaf

salt and milled pepper

cornflour

To marinade:

1. Place the vinegar, olive oil, sliced vegetables, garlic, herbs and seasoning in a suitable non-metallic dish.

2. Place the prepared shoulder in the marinade and leave to soak overnight. Turn occasionally to ensure the joint marinades evenly.

To cook:

1. Drain and place the joint on a trivet in a suitable casserole and pour over the marinade.

2. Place in a hot oven 170C and roast for 1-1¹/₂ hours or until cooked, basting at 20 minute interludes with the marinade. Reduce the heat if it browns too quickly.

3. When cooked remove the meat and keep warm. Remove the trivet and pour the juices (the marinade) into a saucepan and allow to stand for a few minutes to allow the fat to come to the surface.

4. Skim off any excess fat.

5. Reheat the juices and lightly thicken with a little

corn flour mixed with cold water. You may need to add a little stock to make sufficient gravy.

6. Strain the gravy to remove the vegetables.

7. Remove strings from the meat and carve into slices and serve with a little gravy. Serve the remainder in a sauce boat.

Helpful tip:

If you use any metal containers or implements with this recipe you will get an unpleasant metallic taste to the dish. This is because the vinegar will react with the metal.

FELL 'N' TARN

The Cumbrian alternative to Turf 'n' Surf. The gentle flavours of Borrowdale trout are subtly intensified by a marinade of white wine and dill. The combination of the trout and the natural flavours of the Herdwick wrapped in a light puff pastry and served with a sauce made from the marinade, makes a dish for that special occasion.

8 fillets of Herdwick trimmed of excess fat
8 skinned small fillets of Borrowdale trout or 4 skinned fillets cut in half
30 g (1 oz) fresh dill washed and chopped
30 g (1 oz) fresh chopped parsley
8 sprigs fresh dill
250 ml (½ pint) fresh double cream
250 ml (½ pint) white wine
1 dessert spoon red currant jelly
60 g (2 oz) finely chopped onion
salt & milled pepper
Puff pastry: 480 g (1 lb)

Note:

You can always buy a ready-made pack of puff pastry.[1]

---

[1] Or use our recipe on page 153

Marinading the meat and trout:

1. Place the prepared meat, trout, herbs, onions, salt and pepper into a casserole dish and cover with the white wine.

2. Cover the casserole dish with a lid and place in the refrigerator overnight to marinade.

Method of cooking:

1. Lift out the meat and the trout from the marinade and leave to drain.

2. Roll out the puff pastry thinly, and cut into 8 rounds using a saucer.

3. Place the meat in the centre of the pastry; place one folded fillet of trout on top of each of the fillets of Herdwick.

4. Place a sprig of dill on top of the trout.

5. Fold the pastry, opposite sides to the centre and seal the edges with water. You should end up with eight square parcels. Make a small hole in the pastry for the steam to escape.

6. With any left overs of pastry, roll out and cut into diamond shapes and serrate to resemble leaves.

7. Arrange a few of these on the top of each parcel as decoration. Take care not to cover the steam hole.

8. Brush the parcels with egg wash. Lightly grease a baking sheet and place on the parcels.

9. Place in the refrigerator for one hour to relax the pastry.

10. Place the tray in a pre-heated oven 200C. Cook for 20 minutes.

11. Place the marinade in a saucepan and bring to the boil. Add more wine if more sauce is required.

12. Simmer gently until the onion is cooked. Add one dessert spoon of red currant jelly and mix in well.

13. Just before serving add the cream and whisk in well. Check the seasoning.

14. Serve the sauce separately in a sauce boat.

Serving suggestion:
Serve with parsley potatoes, fresh minted peas and grilled mushrooms.

HERDWICK COBBLER

A tasty stew with alternative toppings. Choose from herb and cheese scone or a baked suet topping.

720 g (1¹/₂ lb) diced Herdwick in 2¹/₂ cm (1") dice

90 g (3 oz) diced onion

45 g (1¹/₂ oz) flour

62 ml (¹/₈ pint) olive oil

750 ml (1¹/₂ pint) stock or water

1 dessert spoon tomato puree
1 bay leaf
1 clove of garlic
salt and milled pepper

1. Heat the oil in a saucepan. Fry the meat quickly to brown all sides.
2. Add the diced onion and crushed garlic and fry together for 2 or 3 minutes.
3. Add the flour, mix in well and cook until the flour is a light brown colour. Add the tomato puree and mix in well.
4. Add the water or stock and a little gravy browning. Stir until boiling; add the seasoning and the bay leaf.
5. Transfer to an oven-proof dish with a lid and cook in a moderate oven, 140C for 1¹/₂-2 hours or until the meat is cooked.
6. Remove the bay leaf and check the seasoning. The sauce should not be too thin otherwise the cobbler will sink.

Cobbler, version one:
60 g (2 oz) butter or margarine
240 g (8 oz) self raising flour

1 teaspoon baking powder
1 egg
milk to mix
90 g (3 oz) Cumberland farmhouse cheese
1 dessert spoon fresh, finely chopped marjoram
milled pepper (no salt required as the cheese is salty enough)

1. Sieve the flour and baking powder together. Rub in the fat.
2. Add the grated cheese, the chopped marjoram and a few twists of pepper mill.
3. Make a well in the centre and add the beaten egg and enough milk to make into a soft dough.
4. Roll out to 1cm (¹/₂") thickness and cut into 5 cm (2") circles.
5. Place these slightly overlapping on top of the meat. Brush with egg wash.
6. Return to the oven at 180C for 10 minutes or until golden brown.

Cobbler, version two:
120 g (4 oz) vegetable suet
120 g (4 oz) bread crumbs
120 g (4 oz) self raising flour
1 teaspoon baking powder
90 g (3 oz) Cumberland farmhouse cheese
water to mix to a soft dough
milled pepper (no salt required as the cheese is salty enough)
1 dessert spoon fresh, finely chopped marjoram

1. Sieve the flour and the baking powder and mix in the bread crumbs. Add the suet and mix in.
2. Add the grated cheese, marjoram and pepper.
3. Add enough water to mix to a soft dough. Roll and cut out as for Cobbler 1.
4. Cook in a preheated oven 160C for approximately 40 minutes.

HARDKNOTT LEG WITH CAPER SAUCE

A simple dish and one the Romans would have enjoyed. Tasty and easy to make.

1 small leg of Herdwick
2 whole carrots
2 whole onions
1 small stick of celery
1 bay leaf
1 sprig of thyme
60 g (2 oz) flour
60 g (2 oz) margarine
$\frac{1}{2}$ lt (1 pint) cooking liquor from the Herdwick
2 dessert spoons capers
salt and milled pepper

1. Ask the butcher to remove the aitch bone.
2. Tie the joint round with string. This will keep the leg firm and make it easier to carve.
3. Place the leg into boiling salted water. Bring back to the boil, skim and allow to simmer.
4. Add the prepared whole carrot, onion, thyme and bay leaf. Simmer until the meat is cooked - allow 20 minutes per 480 g (1 lb) plus 20 minutes over.
5. Allow to cool before carving. Serve with a little cooking liquor and the vegetables cut into pieces and caper sauce.

Caper sauce:
1. Make a white sauce with the margarine, flour and stock. Allow to cook out.
2. Rinse the capers under cold water to remove the vinegar and add to the sauce.
3. The capers may be left whole or chopped. Serve in a sauce boat.

CUMBRIAN LEEK HOT POT

A heart warming, traditional type dish served with a fruity, braised red cabbage. Cumbria's answer to the Lancashire Hot Pot! The perfect meal after a day on the bracing Cumbrian fells.

4 good sized Herdwick loin chops
1 kg (2 lb) potatoes
480 g (1 lb) leeks
plain flour
$\frac{1}{2}$ lt (1 pint) lamb stock or 1 stock cube and water
seasoning
1 dessert spoon chopped parsley
60 g (2 oz) butter

1. Peel and slice the potatoes 6 mm ($\frac{1}{4}$ inch) thick and wash off the surplus starch.
2. Wash and chop the leeks and lightly cook in a little butter.
3. Place the leeks on the bottom of a large, deep casserole.
4. Lightly season the chops and coat with flour and place on the bed of leeks.
5. Arrange the sliced potatoes on the top and dot with knobs of butter or margarine.
6. Bring the lamb stock to the boil and just cover the Herdwick chops.
7. Place in a preheated oven 160C and cook until the potatoes are a golden brown and the meat is tender about 1-1$\frac{1}{2}$ hours.
8. Sprinkle with chopped parsley. Serve with braised red cabbage.[1]

WESTMORLAND ROAST WITH SAVOURY POTATOES

An adaptation of a classical dish. The juice of the roast Herdwick adds a delicious flavour to the potatoes. A tasty dish suitable for all occasions.

[1] See page 135

Helpful notes:

You may use the following joints for this dish: a leg, loin or shoulder, boned and rolled, or a best end. If you use a best end, you may require two joints

Initially the potatoes and the joint are cooked separately. In the final stages of cooking, the joint is placed on top of the potatoes for approximately 15 minutes.

If you use a best end, start to cook the potatoes half an hour before you start to cook the meat. If you use a loin or a shoulder the potatoes and meat can go in the oven at the same time.

A loin will take approximately one hour, a shoulder or leg about 1½ hours, a best end 35-45 minutes. Allow 20 minutes per 480 g, plus 20 minutes over.

1 Herdwick joint chosen from above
1 kg (2 lb) potatoes
240 g (8 oz) onions
½ lt (1 pint) stock or water or use a lamb stock cube
30-60 g (1-2 oz) butter or margarine
salt and milled pepper

Savoury potatoes:

1. Peel and slice the potatoes thinly and place in a bowl of cold water to remove the starch.

2. Peel the onions, cut in half and slice thinly.

3. Butter an oven proof dish large enough to hold the potatoes, onions and the joint of meat.

4. Arrange the potatoes and the onions in layers lightly seasoning each layer as you go. Finishing with a layer of potatoes. Leave room to place the joint of meat on top.

5. Add the stock to just below the last layer of potatoes. Place the butter in small knobs over the top of the potatoes.

6. Place in a preheated oven. Cook for approximately 1½ hours at 160C.

7. If the potatoes brown too quickly reduce the heat. When cooked most of the liquid will have been absorbed by the potatoes.

Roasting the Herdwick:

1. Roast the joint in the normal manner.

2. When the joint is nearly cooked, remove from the roasting tray and place on the dish of nearly cooked potatoes.

3. Return to the oven to finish cooking.

4. Serve the carved joint on a bed of the potatoes with a roast gravy made in the usual way. The braised red cabbage is a tasty accompaniment to this dish.[1]

WITHERSLACK SURPRISE

Damsons are grown in the Lyth Valley in south Cumbria and are noted for their strong nutty flavour. They were probably introduced by the Romans. They combine beautifully with Herdwick, making a really fruity stew. This recipe is based on the Belgian Carbonnade

1 kg (2 lb) shoulder of Herdwick
30 g (1 oz) fresh chopped herbs, mint, thyme and rosemary
1 lt (2 pints) damson beer
240 g (½ lb) damsons, (stones removed)
2 cloves of garlic
240 g (8 oz) onions finely sliced
2 tablespoons double cream
2 teaspoons honey
salt and milled pepper
60 g (2 oz) margarine
60 g (2 oz) flour

1. Stone the damsons keeping 12 aside for garnishing.

2. Cut the meat into 2½ cm (1") cubes.

[1] See page 135

3. Fry off in the margarine until the meat is seared, adding the salt and milled pepper to taste. Add the onions and crushed cloves of garlic and continue to fry until the meat and onions are golden brown.

4. Add the flour and mix in. Allow to cook out on a low heat for three minutes stirring occasionally.

5. Slowly add the damson beer, mixing in slowly to prevent any lumps forming.

6. Bring to the boil stirring frequently, add the chopped herbs and seasonings. Add the honey.

7. Cook in a slow cook pot on low for 6-7 hours or in a conventional oven 140C for 1½-2 hours or until tender.

8. Add the damsons 15 minutes before serving. Before serving check the seasoning, adding more honey if it is too sharp for your taste.

9. Remove from the heat for a few minutes add the cream just before serving.

CUMBERLAND FLAN

An unusual alternative to the traditional savoury cheese flan. Slices of smoked Herdwick are cut into neat pieces. The "stumpy", the local name for delicately flavoured Cumbrian goats' cheese is cut into thin slices. This dish can be served hot or cold, as a starter or a main course. A variation is included omitting the goats' cheese.

Pastry
240 g (8 oz) plain flour
60 g (2 oz) margarine
60 g (2 oz) white fat/lard
water to mix
pinch of salt

1. Sieve the flour and salt into a bowl. Rub in the fats. Add cold water and mix to a dough.

2. Roll out and line a greased flan dish.

3. Bake blind but do not prick the base. .Bake for 10 minutes 180C to set the pastry

Filling:
60 g (2 oz) washed finely chopped leek
60 g (2 oz) finely chopped onion
90 g (3 oz) goat cheese
60 g (2 oz) Crofton cheese
120 g (4 oz) Cumberland farmhouse cheese
salt & milled pepper
30 g (1 oz) margarine
4-6 slices of smoked Herdwick
2 eggs
250 ml (½ pint) milk
1 dessert spoon fresh chopped/or ½ dessert spoon dried sage

1. Sweat off the onions and leeks in the fat without colouring.

2. Drain off excess fat and place evenly over the base of the flan ring.

3. Cut the goats' cheese into 8 slices and place on the leek and onions.

4. Add the pieces of Herdwick, a little milled pepper, and the sage.

5. Grate the two cheeses and mix together. Sprinkle over the Herdwick keeping back about 30 g (1 oz) for the top.

6. Heat the milk, it must be hot, but not boiling. Remove from the heat.

7. Beat the eggs in a bowl and add a little salt, not too much as the meat and the cheeses are quite salty.

8. Strain the egg and milk mix into the flan. Sprinkle the top with the remaining grated cheese.

9. Bake in a preheated oven 140C for 45 minutes or until the egg mixture is firm and set and the pastry is cooked.

Variation:

1. Using the same ingredients as above but omit the

goat's cheese. Add 30 g (1 oz) chopped red/green peppers and add to the flan.

BAKED FILLETS IN PUFF PASTRY WITH MUSHROOM STUFFING

An unusual combination that creates a mouth-watering meal full of succulent flavours.

8 fillets/noisettes of Herdwick
240 g (8 oz) mushrooms
120 g (4 oz) onions
1 tablespoon chopped parsley
1 garlic clove
30 g (1 oz) white bread crumbs
480 g (1 lb) puff paste
olive oil
salt and milled pepper

1. Finely chop the onion and the parsley. Cook off the onions in the olive oil without colouring them.
2. Add the crushed garlic and chopped mushrooms and cook until the moisture is removed.
3. Add the seasoning, chopped parsley and the bread crumbs and mix well. Allow to get cold.
4. Brown both sides of the fillets/noisettes in a frying pan. Allow to cool.
5. Roll out the puff paste very thinly, 2 mm (less than ¹/₈") to a square approximately 50 cm by 50 cm (20" by 20") and cut 8 squares 12¹/₂ cm by 12¹/₂ cm (5" by 5")
6. Place a little of the mushroom mixture in the centre of each square and place the meat on top.
7. Place a little more of the mushroom mixture on the top of the meat.
8. Carefully wrap the paste round the meat to form a parcel.
9. Moisten the overlaps with a little water and seal. Place them on a greased tray with the folds of the

paste underneath.
10. Make a small steam hole on the top. Allow to relax for one hour in a refrigerator.
11. Brush with egg wash and place in a preheated oven. Bake at 200C for 15-20 minutes or until the paste is golden brown and the lamb is cooked.

ROSTHWAITE ROAST

A tempting, tasty treat! A recipe based on the classical Tornedos Rossini but using Herdwick products. The paté can be bought ready made from Yew Tree Farm, Borrowdale.[1] This recipe makes four portions with three cutlets per portion.

2 racks of Herdwick - best end necks
1 pot Herdwick paté or 120 g home made paté
12 pieces fried bread
fresh redcurrants/raspberries/oranges as available
12 mint leaves
Cumberland sauce
olive oil
salt and milled pepper

1. Preheat the oven. Score the fat side of the meat. Place the racks on a trivet in a roasting tray. Season with salt and lightly brush with olive oil.
2. Roast for 35 minutes in a hot oven 200C or until the meat is cooked. (Herdwick can be served pink)
3. Prepare 12 oblongs of fried bread. When cold, spread the fried bread with the paté and put to one side.
4. When the meat is cooked, allow to set then cut into cutlets.
5. Place a cutlet on top of each piece of fried bread.
6. Garnish the top of each cutlet with fresh fruit, either redcurrants/raspberries/an orange segment plus a mint leaf.
7. Serve with homemade Cumberland Sauce.[1]

[1] Or you can make your own using our recipe, see page 95

LAKELAND SAUSAGE MEAT

For those who have a mincer this recipe enables you to make your own tasty sausages. Alternatively buy Herdwick sausages from a supplier. Ask your local butcher for the sausage skins they are only a few pence. Other chapters include recipes using the sausage meat.

480 g (1 lb) Herdwick meat
120 g (4 oz) pork fat
¼ teaspoon ground nutmeg
¼ teaspoon ground cinnamon
¼ teaspoon ground ginger
¼ teaspoon ground cloves
½ teaspoon ground white pepper
1 teaspoon salt
finely chopped herbs

1. Remove all sinews and skin from the meat. Leave the fat on unless excessive.
2. Mince the meat and the pork fat through the coarsest mincer plate first. This will break the meat down and make subsequent mincing easier.
3. Mince the coarsely minced meat through the medium mincer plate.
4. Add the seasonings and spices to the meat.
5. Mince the meat through the finest mincer plate. (The meat is minced three times)
6. Add finely chopped herbs of your choice to the meat e.g. one dessert spoon to one pound of meat, or any, or a combination of the following - mint, thyme, parsley, rosemary, basil or oregano.

Variation:
Add 60 g of chopped apple or apricot to the mixture.

HONEY, MUSTARD ROAST SHOULDER

A favourite traditional dish with the mustard adding piquancy softened by the sweetness of the honey.

1 small leg, rolled loin or shoulder of Herdwick
1 tablespoon Cumberland crunchy mustard
6 tablespoon clear Cumberland honey
salt
olive oil

1. Lightly score the joint with a sharp knife.
2. Place on a trivet or roasting rack. Lightly brush the meat with oil and sprinkle with salt.
3. Place in a hot oven, 200C to seal for twenty minutes.
4. Mix the honey and mustard together in a basin and pour over the joint.
5. Reduce the heat of the oven to 160C and continue to roast the joint allowing 20 minutes per 480 g (1 lb).
6. Baste frequently with the juices in the roasting tray until cooked.
7. Remove the meat and keep warm, remove the trivet or rack and allow the juices to settle. Skim off any excess fat.
8. Add a little flour or gravy mix and sufficient water or stock to make a gravy. Allow to cook for five minutes.
9. Carve the meat and serve with a little gravy.

KESWICK BRAISE

You really must use the Cumberland Raspberry Vinegar for this dish as it is the only one we've found that adds that special, fruity flavour, others are too acidic. The black olives hint at Mediterranean summer days with a sharp, tangy sauce. The sweet, buttery flavour of the parsnips complements the other ingredients.

[1] See recipe page 130

4 large/8 small Herdwick chops
375 ml ($^3/_4$ pint) Cumberland raspberry vinegar
125 ml ($^1/_4$ pint) olive oil
250 ml ($^1/_2$ pint) stock/water
60 g (2 oz) sliced carrot
60 g (2 oz) sliced onion
30 g (1 oz) sliced celery
480 g (1 lb) parsnips
1 dessert spoon corn flour
$^1/_4$ teaspoon thyme
$^1/_4$ teaspoon rosemary
1 small clove garlic
1 bay leaf
1 teaspoon tomato puree
gravy browning
16 stoned black olives
salt and milled pepper

The marinade:

1. Place the raspberry vinegar, olive oil, sliced vegetables, herbs and seasoning in a suitable dish (not metal) and mix together.
2. Place the chops into the marinade and leave for 4-6 hours or overnight.
3. Turn the meat occasionally if not fully covered to ensure even soaking. Cover with a lid or cling film.

To cook:

1. Drain the meat and seal on both sides in a hot frying pan. There should be sufficient oil on the meat from the marinade to aid the frying.
2. Place meat in a suitable casserole. Add the marinade with the vegetables to the pan used to seal the meat with the stock or water, tomato puree and a little gravy browning..
3. Bring to the boil and stir to dissolve the juices from the base of the pan.
4. Pour over the meat and cover with a lid and cook in the oven 140C for $1^1/_2$ hours or until cooked.

5. Remove the meat and place in a clean, hot dish. Put the cooking liquor with the vegetables into a saucepan, bring to the boil, thicken with the corn flour, mixed with a little cold water, cook for 5 minutes.
6. The sauce should be thick enough to coat the back of the spoon. If too thick add a little stock or water. If too sharp add a pinch of brown sugar.
7. Strain the sauce over the meat. Add the stoned olives and return to the oven to keep hot.
8. Serve on a bed of pureed parsnips seasoned with salt, milled pepper, nutmeg and mix with a little butter. Sprinkle with chopped parsley.

ESKDALE STEW

Herdwick served in a smooth, creamy cider sauce with that delicate hint of mint.

1 kg (2 lb) Herdwick shoulder in $2^1/_2$ cm (1") cubes
500 ml (1 pint) dry cider
500 ml (1 pint) white lamb stock
90 g (3 oz) butter/margarine
90 g (3 oz) plain flour
4 tablespoons single cream
8 button onions optional
8 button mushrooms optional
salt and milled pepper
rosemary fresh/dried
chopped parsley
4 triangles of fried bread

1. Melt the butter/margarine in a saucepan and add the prepared meat. Fry gently without colouring.
2. Add the flour and carefully mix in. Cook for two minutes over a low heat
3. Slowly add the cider and stock stirring well until the mixture is smooth and boiling.
4. Allow to simmer and add the chopped rosemary, salt and milled pepper.

5. Simmer gently over a low heat until cooked, stirring occasionally to prevent burning. Cook for approximately 1½ hours.

6. Add the onions and mushrooms 15 minutes before the meat is cooked

7. Add a little of the sauce to the cream, mix well, then pour back into the saucepan and stir in thoroughly.

8. Do not boil after adding the cream or the sauce may curdle.

9. Serve sprinkled with chopped parsley and a triangle of fried bread.

Note:

This is cooked on the top of the stove and not in the oven. If it is cooked in the oven the sauce may turn a brown colour. This dish is an ivory coloured stew.

BOETHAR'S BRAISED RICE

A novel way to use up those left overs. A quick, tasty lunch or supper dish. We have also used smoked Herdwick in this dish and it gives a light, smokey flavour. Earl Boethar was the Cumbrian leader who fought in the Battle of Rannerdale.

2 cups long grain rice
4 cups stock/water
1 small finely chopped onion
4 sliced mushrooms
240-480 g (8 oz-1 lb) cooked diced Herdwick/smoked Herdwick
25-30 g (1 oz) butter
1 stick chopped celery
salt and milled pepper
bay leaf
½ teaspoon marjoram
grated mature stumpy cheese (this is as good as parmesan!) (optional)
small piece of butter

¹ Or use our recipe on page 112

1. Select a pan with a lid that can go in the oven. Melt butter in the pan and gently fry the onions and celery without colouring.

2. Add the rice and stir well. Cook for a few minutes until the rice starts to look chalky.

3. Add the stock, mushrooms and cooked diced meat, herbs and seasoning and bring to the boil.

4. Cover with a lid, cook in a hot oven 180C for 17 minutes, no longer.

5. The rice should be cooked, light and fluffy and all the liquid absorbed. Add a little butter and stir in with a fork.

6. Sprinkle with a little grated stumpy cheese if desired.

7. Serve immediately with a green or mixed salad.

Note:

If you use smoked Herdwick add the diced meat to the rice just before serving and stir in well.

SAUSAGE MEAT LOAF

You can buy ready made Herdwick sausage meat.[1] Our original sausage meat loaf recipe has been a family favourite for over 30 years. Using Herdwick sausage meat it seems an even tastier and more succulent dish. Any left overs are beautiful served with a salad.

480 g (1 lb) Herdwick sausage meat
120 g (4 oz) chopped onions
120 g (4 oz) chopped Cumberland bacon
120g (4 oz) chopped cooking apple
1 egg
½ tin drained tomatoes
1 tablespoon chopped marjoram
olive oil
salt and milled pepper

1. Fry off the bacon in a little olive oil, add the chopped onion and continue to fry without colouring. Allow to cool.

2. Place the sausage meat in a basin large enough to take all the ingredients.

3. Add the cold, cooked onions and bacon the chopped cooking apple, the drained, chopped tomatoes, marjoram and the beaten egg. Mix well together.

4. Place into a greased loaf tin and bake in a preheated oven 180C for 45 minutes or until cooked.

5. The remainder of the tomatoes and the juice can be used as a gravy to serve with the loaf.

Note:

This dish can be served cold with a mixed salad and chutneys or pickled damsons.

CUMBERLAND PIZZA

Forget about Italian Pepperoni! Smoked Herdwick and smoked Cumberland ham in a tangy tomato sauce with mushrooms, red peppers, onions, garlic, black olives and herbs rivals the real Macoy; truly delicious and easy to make. We include an easy pizza base recipe or you could buy a ready made base.

Pizza base:

130 ml (¹/₃ pint) warm water
240 g (¹/₂ lb) plain, strong, white flour
¹/₂ tablespoon dried yeast
1 tablespoon olive oil
¹/₂ teaspoon Muscavado sugar
pinch of salt

1. Put the water in a jug with the sugar and sprinkle the yeast over the top. Leave in a warm place to froth up, about 15 minutes.

2. Place the flour and salt in a mixing bowl and leave in a warm place. When the yeast mixture is frothy add the oil.

3. Make a well in the centre of the flour and add the yeast mixture. Mix to a dough, add extra water if necessary.

4. Turn out onto a floured surface and knead thoroughly until the dough is soft and pliable.

5. Put the dough back into a lightly greased bowl, cover the bowl with cling film and leave in a warm place for about one hour or until it has doubled its size.

6. Knead briefly again and press out into one large/2 medium/4 small circles and place on a greased tray.

7. Cover with cling film and leave in a warm place for about ¹/₂ hour.

8. Place in a preheated oven 180C and bake for 5 minutes to set the dough.

9. Remove from the oven and put the prepared topping on top. Return to the oven and bake for a further 10-15 minutes.

Topping:

1 tin tomatoes
120 g (4 oz) finely diced onion
60 g (2 oz) sliced mushrooms
¹/₂ large red pepper
2 cloves garlic
120 g (4 oz) air dried Cumberland ham
120 g (4 oz) smoked Herdwick
30 g (1 oz) sliced Crofton cheese
90 g (3 oz) Cumberland farmhouse cheese
15 g (¹/₂ oz) chopped fresh marjoram
olive oil for frying
12 stoned olives

1. Cook the onions and crushed garlic off in a little oil without colouring.

2. Add the tin of tomatoes and sliced pepper. Cook off for about 10 minutes.

3. Add the sliced mushrooms and cook for a further

5 minutes.

4. Chop the smoked meats into large dice and chop the marjoram.

6. Add these to the tomato mixture; stir in well over the heat and place onto the pizza base.

7. Grate the farmhouse cheese and slice the Crofton cheese. Arrange the stoned olives and the sliced Crofton on the top of the pizza.

8. Sprinkle the grated farmhouse cheese over the top. Return to the oven and bake for a further 10-15 minutes.

9. Serve with a mixed salad.

Note:

No additional salt or pepper was needed with this filling.

THURSBY THINGMOUND

A Thingmound was a Norse meeting place and Thursby is where Crofton cheese is made. In this recipe we have a meeting of unusual flavours - chicory, smoked Herdwick and Crofton cheese. Chicory is a slightly bitter vegetable which combines well with air dried ham and smoked Herdwick, mingled with the delicate flavour of Crofton cheese, sets the taste buds tingling. (If this cheese is not available, try a delicate blue cheese.)

4 heads of chicory
½ lt (1 pint) white sauce
90 g (3 oz) Crofton cheese
60 g (2 oz) bread crumbs
4 slices air dried Cumberland ham
8 slices smoked Herdwick
1 lemon

1. Wash and trim the chicory. Place in an oven proof dish with a lid.
2. Squeeze the lemon and sprinkle the juice over the chicory.

3. With the lid on, place in a preheated oven 160C for 25- 30 minutes or until cooked.

4. Allow to cool and wrap the chicory with the ham and smoked Herdwick.

5. Place these in a greased oven proof dish or casserole.

6. Add 60 g of cheese to the white sauce and pour over the rolls.

7. Slice the remaining 30 g of cheese and lay over each roll.

8. Sprinkle with the bread crumbs place in a hot oven until the cheese has melted and is a golden brown.

9. Make sure that this dish has been properly heated through.

10. Serve with delicately flavoured vegetables, eg., mange tout, green beans and mushrooms and buttered new potatoes.

SHEPHERDS' PIE

A popular, traditional dish using up cooked meat. Finished with a tasty topping of potatoes, leeks and Cumberland cheese crisped up to a nutty brown crust in the oven.

480 g (1 lb) cooked minced or finely chopped Herdwick
120 g (4 oz) chopped onion
60 g (2 oz) butter
480 g (1 lb) peeled potatoes
60 g (2 oz) grated Cumberland farmhouse cheese
120 g (4 oz) chopped leeks
125 ml (¼ pint) milk
125-250 ml (¼-½ pint) thickened gravy to bind the meat
olive oil
¼ teaspoon grated nutmeg
30 g (1 oz) butter (for leeks)

1. Sweat the onions off in the oil without colouring. Add the minced cooked meat and sufficient gravy to bind.

2. Bring to the boil and simmer for 15 minutes. Place the mixture in a suitable oven-proof dish.

3. Cook the potatoes, drain and return to the pan and place over the heat to dry them off.

4. Mash the potatoes and add the butter, milk and nutmeg. Beat well with a wooden spoon to make a creamy mixture.

5. Cook off the leeks in a little butter, mix well with the potatoes.

6. Place the potato mixture on top of the meat and spread evenly. Sprinkle with the grated cheese.

7. Brush with a little melted butter and place in a hot oven 180C to lightly colour and ensure the dish is very hot.

Note:

This dish must be heated through thoroughly as you are reheating cooked meat.

MILLBECK BURGERS IN A BROWN ONION SAUCE

These are traditional burgers because the original Hamburg steak was 100% meat and thick! These burgers are 7½ cm (3½") diameter by 2½ cm (1") thick. Not your fast food variation! This recipe is full of tasty goodness served with a rich brown onion sauce.

720 g (1½ lb) minced Herdwick
2 eggs
120 g (4 oz) diced onions
2 tablespoons chopped fresh mint
2 tablespoon chopped fresh parsley
½ teaspoon ground nutmeg
60 ml (⅓ pint) olive oil

½ lt (1 pint) brown sauce or gravy
4 tablespoons raspberry vinegar
180 g (6 oz) shredded onion
2 tablespoons olive oil

1. Fry the diced onion without browning in a little olive oil. Allow to get cold.

2. Keep back some of the chopped parsley for garnish.

3. Place the minced Herdwick in a bowl, sprinkle the chopped mint, parsley, ground nutmeg, salt, milled pepper and the cold onions over the surface.

4. Whisk the eggs together and pour over the mixture.

5. Carefully mix together with a fork, ensuring that all the ingredients have been mixed through evenly. Divide the mixture evenly into four.

6. On a lightly floured surface, shape the balls into rounds approximately 8 cm (3") diameter and 2cm thick (1").

7. Heat the olive oil in a frying pan and when hot fry the burgers turning carefully after 5 minutes and cook the other side for 5 minutes.

8. They can be finished off in the oven to ensure they are properly cooked without burning them.

Brown Onion Sauce:

1. Fry the onions off in the olive oil until cooked.

2. Drain off any excess fat and add the raspberry vinegar. Place the pan on the stove and evaporate most of the vinegar.

3. Add the brown sauce or gravy, bring to the boil and simmer for 10 minutes.

4. Serve the burgers with the sauce poured over them. Sprinkle with chopped parsley.

ROAST BEST END WITH A SAVOURY CRUST

A novel way of serving up the favourite Sunday roast. The herb flavoured bread crumbs form a tasty, crunchy, crust to this dish.

2 best ends of Herdwick (3 cutlets per portion allowed)
120 g (4 oz) fresh bread crumbs
60-90 g (2-3 oz) butter
2 tablespoons chopped parsley
1 tablespoon thyme
olive oil for roasting
salt and milled pepper
zest of lemon

1. Skin and score the fat side of the best end, ie., with a sharp knife cut a trellis pattern just through the fat. Be careful not to cut too deep, as you do not want to cut into the meat.
2. Place the best ends on a trivet in a roasting tray. Season and lightly brush with olive oil.
3. Roast for 20 minutes in a hot oven 200C.
4. Mix the bread crumbs with the lemon zest, parsley, thyme and melted butter.
5. After 20 minutes remove the best ends from the oven and cover the fat surface of the meat with the breadcrumb mixture, pressing on lightly.
6. Return to the oven to complete cooking, browning the crust to a golden brown colour.
Approximately 10-15 minutes or until cooked (this joint may be served pink)
7. Allow the meat to rest before cutting between the bones into portions, or cut into one thick piece for each portion (three bones per portion)
8. Serve with fresh mint sauce and gravy.

[1] OS map Leisure 19, Howgill Fells, grid ref 809991

MINT SAUCE

30 g (1 oz) chopped mint
1 teaspoon demerara sugar
2 tablespoons raspberry vinegar
2 teaspoons water

1. Chop the washed mint leaves with the sugar.
2. Place into a china or glass basin and add the raspberry vinegar and water and mix well.
3. Serve in a sauce boat.

HUGH'S POT ROAST IN A MULLED WINE SAUCE

Hugh was something of a scoundrel. He gained notoriety as one of the murderers of Thomas a Becket on 29 December 1170. Hugh de Morville owned large estates in Westmorland including Appleby Castle. Part of his land included Mallerstang Edge on the North Yorkshire border. Here he erected a border stone called Hugh's Seat which is still marked on the map.[1]

We serve this mulled wine recipe at Christmas with cheese éclairs, sausage rolls and savoury parcels (see Chapter 10). Here it is used in an innovative way to accentuate the gamey flavour of pot-roasted Herdwick. Something different for Boxing Day lunch!

1 kilo (2 lb) loin boned and rolled
120 g (4 oz) carrots
120 g (4 oz) onions
1 bay leaf
1 teaspoon thyme
60 g (2 oz) butter
4 slices each of fresh lemon and orange
1 bottle damson wine
4 cloves
$^1/_2$ stick cinnamon

1 cup red grape juice
15 g (¹/₂ oz) dark brown sugar
1 dessert spoon corn flour

1. Wash peel and slice the carrot 1 cm thick. Peel and slice the onion 1 cm thick.
2. Use a casserole or a saucepan suitable for using in an oven for this recipe. Place the sliced carrot, onion, bay leaf and thyme in the bottom of the pan.
3. Place the loin on the bed of vegetables and coat the loin with butter.
4. Place in a preheated oven 150C and cook for 1-1¹/₂ hours, or until cooked.

To prepare the sauce:
1. Place the red grape juice in a saucepan with the dark brown sugar.
2. Heat gently stirring all the time until the sugar has dissolved.
3. Add the cloves and cinnamon and simmer for 5 minutes to extract the flavour.
4. Add the slices of fresh fruit. Add the damson wine and slowly bring to the boil. Do not allow to boil. Remove the orange and lemon slices.
5. Dilute the corn flour with a little cold water.
6. Bring the wine mixture to the boil and add the corn flour to lightly thicken the sauce.
7. Bring to the boil and cook out for two minutes. It should coat the back of a spoon.
8. Strain and remove the spices. Place the sauce to one side and keep hot.

To finish the dish:
1. Remove the strings from the meat and keep it warm.
2. Slice the meat and serve with a little of the mulled wine sauce over the meat.
3. Serve the remainder of the sauce in a sauce boat.

LAKELAND STEAMED MEAT PUDDING IN CUMBERLAND ALE

A heart warming meal. Ideal for those cold Cumbrian days and the best way to end a day on the fells.

Filling:
720 g 1¹/₂ lb Herdwick cut into 1 cm (¹/₂") dice
60 g (2 oz) chopped onions
1 dessert spoon chopped parsley
1 bottle Cumberland ale
salt and milled pepper
dash of Worcester sauce
500 ml (1 pint) thickened gravy

1. Place the diced meat in a basin with the salt and pepper, chopped onion, chopped parsley and just cover with the beer.
2. Allow the meat to marinade for six hours or overnight if possible.

Suet pastry:
180 g (6 oz) plain flour
60 g (2 oz) fresh bread crumbs
120 g (4 oz) chopped vegetable suet
1 teaspoon baking powder
1 dessert spoon chopped thyme
125 ml (¹/₄ pint) approx. cold water
pinch of salt

1. Sieve the flour, baking powder and salt into a bowl.
2. Mix in the suet, bread crumbs and thyme. Add sufficient water to make a pliable dough, knead lightly.
3. Grease a 1 lt (2 pint) pudding basin; cut a circle of grease proof 2 inches larger than the top of the basin. Grease this. Put aside for covering the top.
4. Cut a circle of tin foil a little larger than the grease proof top.

5. Cut off ¼ of the suet pastry and keep it aside for the top of the pudding.

6. Roll out the rest of the pastry to a circle 3 mm (⅛") thick.

7. Line the greased basin. Ensure there are no holes or breaks in the pastry.

8. Work the pastry up (thumb up) to just above the top of the basin.

9. Strain the meat and place into the pudding and barely cover with the marinade.

10. Roll out the pastry for the top the same thickness as the base. Moisten the edges, place on the top of the pudding and seal firmly.

11. Make a fold in the circle of grease proof paper (to allow for the pudding to rise) and place over the pudding. Place the tin foil over the top and seal firmly.

12. This dish can be cooked successfully in a slow-cook pot; refer to the manufacturers instructions.

13. Or steam for 4-5 hours topping up the water in the steamer when necessary; or use a pressure cooker and follow the manufacturer's instructions.

14. The left over marinade can be added to the thickened gravy to serve with the pudding.

ROAST LEG WITH GARLIC AND ROSEMARY SERVED WITH A BRANDY AND ROSEMARY SAUCE

The ever popular roast with the flavours of garlic and rosemary permeating the meat, served with a delicious brandy and rosemary sauce.

1 leg of Herdwick
olive oil
4 small garlic cloves
2 sprigs rosemary
salt and milled pepper

1. With the point of a sharp knife, make 8 incisions on the meat and insert the peeled, halved garlic cloves.

2. Lightly season the meat and place on a trivet in a roasting tray.

3. Pour a little olive oil over the joint and place in a hot oven to seal the meat 190-200C for approximately 30 minutes.

4. Reduce the heat to 160C and place the sprigs of rosemary on the joint.

5. Continue roasting, basting frequently to keep the meat moist. Allow 20 minutes per 480 g (1 lb).

6. When cooked keep warm and allow meat to set before carving.

BRANDY AND ROSEMARY SAUCE

60 g (2 oz) flour
60 g (2 oz) butter/margarine
500 ml (1 pint) chicken stock/1 cube
2 tablespoons brandy
1 dessert spoon finely chopped rosemary
salt and milled pepper if you use fresh stock

1. Melt butter/margarine in a saucepan. Add flour

Cumberland Flan

and mix well to make a roux.

2. Cook out over a low heat until dry and sandy. Do not brown.

3. Allow to cool. Gradually add the hot stock, whisking well all the time to prevent lumps.

4. Bring to the boil and allow to simmer over a low heat for 30 minutes then strain.

5. Add the chopped rosemary and brandy, mix well and re-boil for 2 minutes.

6. Finish with a little fresh cream or plain yogurt. Serve with the roast.

Helpful tip:
Add hot stock to a cold roux or vice versa then you shouldn't get a lumpy sauce!

SAUSAGE TOAD IN THE HOLE

A traditional dish, but the addition of the honey and mustard adds a new dimension to the flavours. Served with apple sauce and braised red cabbage, it makes a very tasty meal.

8 Herdwick sausages
Yorkshire pudding batter
2 eggs
120 g (4 oz) plain flour
250 ml (½ pint) liquid, use ½ milk and ½ water
8 teaspoons Cumberland clear honey
8 teaspoons Cumberland mustard
olive oil
pinch of salt

Helpful tip:
A successful Yorkshire pudding depends upon the following:
- Make a few hours before you need it and place in the refrigerator.
- Use plain flour. Use ½ milk and ½ water.
- Aerate (whisk vigorously) once you have finished adding the liquid. You should see lots of tiny bubbles on the surface.
- Leave in the refrigerator undisturbed for at least 1 hour.
- Just before pouring over the sausages whisk briefly again.

1. Sieve the flour and salt into a basin. Make a well in the centre.

2. Break in the eggs, and beat into the flour. Slowly add the milk and water mixture whisking vigorously to prevent any lumps.

3. Continue until all the liquid has been used. Then whisk vigorously to aerate the mixture for about 3 minutes. Place in the refrigerator for about one hour.

4. Heat the oil in a suitable pan or roasting dish. Place the prepared sausages in the pan.

5. Brown the sausages in the oil. Place one teaspoon of honey and 1 teaspoon of mustard over each sausage.

6. Pour the batter over the sausages and place in a hot oven 180C for 15-20 minutes.

7. Serve with a gravy and apple and mint sauce or apple sauce. Braised red cabbage is a tasty vegetable to serve with this dish.

APPLE SAUCE

480 g (1 lb) cooking apples
Juice and rind of 1 lemon
90 g (3 oz) light brown sugar
½ teaspoon ground cloves
½ teaspoon ground mace
knob of butter

1. Peel and core the apples, cut into quarters. Place in a saucepan with the juice, rind of the lemon, the sugar and the spices.

2. And a little water to prevent burning. Cook until

soft then beat in the butter.

3. Serve hot in a sauce boat.

FILLETS SERVED WITH AN ORANGE SAUCE.

A prime cut of Herdwick served with a delicately flavoured sauce. A mouth-watering dish.

8 fillets of Herdwick (cut from a boned loin or fillet)
4 slices bread for fried croutes (8 x ¹/₂ fried slices of bread)
¹/₂ litre (1 pint) lamb stock
olive oil
salt and milled pepper
juice of one lemon
zest of 1 orange
juice of 4 oranges
1 tablespoon fresh mint chopped with a little demerara sugar
corn flour (approximately 1 tablespoon)
1 dessert spoon chopped parsley for garnish

Croutes:

1. To prepare the croutes, remove the crusts from 4 slices of bread and cut in half diagonally. Trim them to the shape of the fillets.

2. Fry the bread in hot olive oil until golden brown. Drain and place on one side.

To prepare the sauce:

1. Remove the peel from 1 orange and keep the peel aside. Remove the segments, keep for garnish.

2. Place the lamb stock in a saucepan with the orange and lemon juice.

3. Bring to the boil and simmer for 5 minutes.

4. Lightly thicken with the corn flour mixed to a paste with a little cold water. The sauce should coat the back of the spoon.

5. Remove the pith from the peel leaving just the zest.

6. Cut the zest into fine strips. Place the shredded zest in a little boiling water for 2 minutes.

7. Drain and add to the sauce with the finely chopped mint leaves.

9. Adjust the colour of the sauce if necessary by using gravy browning.

10. The sauce should be a rich brown colour. Check the sauce for seasoning.

To cook the meat:

1. Lightly season the fillets and fry them in hot olive oil turning them to cook evenly.

2. To serve, place each fillet on a fried croute and pour a little sauce over each.

3. Place an orange segment on each fillet. Sprinkle a little chopped parsley over each one. Serve the remaining sauce separately.

SHALLOW FRIED LEG STEAK WITH CAPERS AND APRICOTS

The succulent flavours of the meat are locked in by the crispy crust of the bread crumbs. The sweetness of the apricots and the sharpness of the capers makes an unusual combination.

4 x 180 g (6 oz) leg steaks
1 egg
2 dessert spoons capers
8 dried apricots
plain flour
bread crumbs
salt and milled pepper
olive oil for frying

1. Soak the apricots in boiling water. Leave to soak for at least an hour.

Pictured top Shallow Fried Leg Steaks and below, Fell 'n'
Tarn

Rosthwaite Roast

2. Remove the pieces of bone from the leg steaks and lightly flatten the meat.

3. Coat the steaks with seasoned flour, beaten egg and bread crumbs.

4. Heat the oil in a thick frying pan, and gently fry the steaks on both sides until cooked, approximately 10-15 minutes.

5. Fill the soaked apricots with the capers. Place in a small oven proof dish with any remaining capers.

6. Barely cover with the liquid used for soaking the apricots. Heat through in the oven.

7. To serve place two apricots by the side of each steak.

STUFFED PEPPERS

Make your own Herdwick sausage meat or buy from a local supplier. The sweet, spicy flavour of the red peppers adds a Mediterranean touch to your menu and complements the gamey taste of the sausage meat.

4 large red peppers
480 g (1 lb) Herdwick sausage meat
120 g (4 oz) Cumberland fat bacon
120 g (4 oz) diced onion
1 teaspoon chopped rosemary
60 g (2 oz) sliced carrot
60 g (2 oz) sliced onion
30 g (1 oz) butter
salt and milled pepper
olive oil for frying

1. Wash and cut off the stalk end of the peppers. Remove all seeds and the white ribs.

2. Lightly season the inside of the peppers with a little salt and pepper.

3. Cut the bacon into small dice and fry off in the olive oil. Add the diced onion and fry without colouring.

4. Place the sausage meat in a basin and mix in the onion, bacon and the rosemary.

5. Divide the meat mixture into 4 and fill the peppers.

6. Place the sliced onion and carrot in the bottom of an oven-proof dish and place the peppers cut end down onto the vegetables.

7. Melt the butter and pour evenly over the peppers. Cook in a preheated oven 150C for 40 minutes or until cooked.

8. To serve: they may be left whole or cut in half length ways and garnished with the slices of carrot and onion.

9. Use the juices left in the dish to make the gravy to accompany the red peppers.

CUMBERLAND PASTY

A dish suitable for lunch, packed lunch or a snack with a blend of flavours to tempt the taste buds. A meal in itself.

480 g (1 lb) short crust pastry
120 g (4 oz) finely diced raw potatoes
60 g (2 oz) finely chopped raw onion
240 g (8 oz) finely diced/minced/raw Herdwick
60 g (2 oz) chopped raw leek
1 dessert spoon chopped parsley
1 dessert spoon chopped mint
2 teaspoons clear Cumberland honey
1 teaspoon crunchy Cumberland mustard
1 tablespoon Cumberland raspberry vinegar
salt and milled pepper

1. Prepare the short crust pastry. Place in the refridgerator until ready to use.

2. Mix the meat with the honey, mustard, raspberry vinegar and allow to marinade for about 1 hour.

3. Mix the meat mixture with the onions, herbs, salt, pepper, leeks and potatoes.

4. Roll out the short crust pastry to 3 mm (¹/₈") thick

and cut 4, 15 cm (6") diameter rounds.

5. Place the meat mixture on half of each round, moisten the edges with water, fold over and press edges lightly together.

6. Brush with beaten egg and place onto a greased baking sheet.

7. Bake at 160C for 30-40 minutes or until cooked.

8. Serve hot with gravy, or cold with a salad or for a packed lunch.

RHEGED HOT POT

This is a dish named after the ancient kingdom of Rheged. We have sourced recipes for wild sheep written by the 1st century Roman cookery expert Apicius. Using ingredients that would probably have been available to the Romans in Cumbria, we have devised an exciting recipe to tempt the taste buds. Ingredients include, wine, damsons, honey, mint, thyme, rosemary, marjoram and ginger. A truly autumnal dish that leaves you glowing from the inside out!

1 kilo (2 lb) shoulder of Herdwick cut in 2$^{1}/_{2}$ cm (1") cubes
170 ml ($^{1}/_{3}$ pint) damson wine
170 ml ($^{1}/_{3}$ pint) lamb stock
240 g ($^{1}/_{2}$ lb) washed damsons
180 g (6 oz) finely chopped onions
125 ml ($^{1}/_{4}$ pt) single cream
30 g (1 oz) fresh chopped herbs (mint, thyme, marjoram and parsley)
$^{1}/_{4}$ teaspoon rosemary
2 cloves crushed garlic
2 teaspoons Cumberland honey
15 g ($^{1}/_{2}$ oz) finely chopped stem ginger
salt and milled pepper

1. Place the prepared herbs, garlic, ginger, onions, honey, salt and pepper into a large casserole dish.

2. Choose 8 firm damsons for the garnish and set aside.

3. Stone the remaining damsons, add to the casserole dish and cover with the damson wine.

4. Add the prepared meat to the casserole dish. Cover and leave to marinade for at least 4 hours (preferably overnight stirring occasionally.)

5. Preheat the slow cooker on high or the oven on 140C

6. Place all the ingredients from the casserole into a saucepan add the lamb stock and bring to the boil. Transfer to the slow cooker pot or a casserole with a lid.

7. Cook in the slow cooker for approximately 4$^{1}/_{2}$ hours or in the oven for approximately 1$^{1}/_{2}$-2 hours 140C or until the meat is tender.

8. Thicken with a little diluted corn flour and check the seasoning.

9. Serve sprinkled with chopped mixed herbs.

Serving Suggestion:

Serve with a selection of winter vegetables eg., sprouts, parsnips, carrots and parsley potatoes.

PORTINSCALE TIT BITS SERVED WITH CUMBERLAND SAUCE

Portinscale is a small hamlet on the outskirts of Keswick. The name Portinscale means the harlot's hut! This recipe is an innovative way of using a cheap cut of meat. It can be prepared in advance ie., the day before. It is a tasty dish with a crispy crust that can be served with a refreshing salad or hot vegetables and a tangy Cumberland Sauce. Children love it with baked beans or spaghetti in tomato sauce. It is also ideal as a starter with the Cumberland sauce served as a dip.

2 whole Herdwick breasts
1 bay leaf
1 teaspoon each of thyme and rosemary

Smoked Cumberland Pizza

Crummock Cutlets with Spaghetti in Tomato Sauce

¹/₂ **small onion**
¹/₂ **small carrot**
2 eggs
flour
bread crumbs
oil for cooking

1. Choose breasts with a good proportion of meat to fat.
2. Remove the skin, bones and any excess fat from the breasts of Herdwick.
3. Place in a casserole with salt, milled pepper, bay leaf, thyme, rosemary, half a small onion and half a small carrot and just cover with boiling water.
4. Cover the casserole with a lid and cook the breasts in the oven at 140C for about 2 hours.
5. Drain and press the meat between two clean plates and place a weight on the top one to compress the meat. Leave until cold.
6. Cut the breast into strips, triangles or leave as irregular shapes, remove any excess fat.
7. Coat each piece with flour, beaten egg and bread crumbs.
8. Heat the oil in a frying pan and fry the pieces of breast until golden brown on each side and hot in the centre.
9. Drain and serve with the Cumberland Sauce

CUMBERLAND SAUCE
240g (8 oz) red currants or 1 jar of red currant jelly
1 orange
1 tot of port
water to cover the meat

1. Stew the redcurrants with a little water until cooked. Pass through a sieve or liquidise.
2. Place in a pan with the grated rind, juice of the orange and the port. Bring to the boil.

3. Thicken with the corn flour mixed with a little cold water.

Note:
If you use the jar of redcurrant jelly then just place all ingredients in a pan and bring to the boil and thicken with the corn flour if necessary. Serve hot as a sauce or as a dip.

Other Garnishes:
- Haricot beans in a tomato sauce.
- Spaghetti in tomato sauce with chopped tomato on top and grated matured, stumpy cheese, (when grated the stumpy cheese resembles parmesan with a stronger flavour.)

SKIDDAW SALAD
Herdwick served cold is unlike other lamb. There should be no cloy or fatty taste on the palate. It is ideal to serve cold as a sliced meat. This dish is different; a refreshing medley of meat and fruit mixed with yogurt served with a salad and an orange dressing.

480 g (1 lb) cooked Herdwick
2 skinned tomatoes
1 dessert apple
2 small cooked beetroot
1 tablespoon sultanas
2 celery sticks
1 x 300 g (¹/₂ pint) carton fresh plain yogurt
1 dessert spoon chopped marjoram
salt and milled pepper

1. Trim any surplus fat, and skin from the meat and cut into 1 cm (¹/₂ ") dice.
2. Cut the tomatoes, beetroot, apple and celery into 1 cm (¹/₂ ") dice.

3. Place the meat, sultanas and other diced ingredients into a basin.

4. Add the marjoram and seasonings. Mix carefully together.

5. Bind with the yogurt and place in a salad bowl.

6. Serve with a mixed green salad with a fresh orange and oil dressing.

ORANGE AND OIL DRESSING

1 teaspoon Cumberland honey mustard
1 tablespoon freshly squeezed orange juice
3 tablespoon olive oil
salt and milled pepper

1. Place mustard in a small bowl. Add the orange juice, olive oil and seasoning.

2. Whisk well together. Shake/stir well before serving with the salad.

SPICED LAKELAND STEW

The strong flavour of Herdwick meat is enhanced by the bitter-sweet tang of paprika. A robust stew for cold winter days.

1 kilo (2 lb) diced Herdwick 2½ cm (1")
120 g (4 oz) diced onions
750 ml (1½ pints lamb stock
60 g (2 oz) flour
3 fresh peppers - yellow, green and red
55 ml (⅛ pint) vegetable oil
1 dessert spoon tomato puree
2 tablespoon plain yogurt
salt
1 dessert spoon paprika pepper

1. Heat the oil in a thick-bottomed saucepan and fry off the diced Herdwick until lightly browned.

2. Add the onions and cook without colouring. Add the flour and paprika and mix in well.

3. Cook over a low heat for 2 minutes, stir occasionally. Slowly add the cold stock, mixing well over a low heat.

4. When all the stock has been added bring to the boil and season with salt.

5. Transfer the stew to a casserole with a lid and cook in a preheated oven at 140C for 1½-2 hours or until the meat is cooked.

6. Check the seasoning and consistency of the sauce. The consistency should resemble double cream.

7. Mix the yogurt with a tablespoon of the sauce and pour this into the stew just before serving.

8. Sprinkle with finely shredded peppers. This will give a fresh, crunchy texture to the dish, or they can be lightly poached in boiling salted water.

CUMBERLAND HAM

Traditional Cumbrian recipe tested by authors.

1 kilo (2 lb) gammon
1 tablespoon Cumberland honey
1 onion
1 carrot
1 stick of celery
demerara sugar
cloves
fresh mixed herbs eg., bay leaf, thyme, marjoram
cider to cover meat
6 peppercorns

1. Soak the ham overnight to remove the excess salt.

2. Roughly chop the washed vegetables and peeled onion. Place in a large saucepan or stock pot.

3. Add the fresh chopped herbs, peppercorns and the cloves.

4. Place the ham on top and cover with cider; add the honey.

Herdwick Stuffed Peppers

5. Simmer gently until cooked. Allow for 20 minutes to 480 g (1 lb).

6. Allow to cool back before carving.

Note:

This is traditionally served with another Cumberland delicacy, Cumberland Sauce.[1]

STUFFED BREAST OF MUTTON

The following Cumbrian recipe is a slight adaptation of one which is almost a 100-years-old and one we have used for nearly 40 years:

1 boned breast mutton
240 g (8 oz) pork sausage meat
1 carrot sliced
1 onion sliced
1 dessert spoon fresh chopped thyme
$^1/_2$ lemon (juice and zest)
oil for cooking

1. Add the herbs, zest and juice of the lemon to the pork sausage meat.

2. Remove the bones and any sinew from the breast. Place the breast on a board with the meat side up.

3. Cover with the sausage meat spreading evenly. Roll up and tie first in the centre then work to each end with the ties 2$^1/_2$ cm (1") apart.

4. Place the sliced vegetables in the bottom of a casserole and place the stuffed breast on top.

5. Brush with a little oil. Cover with a lid and place in a preheated oven 150C and cook for 1$^1/_2$-2 hours or until cooked.

6. The meat is served sliced. Serve with gravy and red currant jelly.

Note:

We do not add any more salt and pepper as the sausage meat is highly seasoned.

[1] See page 130 for recipe.
[2] *Lakeland Recipes Old and New* by Joan Poulson.

ROAST VENISON

1$^1/_2$ kilo (3 lb) leg or loin of venison
240 g (8 oz) slices of pork fat
750 ml (1$^1/_2$ pint) red wine
125 ml ($^1/_4$ pint) raspberry vinegar
1 onion
1 carrot
1 stick celery
2 tablespoon olive oil
1 bay leaf
1 teaspoon each fresh chopped thyme and parsley
6 peppercorns
$^1/_2$ teaspoon salt

1. Wash and slice the vegetables. Place in a china or glass dish large enough to take the venison joint. Add the wine, vinegar, oil, herbs and seasonings.

2. Place in the venison and allow to marinade for two days turning regularly.

3. Remove the venison from the marinade and dry. Place the slices of pork fat over the joint.

4. Place the joint on a wire rack in a roasting tray. Roast in a preheated oven 190C and cook to seal the meat for 15 minutes.

5. Reduce the temperature to 160C basting frequently until cooked. Allow 20-25 minutes to 480 g (1 lb). Venison can be served pink

6. When cooked remove the meat from the roasting tray, add the marinade to the roasting dish and make a gravy.

CUMBERLAND SAUSAGE[2]

Traditional Cumbrian dish tested by authors.

1 kilo (2 lb) lean pork
300 g (10 oz) fatty pork
1 teaspoon fresh chopped or ground sage
$^1/_2$ teaspoon fresh chopped or dried marjoram

$^1/_2$ level teaspoon ground nutmeg
$^1/_2$ level teaspoon ground mace
2 twists black milled pepper
$^1/_2$ level teaspoon salt

1. Mince the pork using a coarse mincer plate.
2. Add the other ingredients and mix well.
3. Fill the mixture into sausage skins and make into long lengths.
4. Fry in hot fat until cooked or brush with hot fat and cook in a hot oven.

CUMBERLAND TATIE POT

Traditional Cumbrian dish tested by authors.

1 kilo (2 lb) Herdwick for stewing
1 kilo sliced raw potatoes
1 whole black pudding sliced
360 g (12 oz) sliced onions
360 g (12 oz) sliced carrots
1 bay leaf
fresh/dried thyme
salt and milled pepper
30g (1 oz) butter

1. Place a layer of sliced potatoes in the bottom of a casserole dish.
2. Cut the meat into 2$^1/_2$ cm (1") cubes. Place on top of the layer of potatoes.
3. Add the rest of the sliced vegetables, black pudding and seasonings in alternate layers, finishing with a layer of potatoes overlapping like tiles on a roof.
4. Add boiling water to cover all the ingredients except the final layer of potatoes.
5. Place a knob of butter on the top of the potatoes. Place in a pre-heated oven 140C for 2 hours or until the meat is tender.
6. Serve with braised red cabbage.

[1]*Lakeland Recipes Old and New* by Joan Poulson.

SAVOURY SUET PUDDING

Traditional Cumbrian dish tested by authors.

120 g (4 oz) plain flour
120 g (4 oz) bread crumbs
120 g (4 oz) suet
1 egg
$^1/_4$ teaspoon baking powder
2 heaped teaspoon fresh chopped marjoram, thyme, basil and parsley
salt and milled pepper
water to mix
Optional: 120 g (4 oz) chopped streaky bacon

1. Place all the dry ingredients in a bowl and mix together.
2. Add the beaten egg and mix well. Add enough water to mix to a soft dough.
3. Place in a greased basin and steam for 1-1$^1/_2$ hours.

CUMBERLAND SWEET MEAT PIE[1]

720 g (1$^1/_2$ lb) beef suet
480 g (1 lb) minced Herdwick
480 g (1 lb) seeded raisins
720 g (1$^1/_2$ lb) currants
480 g (1 lb) dark brown sugar
480 g (1 lb) prepared cooking apples cut into small dice
120 g (4 oz) candied peel
1 lemon, the juice and grated rind
250 ml ($^1/_2$ pint) rum or brandy
1 teaspoon grated nutmeg
1 teaspoon ground mace
480 g (1 lb) short crust pastry

1. Place the dried fruit and sugar in the rum to soak for a few hours.
2. Mince the meat. Add the spices and suet and mix well.

3. Add the prepared apples and candied peel and the grated rind and juice of the lemon.
4. Add the soaked fruit and rum.
5. Line a deep pie dish with pastry and place in the filling. Cover with a pastry cover.
6. Bake in a preheated oven Mark 6 for 45 minutes.

Note:
For use straight away, you could use mutton chops instead of the minced meat. Place all the ingredients in a pie dish and cover with puff pastry and bake. Eat immediately.

VEGETABLE DISHES

This section contains easy to prepare vegetable dishes that go well with Herdwick meat. Just a little something extra and a few more minutes preparation time is sometimes all that is needed to transform the vegetable into a dish that is a little different
It has been recommended that you should eat five portions of vegetables or fruit a day to maintain healthy bodily functions. We have included a nutrient guide.

BRAISED RED CABBAGE
1 small red cabbage
2 tablespoons sultanas
1 cooking apple
1 medium sized onion
375 ml (³/₄ pint) stock/water
60 ml (¹/₈ pint) cooking oil
¹/₂ teaspoon ground cloves
¹/₂ teaspoon ground cinnamon
2 teaspoons Cumberland honey
125 ml (¹/₄ pint) raspberry vinegar
2 dessert spoons corn flour
30 g (1 oz) butter/margarine
30 g (1 oz) plain flour
salt and milled pepper

1. Cut the cabbage into quarters and remove the centre stalk and wash thoroughly. You will get a lot of red, purplish dye coming out.
2. Shred finely and wash again.
3. Heat the oil in a large saucepan and add the drained red cabbage.
4. Lightly fry for 3 to 4 minutes, turning frequently

with a wooden spoon.

5. Peel and chop the onion and add to the cabbage and continue to cook gently.

6. Peel, core and chop the apple and add to the cabbage. Continue to cook for a further 3 to 4 minutes.

7. Add the sultanas, spices and honey, vinegar, salt and milled pepper and stock.

8. Bring to the boil and transfer to a large casserole dish, cover with a lid and cook in a moderate oven 150C until the cabbage is tender, about 45 minutes.

9. Remove from the oven and thicken either with the corn flour diluted with a little cold water or kneaded butter made from flour and butter. Return to the oven to cook out for 5 minutes.

Kneaded butter:

1. Mix equal quantities of flour and butter together to a smooth paste.

2. Add in small pieces to the cabbage and mix in thoroughly with a wooden spoon until the cabbage has been sufficiently thickened.

3. Serve the red cabbage with the Herdwick and Leek Hot Pot or any other savoury meat dish.

PUREE OF SWEDE

Swede is a vegetable with a delicate flavour providing a cheap and useful source of fibre, vitamins A and C and calcium. Vitamin A helps to prevent night blindness and promotes healthy skin. Vitamin C maintains healthy connective tissue and calcium is necessary for healthy bones.

720 g (1¹/₂ lb) swede
30-60 g (1-2 oz) butter
salt and milled pepper

1. Wash and peel the swede. Cut into 1 cm (¹/₂") dice. Place in cold salted water.

2. Bring to the boil and simmer until cooked.

3. Drain and return to the saucepan and place over the heat to evaporate any moisture.

4. Mash and add the butter and milled pepper to taste. Beat well and check the seasoning

SAVOURY PEAS

Peas are a source of vitamin C necessary for healthy connective tissues, vitamin K assists in blood clotting and carbohydrate for energy.

240 g (8 oz) frozen peas
1 small round lettuce
12 button onions or large spring onions
15 g (¹/₂ oz) butter
15 g (¹/₂ oz) flour
¹/₂ teaspoon caster sugar
salt
250 ml (¹/₂ pint) water

1. Put the water into a saucepan and bring to the boil.

2. Peel the onions. Wash and shred the lettuce. Place the onions into the boiling water.

3. When nearly cooked add the peas and the shredded lettuce. Add salt to taste and the sugar. Bring to the boil.

4. Mix the flour and butter together to form a paste. When the peas come to the boil stir in small pieces of the flour and butter paste until the liquid thickens.

5. Allow to cook for approximately 2 minutes and serve with the thickened liquor.

GLAZED CARROTS

Carrots are a good source of vitamin A, necessary for good eyesight and for maintaining the mucous membranes of the body. Carrots also contain calcium necessary for bone formation and vitamin C necessary for the maintenance of connective tissue.

480 g (1 lb) carrots
30 g (1 oz) butter
15 g (¹/₂ oz) caster sugar
salt

1. Wash and peel the carrots. Cut into 2¹/₂ cm (1") lengths. Then cut again into neat pieces.
2. Place in a saucepan with the sugar, butter and a pinch of salt barely cover with cold water.
3. Cover with a circle of buttered grease proof paper.
Allow to boil gently to evaporate most of the water. At this stage you should have a light, syrupy, consistency in the pan.
4. Check the carrots are cooked. If they are, toss in the syrup and serve.
5. If not quite cooked add a little more water and boil until cooked and toss in the syrupy liquor.
6. Serve sprinkled with chopped parsley.

BUTTERED LEAF SPINACH WITH NUTMEG

Spinach is a good source of calcium and vitamin A. It contains traces of other vitamins and minerals including iron and vitamin C.

1 kilo (2 lb) leaf spinach
30-60 g)1-2 oz) butter
salt and milled pepper
ground/grated nutmeg

1. Thoroughly wash the spinach several times. Remove any excess stalk.
2. Place into a minimum amount of boiling, salted water until tender.
3. Drain well, return to the saucepan over heat to remove excess moisture.
4. Add the butter, a twist of milled pepper and grated nutmeg to taste. Toss well and serve.

SHALLOW FRIED COURGETTES

Courgettes are a source of calcium, vitamin A, vitamin C and other minerals.

4 good sized courgettes
125 ml (¹/₄ pint) olive oil
1 dessert spoon chopped marjoram
1 dessert spoon chopped parsley
salt and milled pepper

1. Wash the courgettes and top and tail them.
2. Slice thinly. Heat the oil in a frying pan and add the sliced courgettes.
3. Fry until just cooked, turning occasionally. Drain well sprinkle with salt and milled pepper and the chopped herbs.
4. Serve immediately.

BRUSSEL SPROUTS WITH CHESTNUTS

Brussel Sprouts are an important source of vitamin B6 and B2 which are good for the metabolism and the utilising of energy from food. They also contain folic acid which works with the B vitamins. Folic acid is an important intake requirement for pregnant women as it can reduce the likelihood of spina bifida in new born babies. Brussel sprouts are also a source of calcium necessary for bone development and muscular contraction. Sprouts contain traces of iron necessary for the production of haemoglobin.

480 g (1 lb) brussel sprouts
240 g (8 oz) chestnuts or 1 tin of chestnuts
30 g (1 oz) butter
salt and milled pepper

1. If using fresh chestnuts, make an incision around the chestnuts to cut the shell. Place in cold water.
2. Bring to the boil. Boil until the skins split, about 5 minutes.

3. Cool slightly. Remove the shells and brown skin whilst warm.

4. Cut into ½ cm (¼") pieces. These can be prepared in advance.

5. Wash and remove the outer leaves of the sprouts. Make a small incision on the base of the sprout, then re-wash.

6. Place in sufficient boiling, salted water and boil until tender, do not over cook.

7. Drain well, melt the butter in the pan add the diced chestnuts and sprouts and a twist of pepper mill and toss together.

BROCCOLI HEADS WITH CHEESE

Broccoli is a source of iron, vitamin C and calcium.

4 broccoli heads
30 g (1 oz) butter
30 g (1 oz) grated farmhouse cheese
salt and milled pepper

1. Wash the broccoli and remove excess stalk.

2. Place the broccoli in boiling, salted water and cook until just tender.

3. Carefully drain so as not to break the heads. Place on a tray.

4. Sprinkle with the melted butter and grated cheese and place under a hot grill to melt the cheese.

5. Serve immediately.

COURGETTES WITH TOMATOES AND GARLIC

Courgettes are a good source of vitamin C and magnesium. Magnesium helps enzymes to function properly.

4 courgettes
1 tin chopped tomatoes
2 cloves garlic chopped
1 small onion chopped
125 ml (¼ pint) olive oil
1 teaspoon chopped basil
1 dessert spoon chopped parsley
salt and milled pepper

1. Wash, top and tail the courgettes and slice thinly.

2. Heat the olive oil in a saucepan, fry the onions and garlic without colouring.

3. Add the sliced courgettes, season with the salt and milled pepper.

4. Add the chopped tomatoes and basil; cover with a lid and cook gently until just cooked.

5. Sprinkle with the chopped parsley and serve.

CAULIFLOWER POLISH STYLE

Cauliflower is a nutritious vegetable containing protein, vitamin B, C and calcium.

30 g (1 oz) white bread crumbs
60 g (2 oz) butter
2 hard boiled eggs
1 medium cauliflower
1 dessert spoon chopped parsley
salt and milled pepper

1. Remove the outer leaves of the cauliflower and hollow out the stem.

2. Wash well. Place into boiling salted water

sufficient to cover the cauliflower.

3. Boil gently, approximately 15-20 minutes or until just cooked. Drain the cauliflower well.

4. Sieve the hard-boiled eggs and mix with the bread crumbs and chopped parsley.

5. Sprinkle over the cauliflower Heat the butter until it just starts to turn brown. Do Not Burn.

6. Pour the nut brown melted butter over the cauliflower.

7. Serve the cauliflower immediately, whole or cut into four portions.

CAULIFLOWER FRITTERS

1 medium cauliflower or 12 frozen florets
120 g (4 oz) plain flour
flour seasoned with salt and milled pepper
125 ml (¼ pint) ½ milk and ½ water
oil for deep fat fryer
1 egg
1 dessert spoon olive oil
salt

To make the batter:

1. Place the flour and salt into a basin.

2. Add the egg and beat in the milk/water to make a smooth batter.

3. Add the oil and whisk in.

Preparation of the cauliflower:

1. Break the cauliflower into florets and remove excess stalk.

2. Blanch the cauliflower by placing into boiling salted water for 2 to 3 minutes.

3. Refresh by placing into cold water. When cold, drain thoroughly to remove all excess water.

4. Place onto a cloth to remove any remaining moisture. Coat with the seasoned flour and dip into the batter.

5. Heat the oil in the deep fryer according to the manufacturer's instructions.

6. Carefully place in the battered cauliflower and cook until golden brown following the manufacturer's instructions.

7. Drain well before serving. Serve immediately.

Note:

If you use frozen cauliflower florets, allow to defrost before coating with the flour and batter.

BRAISED LEEKS

Leeks are a source of fibre, vitamin A, B, C and trace elements of iron, potassium and calcium.

½ lt (1 pint) chicken stock
salt and milled pepper
1 teaspoon tomato puree
gravy browning
4 large leeks/8 small leeks
1 tablespoon corn flour
1 large carrot sliced
1 bouquet garni
1 medium onion cut in rings

1. Carefully trim the root end and remove the green tops of the leeks.

2. Remove any damaged outer leaves. Slit the yellow part of the leek length ways.

3. Wash thoroughly under cold running water ensuring all dirt is removed.

4. Place into boiling water and simmer until limp/pliable.

5. Place into cold water to refresh and then drain. Cut the large leeks in half length ways. Fold in half from top to bottom.

6. Place the sliced vegetables in the bottom of a casserole.

7. Place the leeks white side up onto the vegetables barely cover with the boiling stock.

8. Add the tomato puree, salt, pepper, the bouquet

garni and a little gravy browning.

9. Cover and cook in the oven at 140C for approximately 45-60 minutes or until cooked

10. Remove the leeks and keep warm. Thicken the cooking liquor with the corn flour mixed with a little cold water and cook for 2 to 3 minutes then strain.

11. Serve the leeks coated with the sauce.

LEEKS WITH CARAWAY SEED

4 large leeks
caraway seeds
salt and milled pepper
60 g (2 oz) butter

1. Wash the leeks thoroughly. Rough chop.

2. Melt the butter in a thick-bottomed saucepan. Add the leeks, salt, pepper.

3. Cover the saucepan with a lid and cook gently over a low heat for about 15 minutes. Shake occasionally to prevent burning.

4. Add caraway seeds to taste.

BRAISED CELERY

Celery contains vitamin C, minerals and calcium. The ingredients for this recipe and method are as above substituting one large or two small heads of celery for the leeks.

Preparation of the celery:

1. Trim the celery root and remove any damaged stalks.

2. Cut to approximately 15 cm (6") lengths.

3. Place into boiling water and cook until limp. Refresh as above.

4. Cut the small heads in half and large ones into four. Fold in half and proceed as for braised leeks.

5. Cook for 1-1½ hours as above. Finish as for braised leeks.

CABBAGE WITH CARAWAY AND ONION

Cabbage is a very nutritious vegetable containing vitamins A and C, calcium and iron.

480 g (1 lb) green cabbage
60 g (2 oz) chopped onion
30 g (1 oz) butter
1 teaspoon caraway seeds
salt and milled pepper

1. Cut the cabbage into quarters, discard any damaged or withered leaves.

2. Remove the centre stalk and wash thoroughly and drain.

3. Shred the cabbage and cook in the minimum amount of boiling salted water.

4. Cook until just tender approximately 10 minutes.

5. While the cabbage is cooking fry the onions in the melted butter without colouring. Place on a dish and keep hot.

6. Drain the cabbage, return to the saucepan over the heat and evaporate any excess moisture.

7. Add the cooked onions, caraway seeds and a twist of milled pepper. Mix well and serve.

POTATO DISHES

Much has been written about the humble potato - suffice to say it is a versatile vegetable. It lends itself to all methods of cooking, hence its adaptability. Being related to the deadly nightshade family, it should never be eaten when it is green, as it is poisonous at this stage. Potatoes are a good source of carbohydrate, vitamins B and C and contain a small amount of iodine.

MASHED POTATOES

720g (1½ lb) potatoes
30 g (1 oz) butter
60 ml (⅛ pint) milk
salt and ground pepper to taste
ground nutmeg to taste

1. Cook the potatoes, drain, place back in the saucepan and dry off over a low heat.
2. Mash and add the warmed milk, butter, and mix carefully.
3. Add the nutmeg and seasonings to taste. Beat well with a wooden spoon until light and fluffy.

Variation 1:
To the above mashed potato add:-
60 g (2 oz) cooked chopped pimento
60 g (2 oz) chopped ham
1 dessert spoon chopped parsley and mix in

Variation 2:
Place the mashed potato in an oven-proof dish and sprinkle with grated farmhouse cheese and brown in a hot oven or under the grill.

SHALLOW FRIED POTATOES

720 g (1½ lb) potatoes
vegetable oil for shallow frying
salt

1. Scrub the potatoes well and cook them in their skins in water as for boiled potatoes.
2. Allow to cool and peel. Cut into slices approximately 3 mm (⅛") thick.
3. Heat the oil in a frying pan and fry the potatoes until golden brown.
4. Drain in a colander and season with salt and serve immediately.

Note:
Cooking the potatoes first in their skins improves the flavour of the fried potato.

SHALLOW FRIED POTATOES WITH ONIONS

This is a variation of the previous recipe. Follow the recipe above, adding 360 g (12 oz) of fried onions to the shallow fried potatoes.

SHALLOW FRIED POTATO CUBES

720 g (1½ lb) potatoes
2 cloves garlic - optional
1 dessert spoon chopped parsley
vegetable oil for shallow frying
salt and ground pepper

1. Cut the peeled potatoes into approximately 1 cm (½") dice.
2. Wash to remove the starch. Drain and dry thoroughly on a cloth.
3. Heat the oil in a frying pan and add the potatoes and cook to a golden brown.
4. Add the finely chopped garlic, and finish cooking; drain and season with salt and pepper.
5. Sprinkle with chopped parsley and serve immediately.

Variation:
Add diced bacon to the above recipe.

BRAISED POTATOES WITH BACON

720 g (1½ lb) potatoes
180 g (6 oz) diced bacon
180g (6 oz) coarsely chopped onion
375ml (¾ pint) chicken stock
salt and milled pepper
chopped parsley

1. Cut the prepared potatoes into 1cm ($\frac{1}{2}$") dice and wash to remove starch.

2. Place the potatoes, bacon and onions into an oven-proof dish and pour over the boiling chicken stock.

3. Add seasoning if necessary (with a stock cube you may not need any additional seasoning). During cooking the stock will be partly absorbed into the potatoes and some will evaporate so season with care.

4. Place in a preheated oven 160C for approximately $\frac{1}{2}$ hour or until cooked.

5. Sprinkle with the chopped parsley and serve.

BRAISED POTATOES WITH MILK AND CHEESE

720 g (1$\frac{1}{2}$ lb) potatoes
$\frac{1}{2}$ lt (1 pint) milk
90 g (3 oz) grated farmhouse cheese
salt and milled pepper

1. Cut the prepared raw potatoes into slices 3mm ($\frac{1}{8}$") thick.

2. Wash well and arrange overlapping in a shallow oven proof dish.

3. Lightly season, pour over the milk and sprinkle with the grated cheese.

4. Cook in a preheated oven 160C for approximately $\frac{3}{4}$ hour or until cooked. The cheese should form a golden brown crust.

NEW POTATOES WITH PARSLEY AND LEMON

480 g (1 lb) new potatoes
30 g (1 oz) butter
1 dessert spoon chopped parsley and sprig of fresh mint
1 lemon zest only

salt and milled pepper

1. Wash, scrape and re-wash the potatoes.

2. Cook in boiling salted water with a sprig of fresh mint.

3. When cooked drain, and return to the saucepan over the heat to dry off.

4. Add the butter, lemon zest, chopped parsley and a twist of milled pepper

5. Toss gently in the pan and serve immediately.

POTATO GRIDDLE CAKES

720 g (1$\frac{1}{2}$ lb) potatoes
120 g (4 oz) onions
3 tablespoons flour
salt and milled pepper
oil for shallow frying

1. Grate the peeled potatoes and onions on a medium grater. Use a food processor with a grater attachment if you have one

2. The mixture at this stage should be moist. If too watery squeeze out the surplus liquid.

3. Mix in the flour, and seasonings.

4. Heat the oil in a frying pan and place the mixture in the frying pan using a tablespoon. Press down with a fork to make $\frac{1}{2}$ cm ($\frac{1}{4}$") thick cakes.

5. Fry until the underside is golden brown, turn over and cook the other side.

6. Keep hot whilst cooking the remainder. Serve immediately.

Variation:
Chopped herbs of your choice may be added to the mixture ie., parsley, rosemary, basil, mint and marjoram.

EASTER LEDGER PUDDING[1]

**Equal quantities of Easter Ledger leaves and
young nettles**
**1/2 quantity of Easter Ledger leaves of
cabbage/broccoli leaves**
A few dandelion leaves
1 onion
**1 cup of pearl barley soaked overnight in hot
water and then strained**
3 eggs
salt and pepper to taste

1. Wash all the green leaves and finely chop them.
2. Place in a muslin bag with the prepared pearl barley and boil for 1 1/2 hours.
3. Empty the bag of ingredients into a warm bowl and beat in the eggs.
4. Place in the oven for about 5 minutes. Cut into portions. Serve hot.

NETTLE HAGGIS[2]

This was a popular alternative to Easter Ledger Pudding.

A pan full of young nettles
60 g (2 oz) medium/fine oatmeal
240 g (8 oz) chopped bacon
seasonings

1. Wash the nettle tops and put them in a pan. Add a pint of boiling water and a little salt.
2. Cook with the lid off until tender, about 10 minutes.
3. Strain and put the liquid aside. Place the nettles in a pan and chop up with a knob of butter.
4. Fry the bacon and pour the fat over the nettles. Remove the bacon from the frying pan and keep hot.
5. Add half a pint of the cooking liquor from the nettles to the frying pan and bring to the boil.
6. Sprinkle in the oatmeal and keep stirring until thick.
7. Add pepper to taste and stir in the nettles. Serve very hot with the bacon.

[1] *In Search of Food* by Richard Mabey
[2] *Lakeland Recipes Old and New* by Joan Poulson

SWEET DISHES

Here you will find a selection of sweets to choose from to suit your menu requirements. Some are light and fruity, while others are more substantial. Some are Cumbrian in origin and many of them have been adapted to use Cumbrian produce.

DAMSON AND APPLE TANSY

This is an old North Country sweet which used to be made with the herb tansy.[3] Cumbrian damsons add their own special flavour to this unusual sweet that is something like a soufflé, but easy to make

2 large apples
240 g (1/2 lb) damsons
22 g (3/4 oz) butter
60 g (2 oz) demerara sugar
1/4 teaspoon ground cinnamon
1/4 teaspoon ground cloves
4 eggs
3 tablespoons yogurt

1. Peel, core and slice the apples. Stone the damsons.
2. Place the prepared fruit in a saucepan with the butter and 30 g sugar. Add the spices.
3. Place on a low heat and cook gently, stirring all the time. When cooked remove from the heat.
4. Separate the eggs and mix the yolks with the yogurt.
5. Carefully mix the egg and yogurt mixture into the fruit mixture.
6. Whisk up the egg whites until they hold their own weight.
7. Carefully fold some of the egg white into the fruit mixture then gradually fold in the rest.

[3] This recipe is adapted from a recipe in *The Dairy Book of British Food*.

8. Pour the mixture into a shallow oven-proof dish and cook in the oven 140C for about 15 minutes or until the mixture is set and firm to touch.

9. Sprinkle the remaining sugar over the top and place under a hot grill to caramelise.

10. Serve immediately with yogurt.

CABINET PUDDING

This is an unusual combination based on the popular Bread and Butter pudding, but using sponge cake instead of bread and served with a fruity apricot sauce.

¹/₂ lt (1 pint) milk
60 g (2 oz) caster sugar
120 g (4 oz) plain sponge cake or sponge fingers
30 g (1 oz) chopped glacé cherries
4 eggs
30 g (1 oz) sultanas and currants
1 teaspoon vanilla essence

Apricot Sauce:
240 g (8 oz) apricot jam
a little water

1. Cut the sponge into ¹/₂ cm (¹/₄") dice. Mix with the dried fruit and chopped cherries.

2. Place in greased and lightly sugared, one pint pudding basin. Do not fill more than half full.

3. Beat the eggs, sugar and vanilla essence together. Warm the milk and pour onto the egg mixture.

4. Strain over the sponge and fruit mixture. Allow to stand for 10 minutes

5. Place the basin in a roasting tray half full of hot water (not boiling)

6. Place in a preheated oven 140C and cook for 30-45 minutes or until the egg custard is set. The water in the tray must not boil otherwise the custard will curdle.

7. When cooked remove from the oven and allow to stand for a few minutes. Turn out onto a warm serving dish.

Apricot Sauce:

1. Place the jam in a saucepan with a little water and bring to the boil. Pass through a sieve.

2. Serve hot with the Cabinet Pudding.

COLUMBA CREAM BREAD AND BUTTER PUDDING

Columba Cream is a whisky liqueur with cream and adds a touch of flair to an old favourite.

4 slices buttered bread, crusts removed, cut into quarters
60 g (2 oz) caster sugar
¹/₂ lt (1 pint) milk
60 g (2 oz) sultanas
4 large eggs
1 tablespoon per person Columba cream (a blend of whisky and cream or use Baileys)

1. Ideally this dish should stand a few hours before cooking to allow the bread to soak up the milk and flavouring.

2. Grease a pie dish with butter.

3. Arrange the slices of prepared bread and sultanas in alternate layers finishing with a layer of bread.

4. Pour the Columba Cream or Baileys over the bread and sultanas. Place the milk in a saucepan and heat (hot enough to dissolve the sugar.)

5. Place the sugar and eggs in a basin and beat together.

6. Add the warmed milk and stir until the sugar is dissolved.

7. Strain through a sieve over the bread and sultanas. Allow to stand for a few hours before cooking. When cold place in a refrigerator.

8. Remove from the refrigerator 10 minutes before placing in the oven.

9. Preheat the oven to 140C. Place the pudding in the oven in a roasting tray half full of hot water and cook for approximately 40 minutes or until the egg custard is set. The mixture must not boil otherwise the egg will curdle. Serve hot from the dish

CONVERSATION TART

A tart with a difference. One that will keep your friends guessing and talking!

240 g (¹/₂ lb) puff pastry[1]
240 g (8 oz) icing sugar
1 egg white
60 g (2 oz) ground almonds
60 g (2 oz) caster sugar
60 g (2 oz) butter
1 egg
damson jam

1. Using slightly less than half the puff pastry, roll it out to 3 mm (¹/₄") thick and cut an 18 cm (7") round

2. Place on a lightly greased baking sheet.

3. Spread the base with a thin layer of damson jam leaving a margin of 2¹/₂ cm (1") clear all round the edge.

4. Cream the butter and caster sugar together until light and fluffy.

5. Beat in the egg slowly. Fold in the ground almonds to the egg, fat and sugar mixture.

6. Mix in carefully making sure all the almonds have been folded in completely.

7. Place mixture on the pastry covering the layer of jam, keeping the margin clear.

8. Roll out the remaining pastry slightly larger about 20 cm (8") and place on the top of the mixture and seal down the edges with water.

9. Make a royal icing by beating the icing sugar into egg white. You want a thick consistency that will hold its shape. The mixture should "peak".

10. Spread the icing sugar on the top of the tart to cover the top layer of puff pastry. It should not run off the edges, (the tart is uncooked at this point!)

11. From the scraps of pastry left over cut thin strips to go across the top creating a trellis pattern.

12. Allow to relax in a refrigerator for at least one hour before baking.

13. Place in a preheated oven 160C and cook for 40 minutes.

14. May be served hot or cold with cream. This recipe can also be used to make individual tartlets to serve as an afternoon tea pastry.

DAMSON CHEESE CAKE

A variation of the ever popular cheese cake using a fruit native to Cumbria.

180 g (6 oz) digestive biscuits
90 g (3 oz) butter
120 g (4 oz) Muscavado sugar
390 g (13 oz) soft curd goat's/cow's cheese
375 ml (³/₄ pint) double cream
480 g (1 lb) damsons (bottled or freshly stewed)
A little brown sugar and water to stew the damsons
1 lemon
arrowroot for thickening

1. Place the damsons in a saucepan and gently stew with a small amount of sugar and a little water. Do not over cook as you want to keep them whole.

2. Put half aside for decorating.

3. Pass the remainder through a sieve to make a puree. Allow the puree to become cold.

4. Grease a 24 cm (9") by 3¹/₂ cm (1¹/₂") deep flan dish.

5. Crush the digestive biscuits by placing small amounts in a polythene bag and rolling across with a rolling pin.

6. Melt the butter in a saucepan. Add the crushed digestive biscuits and mix in well.

[1] See page 153, or buy ready made

7. Line the base of the flan dish with the biscuit mix pressing down well.

8. Place the zest and juice of the lemon and the sugar in a bowl and slowly beat in the cheese.

9. Beat until the mixture is smooth. Add the cold damson puree and beat in.

10. Whip the cream until it holds its shape, then fold the whipped cream into the cheese mixture a small amount at first, then gradually fold in larger amounts.

11. Spread the cheese and cream mixture over the biscuit base and smooth the top.

12. Cover with cling film and place in the refrigerator for at least 6 hours to set. Just prior to serving, drain any excess juice off the damsons you have put aside and place the juice in a saucepan.

13. Decorate the top of the cheesecake with the damsons.

14. Bring juice to the boil and thicken with the arrowroot, mixed to a paste with a little cold water. The consistency should coat the back of a wooden spoon.

15. Carefully spoon the arrowroot glaze over the damsons. The glaze should be thick enough to cover the fruit without running off the sides.

16. Place in the refrigerator until ready to serve.

LYTH VALLEY DAMSON COBBLER 1

Here are two recipes that are popular in the north of England, again using damsons grown in Cumbria.

60 g (2 oz) butter or margarine
240 g (8 oz) self raising flour
60 g (2 oz) caster sugar
1 teaspoon baking powder
1 egg
milk to mix
720 g (1½ lb) damsons, stoned
90 g (3 oz) demerara sugar for fruit
1 teaspoon ground cinnamon

1. Stone the damsons and place in a saucepan with demerara sugar and pinch of cinnamon and stew until cooked. Place in a deep pie dish.

2. Sift the flour and baking powder into a bowl. Rub in the fat and add the sugar.

3. Add the beaten egg and enough milk to make a soft, scone dough.

4. Knead lightly, remove from the bowl and roll out to 1 cm (½") thickness and cut into 5 cm (2") circles.

5. Place the circles over the damsons overlapping the edges of the circles. Brush with a little beaten egg.

6. Place in preheated oven 180C and cook for 12 minutes or until the scone topping is brown and has risen.

7. Serve with custard, cream or ice cream.

LYTH VALLEY DAMSON COBBLER 2

This is a variation of the above recipe with a dumpling topping; perhaps more suitable for the cold winter months.

720 g (1½ lb) stoned damsons
1 teaspoon cinnamon
90 g (3 oz) demerara sugar to sprinkle on the fruit
120 g (4 oz) vegetable suet
60 g (2 oz) caster sugar
120 g (4 oz) bread crumbs
120 g (4 oz) self raising flour
pinch of salt
water to mix

1. Cook the damsons as above and place in a deep pie dish.

2. Mix the bread crumbs and flour together. Add the suet and mix in.

3. Add the sugar and mix in. Mix to a soft dough with some cold water.

4. Roll out ½" thick and cut into circles. Finish off as above.

5. Place in a moderate oven 160C and cook for about 25 minutes or until brown and risen. Serve as above.

CUMBERLAND TRIFLE

We first tried the original of this sweet in a farmhouse in Wasdale. In the original recipe the fruit was soaked in red wine. We have changed the recipe to use damson gin, made in Cumbria, and some fruits native to Cumbria. We have also substituted a pastry cream for cream.

8 sponge cakes
125 ml (¼ pint) damson gin
720 g (1½ lb) bleaberries/ stoned damsons or bottled blackcurrants or morello cherries

Pastry cream:
500 ml (1 pint) milk
45 g (1½ oz) plain flour
2 eggs
15 g (½ oz) custard powder
120 g (4 oz) caster sugar
1 teaspoon vanilla essence or vanilla pod
500 ml (1 pint) double cream
30 g (1 oz) melted butter
30 g (1 oz) toasted almonds

1. If you use fresh fruit, stew until just cooked. Place to one side and allow to cool.
2. Cut the sponge cakes into 1 cm dice (½") and place in shallow dish.
3. Pour on the damson gin and allow to soak.
4. Place the eggs, plain flour, custard powder and sugar in a basin and mix to a smooth paste.
5. Place the milk in a saucepan with the vanilla essence or pod and bring to the boil.
6. Slowly add the boiling milk to the egg paste and mix in carefully and thoroughly until smooth.
7. Have ready a clean, thick-bottomed saucepan which has been rinsed out in cold water and not dried (this helps to prevent the mixture from burning)
8. Place the milk and egg mixture in this saucepan and return to a low heat.
9. Cook slowly over a low heat stirring all the time until it thickens. Once thickened pour into a basin.
10. Melt the butter and pour over the surface of the pastry cream, this should prevent a skin from forming. Allow to become cold.
11. Whisk the cream until it holds its shape. Add a small amount of the whipped cream to the pastry cream and fold in.
12. Gradually increase the amount you add until all the whipped cream has been added.
13. Place the soaked sponge, stewed fruit and cream mixture in alternate layers, in a serving dish, finishing with a layer of the cream mixture.
14. Smooth the top and decorate with suitable fruit and toasted almonds.

EDEN VALLEY PUDDING

A spicy apple sweet that goes under the name of Eve's pudding in the south of England but here it is named after a beautiful area of Cumbria.

4 large cooking apples
90 g (3 oz) demerara sugar
2 teaspoons ground nutmeg
120 g (4 oz) self raising flour
120 g (4 oz) butter or margarine
120 g (4 oz) caster sugar
2 eggs
1 teaspoon vanilla essence

1. Lightly grease a deep pie dish.

2. Wash, peel, core and slice the apples into the pie dish sprinkle with the demerara sugar and the nutmeg.

3. Cream the butter and the caster sugar until light and fluffy. Beat the eggs with the vanilla essence.

4. Slowly beat the eggs into the butter and sugar mixture.

5. Fold in the sieved flour. Place the mixture on top of the apples.

6. Bake in a preheated oven 160C for approximately 30-40 minutes

7. Serve hot with custard, cream, yogurt or ice cream.

LEMON MERINGUE PIE

A popular sweet. This recipe has a sharp, tangy flavour.

Pastry:
240 g (¹/₂ lb) plain flour
60 g (2 oz) white vegetable fat
60 g (2 oz) margarine
pinch salt
water to mix

1. Sieve the flour and the salt into a bowl and rub in the fats. Add enough cold water to make a dough.

2. Roll out and line a greased 18 cm (7") flan dish. Prick the base of the pastry and line with grease proof paper and add dried beans as a weight and bake blind in 180C oven.

3. Remove the grease proof paper and beans after 10 minutes. Continue baking for a further 15 minutes or until base is cooked.

4. Remove from the oven and place on a wire rack to cool.

Lemon filling:
250 ml (¹/₂ pint) water
2 lemons
60 g (2 oz) granulated sugar
60 g (2 oz) butter
60 g (2 oz) corn flour
2 eggs
120 g (4 oz) caster sugar

1. Place the water, granulated sugar, butter and the grated zest of two lemons in a saucepan and slowly bring to the boil so that the sugar has dissolved and the butter melted by the time the liquid boils.

2. Do not allow to boil. Remove from the heat. Whilst the mixture is heating up squeeze the juice of the two lemons and put aside.

3. Separate the yolks and the whites of the eggs. Place the whites in a bowl ready for whisking. Put aside the yolks.

4. Mix the corn flour with enough cold water to make a smooth paste.

5. Place the saucepan with the water, lemon zest, sugar and butter back on to the heat and bring back to the boil.

6. Turn the heat down so that the mixture is just simmering.

7. Add the corn flour slowly stirring vigorously all the time until well blended.

8. Once the corn flour has been added, bring to the boil and cook for about 3 minutes stirring all the time

9. Remove from the heat and add the juice of the lemons and beat in well.

10. Add the yolks of the eggs and beat in well. Pour the mixture into the prepared flan case.

11. Whisk the egg whites, adding the caster sugar a little at a time, until all the sugar has been added and the meringue is stiff and peaks.

12. Arrange the meringue over the flan. Sprinkle with a little caster sugar.

13. Place in a preheated oven 120C, leave the door ajar. Allow to dry out for 2 hours or until the meringue is firm to touch and golden brown.

Note:

This method of making the meringue and cooking it on a low heat with the door of the oven slightly open should give you a dry crisp meringue.

FRUIT, NUT AND CHOCOLATE AMBROSIA

A substantial sweet but quick and easy to make. It could also be served as a breakfast dish

60 g(2 oz) rolled oats
1 weetabix
30 g (1 oz) roughly chopped flaked almonds
30 g (1 oz) chopped walnuts
60 g (2 oz) butter
60 g (2 oz) clear Cumbrian honey
30 g (1 oz) sultanas
30 g (1 oz) raisins
120 g (4 oz) stewed bilberries (or bottled)
250 ml (½ pint) cream or yogurt
grated chocolate

1. Melt the fat in a thick-bottomed fry pan.
2. Add the oats, grated nuts and the weetabix, fry over a low heat until slightly brown. Stir occasionally to prevent burning.
3. Add the honey and cook for another 3-5 minutes, stirring all the time.
4. Put the mixture into a bowl, add the dried fruit and mix well. Allow to cool.
5. Strain the excess juice off the bilberries. Add the bilberries and mix in well.
6. Serve with either whipped cream or thick yogurt on the top sprinkled with grated chocolate.

Note:

Other fruit can be used - try chopped fresh strawberries or raspberries. Other nuts can be used eg., roughly chopped hazel nuts. Substitute other cereals eg., cornflakes or shredded wheat.

WORKINGTON RUM BROWN BETTY

A popular North country sweet. Quick and easy to prepare

6 large apples
240 g (8 oz) demerara sugar
240 g (8 oz) fresh brown bread crumbs
90 g (3 oz) rum butter
ground/grated nutmeg for each layer
1 lemon zest and juice

1. Grease a deep pie dish with some of the rum butter. Grate the zest of the lemon into the bread crumbs and mix.
2. Peel and slice the apples. Line the pie dish with some of the bread crumbs.
3. Place a layer of apples in the bottom and sprinkle with some of the sugar, lemon juice and grated nutmeg.
4. Dot with some of the rum butter and sprinkle a layer of bread crumbs over the apples.
5. Repeat the process finishing with a layer of bread crumbs.
6. Bake for approximately 30 minutes at 180C or until the apples are cooked.
7. Serve with fresh whipped cream or yogurt.

ST BEE'S DELIGHT

St Bees is named after St Begha an Irish princess who founded a nunnery at St Bees. According to legend she arrived in Egremont with nowhere to go and was befriended by the Lady of Egremont who requested land from her husband for Begha to build her nunnery. The Lord of Egremont agreed to give Begha as much land as was covered by snow on midsummer's day!

Begha prayed all night and on midsummer's day, to her delight, an area of three miles around St Bees was covered with snow!

This pudding makes an alternative sweet for the festive season.

125 ml (¹/₄ pint) milk
6 egg yolks
150 g (5 oz) soft brown sugar
1 teaspoon vanilla essence
375 ml (³/₄ pint) double cream
30 g (1 oz) currants
30 g (1 oz) sultanas
30 g (1 oz) raisins
30 g (1 oz) quartered glacé cherries
4 tablespoon rum
¹/₄ teaspoon ground cinnamon

1. Place the dried fruits and the cherries in a basin and cover with the rum and leave to soak overnight
2. Bring the cream, milk, vanilla essence and the cinnamon to the boil
3. Whisk the yolks and the sugar together in a basin until light and creamy.
4. Whisk the boiling cream and milk quickly onto the egg and sugar mixture and return to a clean saucepan rinsed in cold water but not dried.(this helps to prevent the base from burning).
5. Place on a very low heat and cook until the mixture coats the back of the spoon. The mixture must not boil
6. Strain into a basin (no more than half full as you still have to add the fruit)
7. Place the bowl in a bowl of cold water and stir until cold and then chill in a refrigerator.
8. Set the freezer to fast freezing or the coldest setting (check maker's instructions). Place the basin in the freezer and stir frequently until nearly frozen. Then add the drained fruits.
9. Continue to freeze stirring frequently until com-

pletely frozen. You can user an Ice cream maker attachment if you have one and follow the maker's instructions.
10. Serve immediately with any rum left over from the fruit served as a sauce.

Note:
1. Use the egg whites up by making home made meringues, much better than the shop ones! Serve with the ice cream.
2. Allow 60 g caster sugar per egg white.
3. Beat in the sugar to the egg whites until the egg whites are stiff and peak.
4. Spoon mould onto a greased tray.
5. Bake in a low oven with the door ajar until the meringues have dried out and are a light brown colour, about 1¹/₂-2 hours.

DAMSON ICE CREAM

This is a variation of the previous recipe, using locally grown damsons. Use the same ingredients as above, but omit the dried fruits, glacé cherries and the rum.

Replace with 240 g (8 oz) damson puree. To make the puree stone the damsons and place in a saucepan with nothing else and cook gently. Then pass through a sieve. Chill well before using.

Proceed using the method for St. Bees' Delight.

STICKY TOFFEE PUDDING

A traditional Cumbrian favourite with a touch of individuality.

Pudding:
120 g (4 oz) muscavado (dark brown sugar)
120 g (4 oz) butter
1 teaspoon bicarbonate soda
240 g (8 oz) self raising flour

1 teaspoon vanilla essence
1 tablespoon golden syrup
240 g (8 oz) chopped dates
2 eggs
125 ml (¹/₄ pint) ginger wine
145 ml (³/₈ pint) single cream

1. Finely chop the dates and leave over night in the ginger wine.
2. Lightly grease a deep oblong or oval pie dish. Drain the dates. Keep back any ginger wine for the sauce.
3. Place the bicarbonate of soda, cream and golden syrup in a basin.
4. Cream the butter, sugar and vanilla essence together until light and fluffy.
5. Add the beaten eggs slowly, beating all the time. Carefully fold in the flour, when almost mixed in add the dates and mix.
6. Add the golden syrup and the cream and mix in. Spoon into the prepared pie dish.
7. Place in a preheated oven 160C for about an hour.

Toffee sauce:
90 g (3 oz) butter
150 g (5 oz) muscavado (dark brown sugar
65 ml (¹/₈ pint) cream
ginger wine from soaked dates

1. Place the butter, sugar, cream and any surplus ginger wine into a thick-bottomed saucepan.
2. Bring to the boil and simmer for 3 minutes stirring to prevent burning.

To Serve:
Cut the pudding into portions and pour over the toffee sauce. Serve with a custard sauce, cream or ice cream.

STRAWBERRY PAVLOVA MERINGUE
The Cumbrian raspberry vinegar adds a special flavour to this popular sweet.

3 egg whites
1 dessertspoon corn flour
180 g (6 oz) caster sugar
¹/₂ teaspoon Cumbrian raspberry vinegar
360 g (12 oz) strawberries washed and tailed
125 ml (¹/₄ pint) double cream

1. Grease a sponge flan tin (one with a sunken centre) with white fat.
2. Sift together equal quantities of corn flour and icing sugar - enough to coat the flan tin. Completely coat the tin with this mixture shaking out any excess.
3. Place the egg whites in a bowl and start to beat slowly; increase the speed and start to add the sugar, beating all the time.
4. Beat in all the sugar. The mixture should be stiff and hold its shape.
5. Add the vinegar and the corn flour and fold in carefully. Spoon into the prepared flan tin and spread out evenly.
6. Place in a preheated oven 120C and cook for 1¹/₄-1¹/₂ hours until the mixture is golden brown and firm to touch. Cook with the oven door slightly ajar; this helps the meringue to dry out.
7. Remove from the oven and place on a wire tray. Allow to cool for a few minutes and then turn out onto a flat serving plate placed on a wire tray, (use a palette knife to loosen round the edges.)
8. When cold decorate with whipped double cream and the prepared strawberries.

HAZEL NUT, STRAWBERRY PAVLOVA MERINGUE

This is a variation on the previous recipe, with the addition of 4 oz of toasted, coarse, ground hazel nuts.

1. Place the hazel nuts in a fry pan with no grease, put on a low heat and allow to colour shaking the fry pan occasionally.
2. When browned, turn out onto a clean oven cloth or towel and rub in the towel to remove the outer skins.
3. Place the nuts in a food processor and chop roughly for a few minutes. You want a coarse ground nut.
4. Add the nuts to the meringue mixture when you add the corn flour. Cook and finish as above.

LAMPLUGH PUDDING[1]

Lamplugh Pudding was specially made for farmers working all hours in the long, dark winters, particularly at lambing time. It was also a traditional Christmas dish.

500 ml (1 pint) old ale
2 lemons
120 g (4 oz) porridge oats
1 teaspoon mixed spice
240 g (8 oz) raisins
$\frac{1}{2}$ teaspoon cinnamon
6 rich tea biscuits
6 cloves
60 g (2 oz) Barbados sugar

1. Place the cloves in a muslin bag.
2. Put the ale in a large saucepan. Place the muslin bag in the ale. Add the spices.
3. Bring to the boil and simmer for 5 minutes.
4. Remove the muslin bag and add the sugar, oats, raisins and crushed biscuits. Stir in well.

[1] *Lakeland Recipes Old and New* by Joan Poulson

5. Add the grated rind and juice of one lemon. Serve hot.

CUMBERLAND RUM NICKY

Traditional Cumbrian dish tested by authors.

Sweet pastry:
480 g (1 lb) plain flour
120 g (4 oz) lard/white cooking fat
120 g (4 oz) butter/margarine
1 egg
60 g (2 oz) light brown sugar
pinch of salt

1. Cream the fats with the sugar until smooth. Mix the beaten egg in a little at a time.
2. Sieve the flour and salt. Lightly mix in the flour to the fat and sugar mixture.
3. Leave in the refrigerator for half an hour to become firm, and to make rolling easier.
4. Put aside enough pastry for the lattice top. Roll out the remainder and line a greased 21 cm (8") flan ring.

Filling:
240 g ($\frac{1}{2}$ lb) each of dates and currants
240 g ($\frac{1}{2}$ lb) raisins
120 g (4 oz) butter
120 g (4 oz) muscavado sugar
60 g (2 oz) chopped crystallised ginger
125 ml ($\frac{1}{4}$ pint) rum
$\frac{1}{4}$ teaspoon mixed spice
1 dessert spoon lemon juice
1 large chopped cooking apple

1. Stone and roughly chop the dates. Soak the dates, raisins and currants in the rum overnight if possible, or for a minimum of 2 hours. Drain and save any rum for serving.

2. Mix the fruit, chopped ginger, mixed spice, lemon juice and chopped apple and place in the flan case.

3. Melt the muscavado sugar and butter and pour over the filled flan.

4. Decorate the top of the flan with a lattice work of pastry.

5. Bake in the oven 170C for ½-¾ hour.

6. Serve with any remaining rum and cream.

CUMBERLAND SPOTTED DOG PUDDING

120 g (4 oz) vegetable suet
180 g (6 oz) raisins
120 g (4 oz) bread crumbs
4 tablespoons rum
120 g (4 oz) plain flour
120 g (4 oz) soft brown sugar
1 egg
1 teaspoon baking powder
milk to mix

1. Soak the raisins in the rum overnight.

2. Sift the baking powder and flour. Mix in the bread crumbs.

3. Add the suet and the sugar and mix in. Add the raisins and any remaining rum.

4. Add the beaten egg and enough milk to mix to a soft dough.

5. Lightly grease a pudding basin and place in the mixture.

6. Cover with grease proof paper and tin foil and seal well.

7. Steam for 1½-2 hours or cook in a pressure cooker following the maker's instructions.

8. Serve with custard or brown sugar and butter.

BREAD, PASTRY AND CAKES

Here you will find a selection of delicious cakes, pastries and bread, many of which are traditional Cumbrian recipes.

PUFF PASTRY

The following ingredients for puff pastry will make sufficient for 4 portions:

240g (8 oz) strong white flour
140-150 ml iced water
240g (8 oz) margarine
1 dessert spoon lemon juice
pinch of salt

1. Sieve the flour and the salt into a cold bowl.

2. Cut the fat up into small even pieces. Place in the bowl with the flour and coat the pieces of fat with the flour

3. Make a well in the centre of the flour and add the water and the lemon juice.

4. Mix to a dough and lightly knead.

5. Roll out to an oblong about 16 cm by 10 cm (6" x 4")

5. Fold the top edge over one third, fold the bottom third over it.

6. Wrap in cling film and allow to rest in a refrigerator for half an hour.

7. Turn the pastry ¼ turn/90 degrees and roll out and fold as before and place in a refrigerator.

8. Repeat the process twice more. Rest in the refrigerator for one hour before use.

Helpful tip:
Every thing must be very cold. The ideal work top to make puff paste on is marble or slate.
Avoid handling any of the ingredients too much. Use

margarine straight from the refrigerator.

When rolling puff paste, roll in one direction only, not backwards and forwards.

Mark each turn with a little mark so you don't forget how many turns you have done and you can also see which direction the next ¼ turn has to be.

BORROWDALE TEA BREAD

A popular tea time recipe

125 ml (¼-½ pint) hot tea
120 g (4 oz) raisins
120 g (4 oz) sultanas
120 g (4 oz) muscavado sugar
1 beaten egg
240 g (8 oz) self raising flour
1 teaspoon mixed spice
1 tablespoon orange marmalade

1. Soak the fruit and the sugar in the tea overnight.
2. Add the marmalade and the beaten egg.
3. Sieve the flour and the spice and fold in to the mixture.
4. Put into a greased 480 g (1 lb) loaf tin and bake in preheated oven 140C for approximately 1½ hours.
5. Allow to cool on a rack and serve sliced spread with butter.

BROWN BREAD

This is an easy bread recipe with only one proving

720 g (1½ lb) wholemeal bread flour (strong)
720 g (1½ lb) brown bread flour (strong)
30 g (1 oz) butter or margarine
5 teaspoons dried yeast
1 teaspoon soft brown sugar
4 teaspoons salt
750 ml (1½ pints) lukewarm water

1. Lightly grease three 480 g (1 lb) loaf tins.
2. Place the yeast in a basin with the sugar and add 250 ml of the warm water.
3. Mix together. Leave to froth.
4. Place both of the flours in a large bowl with the salt and rub in the margarine mixing the flours well together
5. Make a well in the centre of the flour. Add the yeast mixture.
6. Then add the remaining warm water. Mix into a pliable dough. Knead until the dough is soft and smooth.
7. Place in a lightly floured bowl, cover with cling film and leave in a warm place to rise and double its size for approximately 1-1½ hours.
8. Turn out onto a floured surface and lightly knead. Divide into three equal pieces and place into the prepared tins. Leave to rise for ½-¾ of an hour
9. Place in a preheated oven 200C for approximately 30 minutes.
10. When cooked the loaves should sound hollow when tapped on the bottom. Allow to cool.
11. This dough can also be used for making bread rolls.

DOROTHY'S CARAWAY SEED CAKE

Caraway Seed cake is said to have been one of Dorothy Wordsworth's favourite tea time cakes.

180 g (6 oz) butter or margarine
180 g (6 oz) soft brown sugar
240 g (8 oz) self raising flour
3 large eggs
1 level dessert spoon caraway seeds
¼ teaspoon ground nutmeg
a little milk to mix
zest and juice of 1 lemon

1. Lightly grease a loaf tin

2. Cream the butter, sugar and lemon zest until light and fluffy.

3. Add the beaten eggs slowly.

4. Sieve the flour and nutmeg and fold in carefully.

5. Add the caraway seeds and the lemon juice.

6. Add a little milk if necessary to make into a dropping consistency.

7. Place in prepared tin in a preheated oven. Bake at 160C for 45-55 minutes.

8. Leave to cool then turn out.

LAKELAND GINGERBREAD

We have devised a recipe based on traditional ingredients historically used in Cumbria namely muscavado sugar, treacle, oats and spices. The addition of bread crumbs makes a very light mix.

180 g (6 oz) butter
180 g (6 oz) muscavado sugar
120 g (4 oz) black treacle
60 g (2 oz) Cumberland clear honey
135 g (4 1/2 oz) self raising flour
60 g (2 oz) medium oatmeal
75 g (2 1/2 oz) fine, brown bread crumbs
1 egg
1 level tablespoon ground ginger
1 level tablespoon ground cinnamon
375 ml (3/4 pint) natural yogurt
pinch of salt

1. Grease a loaf tin.

2. Place the butter, treacle and the sugar in a thick-bottomed saucepan and place over a low heat.

3. Stir all the time until the butter has melted and the sugar dissolved. Remove from the heat and allow to cool.

4. Sieve the flour, bicarbonate of soda, ginger and cinnamon into a bowl, add the bread crumbs and the oatmeal and mix together well.

5. Add the beaten egg to the treacle and butter mixture. Then add to the dry ingredients mixing thoroughly. Finally add the yogurt and stir in.

6. Pour into the prepared loaf tin and bake in a preheated oven 140C for 45-60 minutes.

MAID OF BUTTERMERE'S TEMPTATION

A special afternoon tea cake also suitable as a sweet.

Cake:
6 eggs
210 g (7 oz) ground almonds
240 g (8 oz) caster sugar

1. Grease two 7" flan rings. Place on a tray lined with greased grease proof paper.

2. Separate the whites from the yolks. Place the whites in a bowl.

3. Place the egg yolks in a basin and cover with cold water (three of the yolks will be used for the butter cream).

4. Whisk the whites briskly adding the sugar slowly whilst whisking until all the sugar has been beaten in. The mixture should be very stiff and hold itself in peaks.

5. Add the ground almonds and carefully fold in using a metal spoon and turning the bowl as you cut the spoon across the mixture in short sharp moves to avoid knocking out the air. The almonds should be thoroughly mixed in with a minimum amount of mixing. Place mixture into the flan rings.

6. Place in a preheated oven at mark 120C and leave the oven door slightly ajar, this allows the mixture to dry out. Leave to cook for about 2 hours or until the mixture is a golden brown and feels firm.

7. Turn out onto a wire tray and remove the grease proof paper. Allow to get cold.

Butter cream:

(This uses egg yolks which may be unsuitable for the elderly and the very young. See alternative recipe.)

240g (¹/₂ lb) fresh unsalted butter at room temperature
3 egg yolks
150 g (5 oz) dark brown sugar
liqueur (optional) to taste
3 fl oz cold water

1. Place the egg yolks, sugar and water in a bowl and place over a saucepan of hot water. Do not allow the water to boil.
2. Whisk until thick and creamy and at the ribbon stage.
3. Take the bowl off the saucepan and continue whisking until cold.
4. Add the soft butter in very small amounts to begin with whisking continuously, until all the butter has been added. The butter and the egg and sugar mixture need to be at the same temperature to prevent curdling.

To Finish:

1. Use approximately one third of the butter cream to sandwich the two halves of the cake together.
2. Spread the top and sides with the butter cream. Keep some for decorative piping on the top.
3. Cover the sides with toasted flaked almonds.

Helpful tip:

We do not add any other flavourings as the sugar gives this cake a lovely rum flavour but you could add a liqueur of your choice to the butter cream.
If the butter cream should curdle, place a teaspoon of boiling water into a basin and whisk the curdled mixture slowly onto it until the mixture is reconstituted.

Alternative Butter Cream:
240 g (¹/₂ lb) butter
240 g (¹/₂ lb) icing sugar
liqueur or spirit to flavour eg., rum, brandy or
30 g cocoa

1. Cream the butter until soft.
2. Slowly add the sifted icing sugar and mix in well and beat to a creamy consistency.
3. Add the required flavouring to the butter cream when finished.
4. Decorate as desired or as above.

Suggested flavourings:

Coffee with Tia Maria or chocolate with rum

ORANGE DRIZZLE CAKE

Lemon Drizzle cake is very popular in Cumbria, and isn't named after the weather! Here is an alternative.

Cake:
120 g (4 oz) butter/margarine
120 g (4 oz) caster sugar/soft brown sugar
240 g (8 oz) self raising flour
125 ml (¹/₄ pint) yogurt
2 eggs
1 teaspoon bicarbonate soda
180 g (6 oz) sultanas
120 g (4 oz) finely chopped walnuts
2 large oranges
1 teaspoon vanilla essence

1. Lightly grease and line with greased grease proof paper an 18 cm (7") loose-bottomed cake tin.
2. Cream the butter and the sugar.
3. Add the grated zest of the oranges. Add the beaten eggs.
4. Sieve the flour and the bicarbonate of soda and

Herdwick Shepherd's Pie

fold into the mixture.

5. Add the walnuts, sultanas and the yogurt and fold in carefully.

6. Place in the prepared tin and bake at 160C for approximately one hour.

Drizzle for the topping:
180 g (6 oz) caster sugar
juice of 2 oranges

1. Squeeze and strain the juice out of the oranges.

2. Add the sugar and allow to stand whilst the cake cooks, stirring occasionally.

3. Turn the cake out onto a wire rack and whilst still warm make some holes in the top of the cake using a skewer (do not pierce right through the cake) pour the drizzle mixture over the cake and allow to soak in.

CHOCOLATE PRUNE CAKE

A substantial cake with a difference. Full of fruity flavours.

Cake:
240 g (¹/₂ lb) butter
240g (¹/₂ lb) Bardados sugar
5 eggs separated
30 g (1 oz) cocoa
120 g (4 oz) self raising wholemeal flour
180 g (6 oz) ground almonds
¹/₂ teaspoon baking powder

Filling:
2 tablespoons damson jam
120 g (4 oz) pitted prunes
1 cup warm tea
1 bay leaf

Topping:
120 g (4 oz) cooking chocolate
toasted flaked almonds to decorate

1. Soak the prunes overnight in the tea with the bay leaf.

2. Grease and line the base of two 18 cm (7") sponge tins.

3. Place tea and prunes in a saucepan and bring to the boil; simmer until the prunes are cooked about 10-15 minutes.

4. Drain the prunes; remove the bay leaf. Roughly chop the prunes. Place to one side.

5. Cream the butter and sugar until light and fluffy. Beat in the egg yolks.

6. Lightly mix the flour, cocoa powder, baking powder and ground almonds together in a separate bowl so they resemble fine bread crumbs

7. Whisk the egg whites until stiff. Fold in the dry ingredients and the egg whites alternately until completely mixed.

8. Spoon the mixture into the prepared tins. Cook for 20-25 minutes 160C. When cooked turn out onto a cooling rack.

9. Once cooled sandwich with the damson jam and prunes.

Topping:
1. Break the chocolate into small pieces and place in a basin and place over a saucepan of hot water.

2. Allow to melt. The water in the saucepan must not boil otherwise the chocolate will become too hot and lose its shine.

3. Once melted pour the chocolate on the top and sides and spread evenly.

4. Before the chocolate sets decorate the top with toasted, flaked almonds.

FRUITY TOFFEE ALMOND SHORTBREAD

These are shortbread biscuits with a difference. Depending on the sugar you use in the topping, you can ring the changes between a toffee finish or a more fruity taste.

Biscuits:
180 g (6 oz) soft unsalted butter
120 g (4 oz) soft brown sugar
240 g (8 oz) plain flour
120 g (4 oz) corn flour
½ teaspoon baking powder
1 teaspoon vanilla essence
pinch of salt
135 g (4½ oz) damson jam

1. Lightly grease a swiss roll tin with butter.
2. Cut the butter into small pieces and place in a bowl with the sugar and the vanilla essence. Beat until well mixed.
3. Sieve the dry ingredients together. Add to the butter and sugar mix; rub in until the mixture resembles fine bread crumbs.
4. Tip the mixture into the prepared tin and spread out evenly and press down - use a rolling pin that just fits the tray and roll the mixture in the tray.
5. Place in the preheated oven 180C and cook for 10 minutes then remove and lightly spread with damson jam.
6. Whilst the biscuit mix is cooking prepare the topping.

Almond topping:
120 g (4 oz) unsalted butter
60 g (2 oz) soft brown/muscavado sugar
1 teaspoon rum (optional)
240 g (8 oz) flaked almonds
65 ml (⅛ pint) milk

1. Place the butter, sugar, rum, double cream and almonds in a thick-bottomed saucepan.
2. Stirring all the time heat slowly until the sugar has dissolved and the butter has melted. Do not boil.
3. Pour the almond, butter, sugar and cream mixture onto the biscuit mix and spread evenly.
4. Replace in the oven to finish cooking at 180C for a further 10-15 minutes.
5. Remove from the oven and place the tray on a wire rack to cool.
6. After 5 minutes cut the biscuits into oblongs.
7. Allow to cool for a further 10 minutes, whilst still warm, carefully remove from the tray using a palette knife. As they become cold they will firm up.

Helpful tip:
Cutting the biscuits into squares needs to be done with care. Use a sharp knife and keep dipping it into a jug of boiling water, shake the excess water off and loosen round the edges first, repeat until you have cut into the required number of pieces.

HAVER BREAD

These oat cakes are a traditional Cumbrian dish tested by the authors.

60 g (2 oz) plain flour
180 g (6 oz) fine or medium oatmeal
1 tablespoon melted lard or butter
pinch of salt and bicarbonate of soda
boiling water

1. Sieve the flour, salt and bicarbonate of soda into a bowl.
2. Add the melted fat with enough water to mix into a soft, pliable dough.
3. Knead well and roll out thinly.
4. Cut into rounds and place on a greased baking sheet.

Pictured left, Damson Cobbler, and inset below. Pictured far left, St. Bee's Delight.

Pictured above, Lemon Meringue Pie

5. Bake in a preheated oven mark 180C until brown and crisp.

6. Serve spread with butter.

WESTMORLAND PEPPER CAKE

480 g (1 lb) self raising flour
1 tablespoon black treacle
120 g (4 oz) raisins
120 g (4 oz) currants
240 g (8 oz) muscavado sugar
30 g (1 oz) candied peel
240g (8 oz) butter or margarine
3 large eggs
$^1/_2$ teaspoon each of ground cloves, nutmeg, cinnamon and ground ginger
$^1/_2$ teaspoon ground black pepper
sufficient milk to give dropping consistency

1. Lightly grease and line with greased grease proof paper a round 20 cm (7") cake tin

2. Sieve the flour, pepper and spices into a bowl. Rub in the fat.

3. Add the sugar, fruit and the peel and mix well

4. Add the treacle to the beaten eggs. Add to the flour mixture and fold in.

5. Put the mixture into the prepared tin. Place in a preheated oven 140C. Bake for 1$^1/_2$-2 hours

6. In Cumbria this cake is traditionally served with Cumberland cheese.

HAWKSHEAD WHIGS [1]

750g (1$^1/_2$ lb) strong plain flour
250 ml ($^1/_2$ pint) warm milk
30 g (1 oz) fresh yeast
7 g ($^1/_4$ oz) caraway seeds
45 g (1$^1/_2$ oz) butter
45 g (1$^1/_2$ oz) sugar
pinch of salt
pinch of pepper

[1] *Lakeland Recipes Old and New* by Joan Poulson
[2] *Lakeland Recipes Old and New* by Joan Poulson

1. Sift together the salt and flour, rub in the butter and add the sugar.

2. Make a well in the centre of the flour and add the pepper and the yeast.

3. Pour on the milk warmed to blood heat. Stir and cover with a cloth.

4. Leave to rise in a warm place for 10 minutes.

5. Knead well for 10 minutes adding the caraway seeds at the same time.

6. Leave to prove for half an hour. Cut into pieces weighing about 90 g (3 oz).

7. Form into rounds and place on a greased tray and leave to prove until lightly risen.

8. Bake in a hot oven until golden brown, about 10 minutes at 220C.

9. Serve split with butter.

RUM BUTTER

Traditional Cumbrian recipe tested by the authors.

240 g (8 oz) butter
480 g (1 lb) soft brown sugar
1 wine glass rum
$^1/_2$ teaspoon grated nutmeg

1. Mix the nutmeg and sugar together.

2. Melt the butter and pour over the sugar mixture.

3. Beat well until well mixed and creamy. Add the rum and beat in well.

4. Pour into pretty dishes and leave to set.

FRUMENTY [2]

240 g (8 oz) new wheat hulled
500 ml (1 pint) milk
dark brown sugar to taste
ground cinnamon and nutmeg to taste
grated lemon and orange
dried fruits to taste
double cream (optional)

1. Wash the wheat and place in a bowl and add three times as much cold water. Leave overnight in a warm place.

2. Drain off the surplus water and place the wheat into a thick bottomed saucepan, cook slowly, stirring frequently until it is soft and thick. At this stage the mixture is called cree-ed wheat and used to be sold from market stalls.

3. Now the cree-ed wheat is ready for making the Frumenty.

4. Place the prepared wheat into a thick-bottomed saucepan with the milk.

5. Bring to the boil and simmer until it thickens. If necessary a little flour, mixed with cold water, can be added.

6. Then add your sugar, fruit and spices. Serve with thick cream.

7. This dish seems very similar to the modern day muesli and is a good Cumbrian alternative. Perhaps it should be revived!

Pictured opposite top left Toffee Almond Shortbread and below, Borrowdale Tea Bread.

Pictured above Maid of Buttermere's Temptation

NUTRITIONAL INFORMATION

THE Herdwick is unique. There is no other English breed like it. Herdwicks are bred primarily for their meat. Their natural diet of ling, heather and bleaberries ensures that the meat has a distinctive flavour. It is a specialist meat an its unique flavour and succulence is highly regarded by gourmets in this country.

The fat of Herdwick dissolves during cooking to form juices. Research by Bristol University (1997) has shown that the chemical make up of the fat is different from other animal fats. It has more unsaturated fats than any other breed of sheep, with superior flavours and a high level of eating quality.

In order to improve the flavour and tenderness, Herdwick should be hung for 7-10 days. This allows the natural enzymes in the meat to develop the flavour and break down the tissues to make the flesh tender.

Herdwick meat has little fat and is therefore very economical, as there is little waste. Traditionally, Herdwick is not sold for the table until it is twelve months old (a shearling, having had its first clipping). This is because the Herdwick is a slow maturing animal. Unlike other breeds the lamb is not ready for the table at three-months-old, so it is unlikely that you will eat Herdwick lamb.

The fact that Herdwick matures slowly allows time for the meat to develop its distinctive flavour, whilst remaining tender and succulent. Careful husbandry by the farmer is necessary to achieve this prime condition. The flavour is such, that it is not overwhelmed in cooking by robust ingredients such as garlic, ginger, oregano and other complementary flavourings.

METHODS OF COOKING HERDWICK

Boiling:
Place the meat into boiling water with a small carrot, onion, and bay leaf. Bring back to the boil and then allow to simmer until the joint is cooked. Allow 20 minutes per 480 g (1 lb) cooking time.

Braising:
A combination of stewing and roasting used for large cuts or joints. The meat is first seared in a frying pan and then cooked in sufficient liquid to cover the meat by two thirds in a casserole with a tight fitting lid. The liquid may be stock, beer, wine or sauce.

Grilling:
Cooking by direct heat where the cuts of meat are brushed with oil and placed on grill bars with trays underneath to catch the juices.

Pot roasting:
Cooking the meat on a bed of root vegetables (onion, carrot and celery) using butter as the moistening agent in a covered casserole. The juices and vegetables are then used to make the required sauce.

Roasting:
Cooking in an oven where the meat is moistened with fat or oil. During the cooking process, the joint should be basted frequently to prevent the meat from drying out. Allow 20 minutes per 480 g (1 lb) plus 20 minutes over.

Shallow Frying:
Cooking in a heavy frying pan with sufficient oil/fat to prevent the meat from burning. The meat should be cooked on both sides turning when necessary to ensure even cooking.

Stewing:
The meat is cut into dice or small pieces and cooked in sufficient liquid - water, stock or sauce - to just cover the meat and allowed to simmer.

JOINTS AND CUTS OF MEAT FROM HERDWICK

THE terminology used for the joints of Herdwick are the traditional ones, (see diagrams A & B). We have also included the terminology used by producers who market their own meat. An explanation of the cuts of meat follows:

Cutlets:
These are cut by cutting between the rib bones of a best end or rack.

Loin Chops:
These are cut from the loin by cutting through the joints between the bones.

Fillets/Noisettes:
To cut the fillets/noisettes from the boned loin/fillet, cut across the joint into pieces 2 cm (³/₄") thick as shown by the dotted line in the diagram. Flatten slightly by pressing down with a knife.

Rosettes:
Roll and tie the boned loin/fillet with string 2¹/₂ cm (1") apart. Then cut into even pieces between the strings, as shown in the diagram. Remove the string after cooking and before serving.

Fillet of leg:
The top half of the leg when cut in half.

Shank of leg:
The bottom half of the leg when cut in half.

Leg steaks:
These are cut across the leg and are best purchased from your supplier because the bone has to be sawn through.

Keswick Braise

JOINTS OF HERDWICK & RECOMMENDED METHODS OF COOKING

Legend	Joints	Braising	Boiling	Pot Roasting	Roasting	Stewing
1 & 2	Scrag & middle neck					✔
3	Shoulder	✔		✔	✔	✔
4	Best End neck/rack				✔	
5	Loin/fillet			✔	✔	
6	Leg	✔	✔	✔	✔	
7	Breast					✔

Diagram A

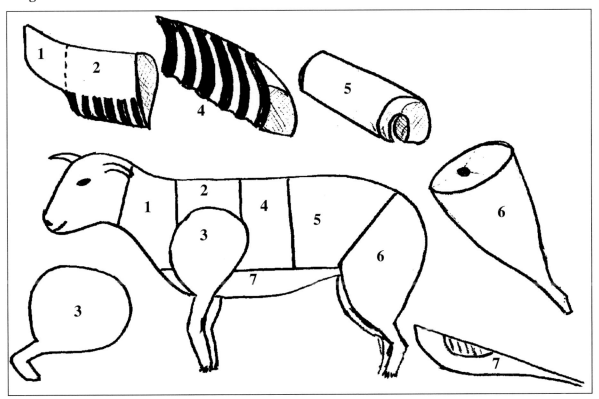

CUTS OF HERDWICK & RECOMMENDED METHODS OF COOKING

Cuts	Braising	Grilling	Shallow frying	Baking
1 Neck chops/cutlets		✔	✔	✔
2 Loin chops	✔	✔	✔	
3 Fillets/Noisettes			✔	✔
4 Rosettes			✔	
5 Leg steaks	✔	✔	✔	

Diagram B

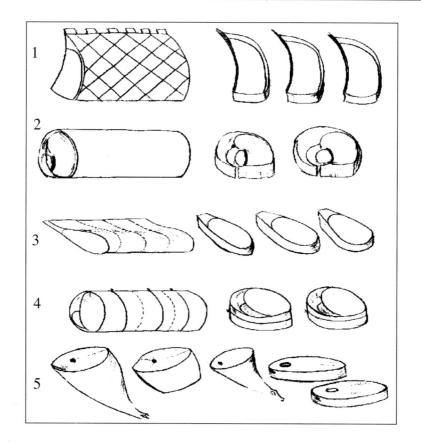

OVEN TEMPERATURE

All the dishes in this book have been cooked in a fan oven which cooks food at a temperature between 10C-20C lower than conventional ovens. It may be necessary to adjust the temperature given in the recipes to suit your oven. Consult your appliance instruction book. Some traditional recipes have not been tested by the authors.

WEIGHTS AND MEASURES

Metric weights have been calculated using 480g to the pound.

Dry measurements:

960 g	2 lb
840 g	1¾ lb
720 g	1½ lb
600 g	1¼ lb
480 g	1 lb
360 g	12 oz
240 g	8 oz
120 g	4 oz
30 g	1 oz

Liquid Measurements

1 litre	2 pints
750 ml	1½ pints
500 ml	1 pint
375 ml	¾ pint
250 ml	½ pint
125 ml	¼ pint
62 ml	⅛ pint

PORTIONS

The number of portions obtained from recipes in this book are sufficient for four normal servings. Some of the dishes are for more than four portions because of the minimum quantity that can made. These are listed below:

Starters

Pate	8 portions
Damson Fruit Ice	6-8 portions
Melon and Tomato Cocktail	8 portions
Cheese Eclairs	6-8 portions
Soups	6-8 portions

Sweets

Cheese Cake	6-8 portions
Conversation Tart	6-8 portions
Sticky Toffee Pudding	6-8 portions
Lemon Meringue Pie	6-8 portions
Cobblers	4-6 portions
Cumbrian Trifle	4-6 portions
Pavlova	4-6 portions
Ice Cream	4-6 portions

The cakes, tea bread and biscuits are sufficient for 8-12 portions.

NUTRITIONAL VALUE OF VEGETABLES[1]

Vegetables	Minerals	Protein	Vitamin A	Vitamin B	Vitamin C	Vitamin E	Vitamin K	Calcium	Magnesium	Iron	Folic Acid	Carbohydrate
Beetroot	✔	✔						✔				✔
Broccoli				✔								
Brussel Sprouts		✔	✔	✔	✔		✔		✔	✔	✔	
Cabbage, green			✔	✔	✔		✔	✔	✔			✔
Cabbage, red												
Carrots			✔	✔	✔							✔
Cauliflower		✔	✔	✔	✔		✔	✔				✔
Celery	✔				✔			✔				✔
Courgettes					✔				✔			
Parsnips		✔			✔			✔	✔			✔
Peas, frozen			✔	✔	✔		✔	✔	✔			
Peppers, red			✔	✔	✔	✔						
Potatoes, old			✔	✔	✔							✔
Potatoes, new			✔	✔	✔							✔
Leeks	✔	✔	✔	✔	✔		✔					
Spinach			✔		✔		✔	✔	✔	✔		✔
Swede			✔		✔			✔				

[1]Information from *The Manual of Nutrition* by MAFF and
The Science of Catering by J. A. Sretch and H. A. Southgate

BODY MAINTENANCE PROVIDED BY VEGETABLES[1]

Minerals: At least 15 elements are essential to man, 8 of which are required in relatively large amounts. They are constituents of bones and teeth, and they help to control the composition of body fluids and cells.

Protein: Protein is necessary for the growth and repair of the body, any excess is utilised as energy.

Vitamin A: Prevents night blindness, maintains the mucous membranes of the body, helps to prevent respiratory disease.

Vitamin B: A diet deficient in B vitamins can lead to multiple deficiency diseases within months.

Vitamin C: Most of our Vitamin C comes from fruit and vegetables. It is necessary for healthy connective tissue. Deficiency can lead to bleeding from the gums and wounds take longer to heal. Prolonged deficiency can lead to scurvy

Vitamin E: Major use is as an anti-oxidant.

Vitamin K: Necessary for the normal clotting of blood.

Calcium: Strengthens bones and teeth, essential for muscular contraction, nerve transmission and blood clotting.

Magnesium: Necessary for normal functioning of nerves and muscles and it plays a part in enzyme reactions, transferring energy.

Iron: Necessary for the production of Haemoglobin.

Folic Acid: Works with Vitamin B, a deficiency can lead to anaemia, increased intake during pregnancy can help reduce the risk of babies being born with neural tube defects eg., spina-bifida.

Carbohydrate: A major source of energy.

RECOMMENDED ADVICE FOR ALL WALKS AND WALKERS

❖ Carry a map and compass and know how to use them.

❖ Wear suitable clothing and footwear.

❖ Good quality walking boots are recommended for all walks described in this book.

❖ Always take waterproofs with you. The weather can change very suddenly in the Lake District.

❖ Carry extra warm clothing.

❖ Take care on uneven and slippery surfaces.

❖ Don't take risks; know your limitations.

❖ Take hot drinks, and water especially in the summer when you can become dehydrated and emergency rations eg., mint cake or chocolate.

❖ Have a rest before a tricky part of the walk.

❖ Take your time and enjoy your surroundings, even in wet weather.

COUNTRYSIDE CODE

❖ **Take nothing but photographs and leave nothing but footprints**

❖ Leave all gates as you find them.

❖ Keep dogs on leads when requested.

❖ Keep dogs under control at all times

❖ Obey notices

❖ Keep to public rights of way or permissive footpaths where necessary.

[1]Information from *The Manual of Nutrition* by MAFF and *The Science of Catering* by J A Sretch and H A Southgate

FOOD TRAIL

ERIC TAYLFORTH
Millbeck Farm
Great Langdale
Nr Ambleside
Cumbria, LA22 9JU
Herdwick meat and other products
Available by mail order:
tel: 015394 37364 ~ e-mail: millbeck@lineone.net

MR AND MRS J RELPH
Yew Tree Farm
Rosthwaite
Borrowdale
Cumbria, CA12 5XB
**Herdwick meat, Herdwick paté, smoked
Herdwick, Cumberland sauce and other sauces**
Available from the tea room or by mail order:
tel: 017687 77675 ~ fax: 017687 77863 ~
web: www.flock-in.co.uk

MR ANDY SHARP
Borough Market
8 Southwark Street
London, SE1 9AH
Herdwick meat
This enterprise includes twenty other Herdwick
farmers. Available retail from Borough Market on
Fridays and Saturdays or order through the web:
www.farmersharp.co.uk

RICHARD WOODALL
Waberthwaite
Nr Millom
Cumbria, LA19 5YJ
**Air dried Cumberland ham, Cumberland ham,
Cumberland sausage**
tel: 01229 717237

FOOD FROM THE FELLS
Rheged Discovery Centre
Redhills
Penrith
Cumbria
**Damsons, Damson beer, wine and gin,
Cumberland mustards, Raspberry vinegar,
Woodalls products, Jennings beer, other
Cumbrian products**
tel: 01768 895598

THORNBY MOOR DAIRY
Crofton Hall
Thursby
Nr Carlisle
Cumbria
**Cumberland farmhouse cheese, Crofton cheese,
Stumpy cheese, other Cumbrian cheeses**
Mail order and purchase from the dairy:
tel and fax: 016973 45555

DEMEL'S CHUTNEYS
The Barn
Arrad Foot
Ulverston
Cumbria, LA12 7SL
Selection of chutneys and pickles
Also available in major towns in the north west.
Orders:- tel and fax: 01229 861012 ~ e-mail:
demels@btinternet.com ~ web: www.speciality-
foods.com

CUMBERLAND MUSTARD
Tyne Willows
Alston
Cumbria, CA9 3HZ
Cumberland mustards, pickled damsons, raspberry vinegar, other products
Orders - tel: 01434 381135

LAKELAND SPECIALITIES
Heathlands
Keswick
Cumbria, CA12 4EL
Lakeland honey, oat cakes and other products
Available from Friars, Keswick, or tel: 017687
79136 ~ fax: 017687 79890 ~ e-mail: lakeland.spe-
cialities@btopenworld.com

STRAWBERRY BANK
Crosthwaite
Cumbria, LA8 8HX
Damson beer, liquers and other products
Orders - tel: 015395 68812

WESTMORLAND DAMSON ASSOCIATION
**Damson wine, bottled damsons, damson jam and
other products**
Available from Food From The Fells, Rheged
Discovery Centre, Penrith

SALKELD FLOUR MILL
Salkeld Flour Mill
Little Salkeld
Penrith
Cumbria, CA10 1NN
**Selection of organically grown flours and oat
meals**
Available from various outlets including Priest's
Mill, Caldbeck and whole food shops or tel: 01768
881523

W. S. AND S. S. EDMONDSON
Borrowdale Fisheries Trout Farm
The Cottage
Seathwaite Farm
Borrowdale
Keswick
Cumbria, CA12 5XJ
Fresh trout and other products
For more information tel: 017687 77293

JENNINGS BROS. PLC
Castle Brewery
The Maltings
Cockermouth
Cumbria
Cumberland ale, Cocker Hoop, Sneck Lifter
Jennings beers are available through retail outlets or
tel: 01900 823214 ~ web:
www.jenningsbrewery.co.uk

BARRATT AND KEEGAN
Cowmire Hall
Crosthwaite
Kendal
Cumbria, LA8 8JJ
Cowmire Hall damson gin
Available from many retail outlets including:-
Fortnum and Mason's, 181 Picadilly, London
Jeroboams, 51 Elizabeth Street, London, SW1 9PP
The House of Bruar, By Blair Atholl, Perthshire,
PH18 5TW, Scotland
Thorpe Farm, Peel House, Greta Bridge, Barnard
Castle, Durham, DL12 9TY
Country Harvest, Ingleton , North Yorkshire, LA6
3PE
Lake Food Store, Keswick, Cumbria
Food From The Fells, Rheged, Penrith
G Richardson and Sons, Whitehaven
Taste of Lakeland, Ambleside
Muncaster Castle, Ravenglass
Windermere Wine Stores, Windermere
Orders can also be taken on tel and fax: 015395
68200 ~ e-mail: cowmire.hall@btinternet.com

WOOLLEN TRAIL

JANE EXLEY
The Woolly Rug Company
The Barn
Elterwater
Cumbria
Speciality rugs

Arts and Heritage Centre
Farfield Mill
Garsdale Road
Sedbergh
Cumbria, LA10 5LP
Herdwick display and products, spinning, weaving, knitwear, textiles and other crafts. Weaving demonstrations
There are retail outlets on site or for more information - tel: 015396 21958 ~ e-mail: farfieldmill@email.com ~ web: www. farfieldmill.freeserve.co.uk

VICTORIA EDMONSON
Robinson Place Farm
Great Langdale
Ambleside
Cumbria, LA22 9JS
Hand knitted Herdwick jumpers, B&B
Orders or more information - tel: 015394 37214 ~ e-mail victoriaedmonson@hotmail.com

MRS RELPH
Yew Tree Farm
Rosthwaite
Borrowdale
Nr Keswick
Cumbria, CA12 5XB
Selection of Herdwick woollen products and sheep skin rugs
For more information tel: 017687 77675

THE WOOL CLIP LTD
The Wool Clip farmers' & craft workers' co-operative
Priest's Mill
Church Terrace
Caldbeck, CA7 8DR
Wide range of rugs, throws, wall hangings, knitwear, hand spun yarns many made from locally produced wool including Herdwick. Workshops in the following available: spinning, weaving, dyeing, felting, hookey rugs, knitting and crochet.
Retail from shop or mail order - tel: 016974 78707 ~ web: www.woolclip.com

ULPHA POST OFFICE
Ulpha
Broughton in Furness, Cumbria
Selection of Herdwick woollen products

MARY BELL
Crookabeck
Patterdale
Cumbria, CA11 ONP
Crookabeck Herdwicks. Selection of Herdwick rugs, throws, wall hangings, hand knitted garments, floor rugs, sheep skins and wool.
Available from the Wool Clip, Priest's Mill, Caldbeck or by mail order or from farm shop by appointment - tel: 017684 82742 ~ web: www.herdwickwool.com

MRS KYLE
Buttermere Landscapes and Crafts
Syke Farm
Buttermere
Cockermouth
Cumbria, CA13 9XA
Selection of Herdwick products and other gifts plus Buttermere Ayrshire's ice cream
For more information tel: 017687 70277 ~ web: www.buttermere-lorton.com

CUMBRIAN WOOL
Pike Side Farm
Ulpha
Broughton-in-Furness
Cumbria, LA20 6EY
Rugs, throws, blankets made from the fleece of fell sheep, including Herdwick
tel: 01229 716188

ORIGINAL CUMBRIAN WOOL
Old Hall Farm
Ulpha
Broughton-in-Furness
Cumbria, LA20 6EY
Range of undyed natural wool products
tel: 01229 716067

THE NATIONAL TRUST
National Trust Information Centre
Church Stile
Grasmere
Ambleside, LA22 9SW
tel: 015394 35621

Sizergh Castle
Sizergh
Nr Kendal, LA8 8AE
tel: 015395 60070

Corner Shop
Hawkeshead
Ambleside, LA22 0NS
tel: 015394 36471

Wordsworth House
Main Street
Cockermouth, CA13 9RX
tel: 01900 824805
All shops selling a selection of Herdwick wool products

SECOND NATURE UK LTD
Soulands Gate
Soulby
Dacre
Penrith, CA11 0JF
Thermafleece sheep's wool thermal insulation, made from British hill sheep wools, including Herdwick and Swaledale
For more information - tel: 017684 86285 ~ fax: 017684 86825 ~ e-mail: info@secondnatureuk.com ~ web: www.secondnatureuk.com

BIBLIOGRAPHY

Herdwick Sheep, Geoff Brown, Herdwick Sheep Breeders' Association

Herdwick Sheep, S Denyer, National Trust Publication

Herdwick research paper, W. Rawling, Whitehaven Records Office

Herdwick Past and Present: History of The Breed, R. H. Lamb

Herdwick Sheep, Ruskin Museum, Coniston (internet)

Old Norwegian Sheep, Trygve Fjarli, Norway (internet)

Lakeland Recipes Old and New, Joan Poulson

In Search of Food, Richard Mabey

The Roman Cookery Book of Apicius, translated and adapted for the Modern Kitchen by John Edwards

Journeys of Celia Fiennes, Ceilia Fiennes

The House of Clifford, Hugh Clifford

Lady Anne Clifford, Richard T. Spence

Food in England, Dorothy Hartley

The Art of Cookery Made Plain and Easy, Hannah Glasse, 1747

The Manual of Nutrition, MAFF

The Science of Catering, A. Stretch and H. A. Southgate

Lake District Life and Traditions, William Rollinson

The Dairy Book of British Food, Milk Marketing Board

Traditional Lakeland Recipes, Cumbria Magazine

Buttermere, Tales of a Lakeland Valley, S. Richardson

Loweswater, Tales of a Lakeland Valley, S. Richardson

Borrowdale, Tales of a Lakeland Valley, S. Richardson *The Langdales, Tales of a Lakeland Valley*, S. Richardson

The Buttermere Valley, National Trust leaflet *Crummock Water*, National Trust leaflet

The Lake District, M. Dunn

Companion into Lakeland, Maxwell Fraser

Highways and Byways in the Lake District, A. G. Bradley

The Lake Counties, W. G. Collingwood

A Companion Guide to the Lake District, Frank Walsh

Around the Lakeland Hills, F. J. Carruthers

Guardian of the Lakes: A History of the National Trust in the Lake District from 1946, Elizabeth Battrick

The Lake District, Roy Millward and Adrian Robinson

Roads and Trackways of the Lake District, Brian Paul Hindle

The Wider Sea: A Life of John Ruskin, John Dixon Hunt

Wordsworth Complete Poetic Works, William Wordsworth

The Illustrated Lakeland Journals, Dorothy Wordsworth

Wainwright's Favourite Lakeland Mountains, A. Wainwright and Derry Brabbs

Lake District Place Names, Robert Gamble

A Dictionary of English Place Names, A. D. Mills

The English Lakes: Tales from History Legend Folklore, David Ramshaw

Tales of Old Cumbria, William Amos

The Secret Valley, Nicholas Size

The Story of the Lakeland Dales, Robert Gamble *Ninety Four Years in Eskdale*, the reminiscences of John Porter of Yattus

The Correspondence of Sir John Lowther of Whitehaven, 1693-1698, edited by D. R. Hainsworth

The Forgotten Trade, Nigel Tattersfield

The Republic, Plato

Bradbury's History of Cockermouth, J. Bernard Bradbury

The Mummies of Urumchi, Elizabeth Wayland Barber

Women's Work, the First 20,000 Years, Elizabeth Wayland Barber

Kendal On Tenterhooks, John Satchell

The Kendal Weaver, John Satchell

Landscape and Society in Mediaeval Cumbria, Angus J. L. Winchester

Diary of Isaac Fletcher of Underwood, Whitehaven Record Office

Anglo Saxon and Viking Crafts - Textiles, Roland Williamson, 1999 (internet)

Revival of Spinning and Weaving in Langdale, Marguerite Blake

The Lake District at Work, Past and Present, J. D. Marshal and M. Davies-Shiel

Wool Is My Bread, M. Davies-Shiel

To The King's Deceit, a Study of Smuggling in the Solway, Ronald T. Gibbon

The Oxford Companion To English Literature, Sir Paul Harvey

The Cambridge Guide To English Literature, Michael Stapleton

Encyclopedia Britannica

Farming and Food, the Curry Commission

Westmorland Agriculture, F. W. Garnett

INDEX

Apple Sauce	122
Beetroot, cheese & cashew	97
Borrowdale tea bread	154
Braise, Keswick	112
Brandy & Rosemary Sauce	120
Bread, brown	154
Broccoli with cheese	138
Broth, Herdwick	100
Brussel Sprouts with chesnuts	137
Burgers in brown onion sauce	117
Cabbage, caraway & onion	140
Cabinet pudding	144
Caraway seed cake, Dorothy's	154
Carrot and apricot Soup	99
Carrots, glazed	136
Cauliflower fritters	139
Cauliflower, Polish style	138
Celery, braised	140
Cheese Eclairs, Crofton	98
Chick Pea, nut & mushroom parcels	94
Chocolate Prune cake	158
Columba Cream pudding	144
Conversation tart	145
Courgettes, shallow fried	137
Courgettes, tomatoes & garlic	138
Cumberland Sauce	130
Curry, Cumberland	103
Cutlets, Crummock	104
Damson and apple tansy	143
Damson cheese cake	145
Damson cobbler, Lyth Valley 1	146
Damson cobbler, Lyth Valley 2	146
Damson fruit ice	95
Damson ice cream	150
Damson soup, chilled	99
Easter Ledger pudding	143
Eden Valley pudding	147
Fell 'n' Tarn	106
Fig Sue	102
Fillets & orange sauce	123
Fillets & mushrooms	111
Flan, Cumberland	110
Fruit, nut & chocolate Ambrosia	149
Fruity toffee almond shortbread	159
Frumenty	162
Gateau, Maid of Buttermere	155
Gingerbread, Lakeland	155
Ham, Cumberland	131
Hardknott leg & caper Sauce	108
Haver bread	159
Hawkshead Whigs	162
Hazelnut, strawberry pavlova	152
Herdwick Cobbler	107
Hot Pot, Rheged	127
Lamplugh pudding	152
Leek Hot Pot, Cumbrian	108
Leeks, braised	139
Leeks, with caraway seeds	140
Leg Steak, capers & apricots	123
Lemon & garlic dressing	94
Lemon meringue pie	148
Lentil soup with tahini	102
Melon and tomato cocktail	97
Mint sauce	118
Nettle haggis	143
Onions, French fried	103
Orange and oil dressing	131
Orange drizzle cake	156
Parsnip and paprika soup	101
Pasty, Cumberland	126
Paté, Patterdale	95
Peas, savoury	136
Pepper cake, Westmorland	162
Peppers, stuffed	126
Pineapple, orange & mint cocktail	97
Pizza, Cumberland	115
Portinscale tit bits	127
Pot Roast in mulled wine sauce	118
Potatoes, braised with bacon	141
Potatoes, braised with cheese	142
Potatoes, fried cubes	141
Potatoes, mashed	141
Potatoes, new, parsley & lemon	142
Potatoes, shallow fried	141
Potatoes, fried & onions	141
Potato and watercress soup	100
Potato, griddle cakes	142
Potato, watercress & pear soup	101
Puff pastry	153
Red cabbage, braised	135
Rice, braised Boethar's	114
Roast best end in savoury crust	118
Roast leg with garlic & rosemary	120
Roast, Rosthwaite	111
Roast shoulder, Derwent	105
Roast shoulder, honey & mustard	112
Roast with savoury potatoes	108
Rum brown Betty, Workington	149
Rum butter	162
Rum Nicky, Cumberland	152
St. Bee's Delight	149
Salad, Skiddaw	130
Sausage, Cumberland	133
Sausage meat, Lakeland	112
Sausage meat loaf	114
Sausage rolls, Herdwick	98
Sausage Toad in the Hole	122
Savoury Parcels	94
Savoury Suet Pudding	
Shepherds' Pie	116
Spaghetti in Tomato Sauce	105
Spinach, buttered with nutmeg	137
Spotted Dog pudding	153
Steamed meat pudding	119
Stew, Eskdale	113
Stew, spiced Lakeland	131
Sticky Toffee pudding	150
Strawberry Pavlova meringue	151
Stuffed breast of mutton	133
Swede and cinnamon Soup	101
Swede, puree	136
Sweet meat pie, Cumberland	134
Tatie Pot, Cumberland	134
Thursby Thingmound	116
Tomato sauce for spaghetti	104
Trifle, Cumberland	147
Venison, roast	133
Witherslack surprise	109

MORE BOOKS FROM HAYLOFT

A Journalist's Journey Around Britain
Roy Maddison (£10, ISBN 1 9045240 6 0)

The Long Day Done by Jeremy Rowan-Robinson
(£9.50, ISBN 1 9045240 4 4)

Odd Corners in Appleby, Gareth Hayes
(£8.50, ISBN 1 9045240 0 1)

The Ghastlies, Trix Jones and Shane Surgey
(£3.99, ISBN 1 9045240 4 4)

A Journey of Soles, Lands End to John O'Groats,
Kathy Trimmer (£9.50, 1 9045240 5 2)

*Changing the Face of Carlisle, The Life and Times
of Percy Dalton, City Engineer and Surveyor, 1926-
1949,* Marie K. Dickens (£8, ISBN 0 9540711 9 0)

*From Clogs and Wellies to Shiny Shoes, A
Windermere Lad's Memories of South Lakeland,*
Miles R. M. Bolton (£12.50, ISBN 1 9045240 2 8)

A History of Kaber, Helen McDonald and Christine
Dowson, (£8, ISBN 0 9540711 6 6)

The Gifkin Gofkins, Irene Brenan
(£2.50, ISBN 1 9045240 1 X)

*A Dream Come True, the Life and Times of a Lake
District National Park Ranger,* David Birkett
(£8.00, ISBN 0 9540711 5 8)

Gone to Blazes, Life as a Cumbrian Fireman,
David Stubbings (£9.95, ISBN 0 9540711 4 X)

Changing Times, The Millennium Story of Bolton,
Barbara Cotton (£12.50, ISBN 0 9540711 3 1)

*Better by Far a Cumberland Hussar, A History of
the Westmorland and Cumberland Yeomanry,* Colin
Bardgett
(Hardback, £26.95, ISBN 0 9540711 2 3)
(Paperback, £16.95, ISBN 0 9540711 1 5)

*Northern Warrior, the Story of Sir Andreas de
Harcla,* Adrian Rogan (£8.95, ISBN 0 9523282 8 3)

A Riot of Thorn & Leaf, Dulcie Matthews
(£7.95, ISBN 0 9540711 0 7)

*Military Mountaineering, A History of Services
Expeditions, 1945-2000,* Retd. SAS Major Bronco
Lane (Hardback, £25.95, ISBN 0 9523282 1 6)
(Paperback, £17.95, ISBN 0 9523282 6 7)

2041 - The Voyage South, Robert Swan
(£8.95, 0 9523282 7 5)

Yows & Cows, A Bit of Westmorland Wit, Mike
Sanderson (£7.95, ISBN 0 9523282 0 8)

Riding the Stang, Dawn Robertson
(£9.99, ISBN 0 9523282 2 4)

Secrets and Legends of Old Westmorland,
Peter Koronka and Dawn Robertson
(Hardback, £17.95, ISBN 0 9523282 4 0)
(Paperback, £11.95, ISBN 0 9523282 9 1)

*The Irish Influence, Migrant Workers in Northern
England,* Harold Slight (£4.95, 0 9523282 5 9)

Soldiers and Sherpas, A Taste for Adventure,
Brummie Stokes. (£19.95, 0 9541551 0 6)

North Country Tapestry, Sylvia Mary McCosh
(£10, 0 9518690 0 0)

*Between Two Gardens, The Diary of two Border
Gardens,* Sylvia Mary McCosh
(£5.95, 0 9008111 7 X)

*Dacre Castle, A short history of the Castle and the
Dacre Family,* E. H. A. Stretton
(£5.50, 0 9518690 1 9)

Antarctica Unveiled, Scott's First Expedition
David E. Yelverton (£25.99, 0 8708158 2 2)

You can order any of our books by writing to: Hayloft Publishing Ltd., South Stainmore, Kirkby Stephen, Cumbria, CA17 4EU, UK.
telephone: +44 (0)17683) 42300
For more information see: www.hayloft.org.uk